Finding Meaning in Civically Engaged Scholarship

Personal Journeys, Professional Experiences

Finding Meaning in Civically Engaged Scholarship

Personal Journeys, Professional Experiences

edited by

Marissa L. Diener
University of Utah

Hank Liese
University of Utah

INFORMATION AGE PUBLISHING, INC.
Charlotte, NC • www.infoagepub.com

Library of Congress Cataloging-in-Publication Data

Finding meaning in civically engaged scholarship : personal journeys, professional experiences / edited by Marissa L. Diener, Hank Liese.
    p. cm.
  Includes bibliographical references.
  ISBN 978-1-60752-111-2 (pbk.) – ISBN 978-1-60752-112-9 (hardcover)
1. Service learning–United States. 2. Civics–Study and teaching (Higher)–United States. 3. Education, Higher–Social aspects–United States. 4. Community and college–United States. 5. Learning and scholarship–United States. I. Diener, Marissa L. II. Liese, Hank.
  LC220.5.F56 2009
  378.1'03–dc22

                                                             2009014748

CONTENTS

PART I

JOURNEYS TO CIVICALLY ENGAGED SCHOLARSHIP

PART II

CIVIC ENGAGEMENT IN ACTION:
COMMUNITY-BASED RESEARCH AND SERVICE-LEARNING

INTRODUCTION

The Journey

Marshall Welch

jour–ney (n.) (a) a traveling from one place to another, usually taking a rather long time; trip; (b) a distance, course, or area traveled or suitable for traveling: a desert journey; (c) passage or progress from one stage to another: the journey to success.

> I believe we are destined to meet the people who will support, guide, and nurture us on our life's journey, each of them appearing at the appropriate time, accompanying us at least part of the way.
>
> I think specific human beings, sometimes only in spirit, will present themselves in such a way that their presence will shape and reshape our hearts until we are more fully who we are. (Walker, 1993, p. 3)

These pages represent a journey, both literally and metaphorically. Like most journeys, it comprises a series of events and stories. It began as a five-hour van trip by six faculty members from the University of Utah. The group, which later would become the Civically Engaged Scholar Cohort and grow to nine members representing eight different disciplines, was making its way to a retreat along the banks of the Colorado River beneath towering red cliffs in the Utah desert. There, they would join 80 other faculty mem-

Finding Meaning in Civically Engaged Scholarship, pages ix–xvi
Copyright © 2009 by Information Age Publishing
All rights of reproduction in any form reserved.

bers from various institutions of higher education from around the state to engage in conversation about service-learning and civic engagement. In this inspiring setting, participants were to share with their colleagues what guides them down the path of service-learning and civic engagement. In a 24-hour period spanning two days, the journey became a passage from one stage of professional work to another for everyone.

The event was being sponsored by Utah Campus Compact, one of the 30-plus state offices of Campus Compact, a national association that assists more than 1,000 member colleges and universities in advancing campus-based civic and community engagement. During the course of the retreat, in large- and small-group sessions, participants shared ideas and strategies related to their teaching, research, and service. The gathering concluded with an opportunity to reflect on what draws faculty to this kind of work. In a 90-minute final session, the reflection began simply enough. The group merely sat in silence, a first step in clearing some of the noise from its collective consciousness. It was simultaneously comforting and unnerving; the act of sitting quietly for nearly 15 minutes runs completely counter to a culture of discourse and lecture. The large group gradually settled into the silence and centered itself.

Participants then turned inward as they wrote out answers to a series of five questions posed by the facilitator, sharing their personal reflections with the person sitting next to them after each question. The first question was, "*Who* am I?", which allowed each participant to reflect on his or her strengths, interests, and challenges. As the facilitator explained, this exploration of personal identity was analogous to asking, "What would things posted on your refrigerator at home reveal about yourself?" The reflection then shifted to a question Parker Palmer (2000) asks, "*Whose* am I?" prompting an examination of stewardship and commitment to family, friends, students, discipline, institution, and beyond. The group then considered, "*Why* do I do what I do?", with a follow-up question, "What would it mean if I *didn't* do this work?" The activity concluded with the question, "How do I *integrate* or *reconcile* my identity and what I do with expectations of the academy?" What emerged was profound, deep, and personal as faculty considered their scholarly work in a context that diverges from the traditional academic model.

Retreat participants collectively discovered and shared that they viewed service-learning as an effective pedagogy. Recognizing the value of applied learning in authentic settings, addressing real issues in the real world, they saw service-learning as a "good way to teach and learn." This seems a typical and logical starting point for academicians, who might naturally be drawn to this dimension of service-learning. Participants noted that, over time and through experience, they have come to see and appreciate the impact of their students' work beyond test scores and grades, vicariously deriving satisfaction from "making a difference" through their students and community partners.

REFINING THE SENSE OF SELF

For many, this discovery was the first real acknowledgment that this type of work was different somehow from other scholarly activities. "Making a difference" with students and the community through some kind of tangible outcome was seen as a significant diversion from traditional academic products that "matter," such as publications, presentations, and positive course evaluations. In essence, faculty at this retreat began to recognize the same rewards that explain the current trend of students' engaging in voluntary service as an alternative to conventional politics (e.g., voting) because they readily see they are making a difference through their efforts (Rimmerman, 2001). Coincidently, some of the motivators for faculty that emerged were similar to what Ann Colby and her colleagues (2003), in their book *Educating Citizens*, identified as motivators for students to becoming civically engaged. These include political, moral, and spiritual factors, as well as issues relating to self-identity.

Through the course of reflection and dialogue at the retreat, it became apparent that most of these factors were intertwined. Many participants in the discussion were unable to separate their political and moral reasons for teaching service-learning from their professional and personal sense of self. To an extent, teaching service-learning became a political act as it facilitated student awareness and action. Similarly, faculty discovered they felt compelled to use their knowledge and expertise to help make a difference. While still creating new knowledge for an academic discipline, faculty began to sense they were also making a contribution to the community; hence, they could claim a moral dimension to their work, without necessarily imposing any particular "morality" on students. In other words, their commitment to facilitating student awareness and action toward important social issues through service-learning reflects *who they are*, not merely *what they do*. Faculty began to discern a sense of personal identity apart from a discipline-specific professional identity. By exploring connections and relationships, faculty suddenly discovered their own sense of self, as well as interest in others and society coupled with intellectual and epistemological activity.

Curiously, all of these factors reflect what might be characterized as a spiritual dimension of learning—not to be confused with a religious dimension; the terms are related but not synonymous. English (2000) characterized three dimensions of spirituality in adult learning: (1) a strong sense of self; (2) care, concern, and outreach to others; and (3) continuous construction of meaning and knowledge. These three dimensions clearly reflect what faculty experienced at the retreat.

A strong sense of self evolves by learning from and with others, an opportunity that service-learning certainly affords. This creates relationships that provide an opportunity to learn about alternative views and ways of being, which in turn provides insights about our sense of self. What could be more scholarly than the Oracle's charge at Delphi to "know thyself?" The group discovered this question is just as appropriate for the teacher as it is the student. Care, concern, and outreach to others are important dimensions as learners acknowledge a world outside the self. Here, service-learning moves from a transactional learning mode of dispensing facts and information to a transformative experience in which students (and hopefully faculty) begin to transcend the self as they meet the needs of others. Students and faculty alike are moved to become civically engaged as global citizens and to discover their place and role in the world. The "continuous construction of meaning and knowledge" is an essential tenet of higher education and contributes to the discovery that life is greater than the self, and we are bound and related to others.

It is important to note what themes did *not* emerge from the collective reflection process in the desert. While non-tenured faculty were sensitive to the political and professional ramifications of their RPT reviews, it became clear that their motivation for doing this work was not entirely driven by these factors. In fact, many participants in the dialogue admitted they had been counseled by peers, department chairs, and deans to avoid the risk of this "seductive activity" (an actual term used) until they had earned tenure. Yet faculty members choose to engage in this work for reasons beyond personal and professional advancement. Simply put, faculty didn't choose this path because they thought it would help earn promotion and tenure—they did it for the reasons articulated above. At the same time, they also recognized taking this path had the potential of facilitating promotion and tenure as long as other scholarly expectations were met. Likewise, strategic and institutional power did not seem to play into personal decisions. Faculty at this retreat did not see that engaging in service-learning and other civic engagement activities would necessarily garner prestige for the department or institution. They didn't see this work simply as good public relations with voters and legislators, although such benefits can certainly result.

Faculty members at this retreat began to see that they were not merely scholars creating and disseminating knowledge. Instead, participants discovered they had a responsibility to others in the local and global community. This discovery complements theoretical tenets of civic engagement articulated by educators such as John Dewey and Ernest Boyer. Service-learning enables faculty to remove their sense of self from the confines of an abstract and theoretical world to become meaningfully engaged within the real world. Service-learning balances and combines an empirically-based pedagogy with something intangible and deeply personal. Service-learning allows individuals to begin to explore the inner geography that often goes uncharted.

THE LEARNING COMMUNITY
OF CIVICALLY ENGAGED SCHOLARS

At the end of the retreat, most attendees quickly packed their things to take advantage of the warm weather and the spectacular setting for hiking and other outdoor activities. As these individuals bid farewell to new colleagues, the same small group of faculty from the University of Utah mentioned at the beginning of this chapter remained at a table. For this group, the retreat had not ended; in some respects, it had just begun. These faculty members did not want the conversation that began in the van ride down to the retreat to end. They were not quite ready to venture back to the lives they had left behind. Over the weekend, personal discoveries had been made and epiphanies shared—and a community had begun to emerge. The Latin root for community, *communis*, means common, and these scholars from diverse disciplines realized they had something in common. For another hour, the group committed to keeping the dialogue and the inner journey alive. The conversation continued in the van ride home.

These individuals—this new learning community—pledged to continue the dialogue through monthly "gatherings"—not formal or scholarly meetings, but informal conversations. The desert setting had been conducive to personal reflection and professional development, and they recognized the need for a venue separate and apart from their daily routines for this to continue. The group agreed to take turns hosting the gatherings in their homes, with the sharing of food being a critical component of the communal experience.

This was a curious development, as the group was fortunate to have a nationally recognized center for service and service-learning at its institution, the Lowell Bennion Community Service Center. There already were considerable infrastructure and financial resources available to promote this type of work; more than 150 courses had been officially designated as service-learning. Despite this history and resource availability, the group felt it was not enough in and of itself. Technical support is important and often a luxury, but the group recognized that another kind of support was required. These individuals confessed they often felt undervalued and misunderstood, primarily by their colleagues and administrators within their own disciplines and departments. They needed a gathering of like-minded scholars as a safe haven and a chance for exchange. They longed for a shared personal community that was their own to continue the journey that began at the desert retreat.

During the remainder of spring semester and into the summer, our group met. We continued to share stories and derive meaning from and about our work. During the gatherings, each of us began to share our own stories. It was a process of both professional and personal affirmation and discovery. We acknowledged there were few other contexts in which professors from

English, Family and Consumer Studies, Social Work, Physical Therapy, Education, Political Science, and Architecture and Planning could find a common interest, language, purpose, and commitment that transcended the constraints of our individual disciplines. As one colleague articulated, "I am drawn to the people who do this work. They bring out the best in me. Interacting with and learning from each other helps me become a better person as well as a better academician."

To mirror what Donald Schoen (1987) characterized as the "reflective practitioner," learning community members decided to provide a quasi-structure to guide the process. A set of "pre-flection" questions was created, and each member was asked to respond to them in writing:

- What does "civically engaged scholarship" mean or look like to you?
- Why do you do this type of work?
- What would it mean if "we" didn't do this type of work?
- Why are you a part of this community of scholars?

Each member was encouraged to use a stream of consciousness approach to the written reflection process and eschew our typical scholarly, structured writing. For many of us, the approach was somewhat "counterculture" in nature and initially difficult. We began to simply "free associate" at the keyboard and attempted to organize our thoughts later with the help and guidance of fellow group members. With time, it became a powerful and liberating process. We all took turns submitting our personal narratives to public reading and discussion at our gatherings at each other's home. Colleagues validated and questioned each other after reading the passages.

Collectively, as these conversations ensued, we decided it was equally important to talk about our service-learning courses and community-based research projects. The intent was not to produce a dry, technical report or formal case study of the class or project, although some demographic information was deemed necessary, but rather to tell the *story* of the class or project. We felt it was important to accompany each of our personal narratives with a professional narrative describing in detail how we translate our personal philosophies into actual classes and community projects.

OUR STORIES

The essays in this volume are a collection of reflective narratives, rather than traditional scholarly treatises. The book is divided into two parts. The first part describes our individual journeys as each of us found our way to civically engaged scholarship and came to see it as critical to our academic endeavors and identity. This section also highlights the interdisciplinary nature of our work as we discuss our journeys through our own disciplinary lenses. The second part presents detailed examples of our civic engagement, including service-learning classes, community-based research projects, and creation of community service-learning spaces. These chapters provide a varied picture of the available avenues for civic engagement for students and faculty in a higher education setting. We provide sufficient details of our projects and classes to enable replication.

The book concludes with a discussion of civic engagement as it is defined in the literature. The conclusion also discusses institutional factors that support and promote civic engagement as well as the importance of community involvement in service learning. Five common themes that emerged across the chapters are described. These themes include the use of service-learning and civic engagement as an effective pedagogy, the relationship between civic engagement and political activism, the importance of partnership and collaboration, the meaning found in civic engagement, and the challenges of civically engaged work.

Our collection of narratives is intended to validate and inspire others who share our passion for this work but may not have the resources or the support that our group has enjoyed. It is our hope that kindred spirits at other colleges and universities will establish and convene gatherings of similar, like-minded affinity groups. Gelmon and colleagues (2001) argue that we must demonstrate the impact of service-learning and do so in the context of the engaged campus. They specifically suggest that "assessment serves a useful purpose as a mechanism to tell the story of what one has learned from one's work—articulating that learning for oneself as well as for others" (Gelmon et al., 2001, p. 4). This is our work. It makes a significant contribution to students, to our disciplines, to the civic mission of the institution, and to our own sense of self.

And so, the journey continues. This collection of personal narratives *is* the journey. Naturally it is important to explore the complex array of administrative, systemic, and cultural factors within academia that promote and impede service-learning and civic engagement if we hope to embed this work within institutions of higher education. But that is not the purpose of this volume, although some insights might be gained from a personal, rather than empirical, perspective. We recognize the value of such research in scholarly journals found elsewhere. Similarly, we acknowledge the need to continue to explore service-learning as a pedagogy and how the act of service can be an effective teaching and learning tool. In particular, we can begin to consider how faculty can incorporate various perspectives such as politics, culture, health, economics, and the environment through the reflection process to broaden students' understanding of their experience. But again, this type of inquiry has ample venues through traditional scholarship. Our purpose and decision in this collection of personal narratives is to continue the dialogue that began in the desert.

Why? Because even the other 80 colleagues at the original desert retreat who are not part of this particular learning community—named the Civically Engaged Scholar Cohort, or CESC—consistently shared in the dialogue and in post-session evaluation surveys that the retreat was both profound and rejuvenating. They, like the members of the CESC, confessed they rarely have the time or opportunity to engage in this type of reflection. It was the entire group attending the retreat that proposed we continue to make time for *conversations* (not just meetings or conference presentations) and for *reflection* (not merely research). We also know this reflective process is an essential component of discovery and new knowledge. So, at the insistence of our other 80 colleagues at the retreat and of ourselves who continue to gather, it seems we must continue to ask some of the same questions that were posed in the desert—specifically asking at least one critical question: "What would it mean if we *didn't* do this work?" The answers have important implications for our selves, our students, our institutions, our disciplinary fields, our society, and the global community.

REFERENCES

Colby, A., Ehrlich, T., Beaumont, E., & Stephens, J. (2003). *Educating citizens: Preparing America's undergraduates for lives of moral and civic responsibility.* San Francisco: Jossey-Bass.

English, L. M. (2000). Spiritual dimensions of informal learning. In L. M. English & M. A. Gillen (Eds.), *Addressing spiritual dimensions of adult learning: What educators can do* (pp. 29–38). San Francisco: Jossey-Bass.

Gelmon, S. B., Holland, B., Driscoll, A., Spring, A., & Kerrigan, S. (2001). *Assessing service-learning and civic engagement: Principles and techniques.* Providence, RI: Campus Compact.

Palmer, P. (2000). *Let your life speak: Listening to the voice of vocation.* San Francisco: Jossey-Bass.

Rimmerman, C.A. (2001). *The new citizenship: Unconventional politics, activism, and service* (2nd ed.). Boulder, CO: Westview Press.

Schoen, D. (1987). *The reflective practitioner: How professionals think in action.* New York: Basic Books.

Walker, A. (1993). Part One: Introduction. In A. Walker & P. Parmar, *Warrior marks: Female genital mutilation and the sexual blinding of women* (pp. 3–4). New York: Harcourt Brace & Company.

PART I

JOURNEYS TO CIVICALLY ENGAGED SCHOLARSHIP

CHAPTER 1

REFLECTIONS ON THE SEARCH FOR MEANING IN ACADEMIA

Marissa L. Diener

IN THE BEGINNING

Why does one child scream in laughter at a haunted house whereas another shakes in fear and yet another walks stoically? I pursued a Ph.D. in developmental psychology because I was fascinated by these questions and others related to individual differences in children's socioemotional development. I found graduate school exciting and stimulating and was motivated to pursue research that would answer questions about children's development and interpersonal processes. My research focuses on basic processes of child development and how family, cultural, and individual factors may shape children's socioemotional development. When I left graduate school, conducting research and creating knowledge were my main goals. I came from a graduate program, one of the top five programs in the country (as defined by *US News and World Report*), that emphasized, above all else, basic research. Success in the program was defined mostly by two main criteria: publishing research and obtaining a tenure-track position at a research university. Students who left academia for applied positions in the corpo-

Finding Meaning in Civically Engaged Scholarship, pages 3–10
Copyright © 2009 by Information Age Publishing
All rights of reproduction in any form reserved.

rate world, or who obtained positions focusing on teaching, rather than research, were not viewed for being as successful as those with research positions.

It was in this context, with this socialization, that I arrived at the University of Utah as an assistant professor. I understood what it would take for me to be successful and planned to focus my attention on research. Although I still recognize the importance of understanding why one child shakes in fear whereas another reacts with laughter to a haunted house, I no longer view basic research as my sole, most important career goal. More and more, I find greater meaning in teaching and service to the larger community. Whereas I previously offered service-learning as an option in one of my courses, I have required it for the past several years. When I recently designed a new course, I included service-learning as an integral part. I cannot envision teaching the material any other way. This chapter represents my reflections on why and how my goals changed dramatically since arriving at the University of Utah 12 years ago.

WHAT HAPPENED?

A number of factors have influenced my shift in priorities. Not long after being at the University of Utah, I recognized that teaching mattered. During graduate school, I served as a teaching assistant and taught several classes as a way to finance my education, but these courses were not very rewarding (I was not a very skilled teacher), and I viewed them as a necessary part of an academic career. The message had always been that teaching would draw attention away from the important task of research. What surprised me was that, over time, I found my research less gratifying and meaningful relative to teaching. I often found research isolating, whereas teaching provided connections with students, both undergraduate and graduate, that I found rewarding.

Women tend to find meaning in relationships more so than in accomplishments (Krefting, 2003; Munn-Giddings, 1998), and this certainly applied to me. As I improved as a teacher, I found mentoring students satisfying and came to view it as an important part of my job, not just a task to be tolerated. Although teaching is often undervalued at research universities, as a woman, I found that relational activities were more compelling than a focus on individual research accomplishments (Krefting, 2003). My own experience mirrors research findings indicating that women in academia tend to focus more on collaboration as opposed to the competitive nature of individual achievement (Munn-Giddings, 1998).

CONCEPTS OF MERIT

As I prepared my materials for my pre-tenure reviews, I reflected on the fact that my own concept of merit did not match the University's concept of merit. Feminist critiques of merit suggest that definitions of merit reflecting individual success rather than shared collective endeavor and community emphasize more masculine than feminine traits (Lyon, 1995), and these critiques resonated with me. As part of our annual merit evaluation, the chair of our department (and dean) requires us to submit a number of "quality indicators." One "quality indicator" that our College (the College of Social and Behavioral Sciences) uses is the extent to which we publish our work independently. A faculty member who publishes articles alone receives a higher merit score (using their formula) than one who publishes with colleagues. This approach is counterintuitive to my own notions of merit and contradicts my sense of what it means to create new knowledge. I do my best work in collaboration with others. In assigning authorship, I want to acknowledge the graduate students and individuals with whom I have worked and who have contributed to the research. Furthermore, I don't like to "sell" my work. I also suffer from the "feminine modesty effect" (Berg, Stephan, & Dodson, 1981; Chrisler, 1998) that inhibits me from touting my own accomplishments to colleagues. Rather than promoting myself, it feels like boasting and makes me uncomfortable. However, this reluctance to self-promote puts me at a disadvantage in a setting in which reputation is an important part of merit (Bagihole & Goode, 2001).

Another quality indicator used by my College is a citation count, the number of people citing our research. In the process of defining my "quality," I conducted a citation count of the article of which I was most proud. I do not recall the exact number, but perhaps about 40 people had cited this particular article. This means that 40 other like-minded scientists in the field of developmental psychology have relied at least partially on my research. Is this sufficient to give my research meaning? Does this fit with my own definitions of success? Is this how I want to define myself? Is the most important impact I can make within the ivory tower? I increasingly find myself answering "no" or "I'm not sure" to these questions. The annual exercise of collecting data on "quality" indicators leads me to reflect on whether there might be a better way to reach people and make my career more meaningful. On the other hand, I still have the desire to succeed within the structure of the university, which is critical to keeping my job. Thus, despite some dissatisfaction with aspects of my position, I am unable to imagine myself working outside of academia. I choose to work within the boundaries of the narrow definitions of success provided, while at the same time, searching for other avenues to pursue meaning. I still conduct basic research; however, since receiving tenure, I have also felt the freedom to explore opportunities to increase my engagement with the larger community.

I do not want a citation count to be my measure of success; a better measure is whether you leave the world a better place. Success should be about improving our world, and helping the community. Service-learning is a way to connect with students and the community and succeed by touching real people's lives directly. I have come to believe that I will have a greater effect on children's well-being and development by serving children and their families and by reaching students, who will then serve their own children, and the children with whom they work. Over time, this ripple effect will have a larger impact on the community. Although many in academia would agree that service is less valued than research and teaching, and does not count much toward tenure, service-learning is an ideal way to provide community service in a way that fits with a merit system that rewards teaching. Service is often defined as service to the profession in terms of serving on committees, editorial boards, and governing bodies; however, service to the community is also important.

IMPORTANCE OF EFFECTIVE PEDAGOGY

Another shift in my attitude arose from my greater awareness of pedagogical theories. As I learned about ways to increase students' retention and understanding of course material, service-learning seemed a way to integrate many of the principles of effective teaching. One program that our University offers is called the University Teaching Assistant program, in which graduate students are mentored by faculty members to become prepared for teaching careers and to improve undergraduate education. I have mentored several graduate students in this program, and each time I learn more about pedagogical techniques as we critically examine the literature on pedagogy together. Mentoring graduate students in teaching also requires me to consciously consider the decisions that I make in my own teaching. Not only did these practices improve my teaching skills, they also increased my knowledge of the philosophy of learning (e.g., Dewey, 1916; Orlich, Harder, Callahan, & Gibson, 1998). As a result, I began to choose certain teaching strategies over others. The philosophy of learning based upon Dewey, Piaget, and others, suggests that students need to construct their knowledge out of personal experiences. Service-learning fits well with this approach because it involves putting the course concepts into action in context.

MOTHERHOOD AND ACADEMIA

Another factor that influenced me to reevaluate my priorities was that I had two children before I received tenure. Thinking about their future increased my desire for my work to have more of an immediate impact on my community, rather than a trickle down effect. The research on women in academia shows that women get tenure-track jobs at a lower rate than men, achieve tenure at a lower rate than men, and are less likely than men to become full professors (American Association of University Professors, 2001, 2004; Wolfinger, Mason, & Goulden, 2008). Contributing to this discrepancy is the difficulty women experience balancing a demanding career and motherhood, so that women with children are less likely to obtain tenure-track positions (Wolfinger et al., 2008). Also, the notion of "greedy institutions" applies: many institutions of higher education demand that women put in long hours and be constantly available and highly committed (Acker, 1983; Leonard & Malina, 1994; Munn-Giddings, 1998). I soon realized that it would be impossible to maintain a high publication rate without sacrificing my personal well-being or spending substantially less time with my children than I preferred. Furthermore, as I weighed the tradeoffs and compromises I had to make, my time became more valuable, and I wanted to ensure that I would use it wisely, in meaningful ways. Thus, at the same time that I felt increasing time demands inherent in raising young children, I also felt increased pressure to make my work count beyond the academy.

I faced another challenge related to time pressures. It was difficult for me to prioritize my needs, and my work, over the competing needs of others—students who needed advice, colleagues who wanted to meet, community members who asked for help addressing challenging social issues. These were important needs, and it seemed selfish to focus time on my scholarship. Other women (e.g., Simeone, 1987; Valian, 1985) have also reported a tension between being accessible to others and promoting one's own scholarship. Civic engagement may be an opportunity to merge these competing demands. Several of my colleagues in the Civically Engaged Scholar Cohort provide models for combining these competing demands. Service-learning is one solution to merging my own work with the needs of the community and students.

REDEFINING SUCCESS DURING THE POST-TENURE PERIOD

I received tenure in 2004, but also had a son who was born earlier that year, so I was in "survival" mode until recently. Consequently, I continued along the path that was already set for me, and that I was already following, because it was the path of least resistance. Doing anything else would have been too much of an effort. Gradually, however, I had more time to actually consider my future goals. In 2005, I had a semester sabbatical, and part of that time was spent reflecting on the question, "What now?" I had received tenure, which had been my focus since I obtained my position as an assistant professor. Finally, I had arrived at a place where I could have more say in the direction my work took and pursue directions that were more meaningful.

Soon after, I attended a Utah Campus Compact conference, which I found incredibly affirming and invigorating. I also became involved in the Civically Engaged Scholar Cohort, the group whose work is represented in this volume. These involvements excited and inspired me at a time, after receiving tenure, that I was questioning whether the sacrifices I had made to achieve tenure were worthwhile, and at a time I was feeling burned out. The timing was perfect, and my involvement with the CESC has been a great experience. My colleagues have shown me alternative paths and routes to success. I admire them greatly and consider them successful, and they have provided me models for how I might achieve a professional identity that fits with my own priorities and values.

Since my involvement in the Civically Engaged Scholar Cohort, I have become increasingly involved in community issues. For example, I developed another service-learning course, and am conducting research that should have more immediate impact on the community where I am working. In connection with my new course, *Parenting Across Cultures*, I created partnerships with University Neighborhood Partners, which other authors in this book also mention. University Neighborhood Partners (UNP) links the University of Utah with seven ethnically and culturally diverse Salt Lake City neighborhoods to create pathways to higher education and address barriers to college attendance, e.g., race, ethnicity, and geography. In one UNP program, the Community Advocate Training Program, my students and I worked with parents to help them advocate for their children's education. We met with a group of parents met once per month on Saturdays for a semester to provide parents with the resources they needed to help their child be successful in school. When parents had questions that weren't answered, students in the class researched the issues and presented what they had found at the following meeting. In another program with UNP, the Family Financial Planning Program, my students provided individualized family financial planning for parents, tailoring the curriculum to the needs and interests of the family. Both of these programs served recent immigrants and fit well with my new course.

My next endeavor will to become engaged in applied research which addresses needs of parents and children in my community. Previously, I was never able to imagine what that research would look like; however, as I become more involved in the community, I gain a better understanding of the types of research that can benefit the community directly. Furthermore, I see that this research can be of high quality and publishable in academic journals, in addition to addressing community needs. Completing this type of research will enable me to bridge the areas of teaching, service, and research on which I am evaluated within my department, College, and the larger University.

CONCLUSION

Although basic ivory tower research can be powerful in shaping people's lives, a direct connection between basic research and the larger community may or may not be present. When that connection is weak, the effects or benefits for the community may take much longer to materialize. Certainly, understanding issues of basic child development is critical to improving children's lives, but I recognize that my research is one small drop in a huge sea of information. Recognizing the importance of teaching, and gaining a better understanding of pedagogy, as well as becoming a mother and achieving tenure, have all motivated me to pursue civically engaged scholarship. As a result, my connection to the community is stronger, and the benefits on both sides of the relationship are more tangible and rewarding.

REFERENCES

Acker, S. (1983). Women, the other academics. *Women Studies International Forum, 6,* 191–201.

American Association of University Professors. (2001). Statement of principles on family responsibilities and academic work. Retrieved 7-7-08 from http://www.aaup.org/AAUP/pubsres/policydocs/contents/workfam-stmt.htm

American Association of University Professors. (2004). Faculty salary and faculty distribution fact sheet. Retrieved 7-7-08 from http://www.aaup.org/AAUP/pubsres/research/2003-04factsheet.htm

Bagihole, B., & Goode, J. (2001). The contradiction of the myth of individual merit, and the reality of a patriarchal support system in academic careers: A feminist investigation. *European Journal of Women's Studies, 8,* 161–180.

Berg, J. H., Stephan, W. G., & Dodson, M. (1981). Attributional modesty in women. *Psychology of Women Quarterly, 5,* 711–727.

Chrisler, J. C. (1998). Teacher versus scholar: Role conflict for women? In L. H. Collins, J. C. Chrisler, & K. Quina (Eds.), *Career strategies for women in academe: Arming Athena* (pp. 107–127). Thousand Oaks, CA: Sage.

Dewey, J. (1916). *Democracy and education.* New York: The Free Press.

Gunew, S. (1990). (Ed). *Feminist knowledge: Critique and construct.* London: Routledge.

Krefting, L. A. (2003). Intertwined discourses of merit and gender: Evidence from academic employment in the USA. *Gender, Work and Organization, 10,* 260–278.

Leonard, D., & Malina, D. (1994). Caught between two worlds: Mothers as academics. In S. Davies, C. Lubelska, & J. Quinn (Eds.), *Changing the subject: Women in higher education* (pp. 29–41). London: Taylor and Francis.

Lyon, K. (1995). The trouble with equal opportunities: The case of women academics. *Gender & Education, 7,* 51–68.

Martin, J. R. (2000). *Coming of age in academe.* New York: Routledge.

Munn-Giddings, C. (1998). Mixing motherhood and academia—a lethal cocktail. In Malina, D. & Malin-Prothero, S. (Eds.) *Surviving the academy: Feminist perspectives* (pp. 56–68). London: Routledge.

Nussbaum, M. (1997). *Cultivating humanity.* Cambridge, MA: Harvard University Press.

Orlich, D. C., Harder, R.J., Callahan, R. C., & Gibson, H. W. (1998). *Teaching strategies: A guide to better instruction.* Boston: Houghton Mifflin.

Simeone, A. (1987). *Academic women: Working toward equality.* South Hadley, MA: Bergin & Garvey.

Tierney, W. G., & Bensimon, E. M. (1996). *Promotion and tenure: Community and socialization in academe.* Albany: State University of New York Press.

Tierney, W. G., & Rhoads, R. A. (1993). *Enhancing promotion, tenure and beyond: Faculty socialization as a cultural process.* ASHE-ERIC Higher Education Report No. 93-6. Washington, DC: The George Washington University.

Valian, V. (1985). Solving a work problem. In M. F. Fox (Ed.), *Scholarly writing and publishing: Issues, problems, and solutions* (pp. 99–110). Boulder, CO: Westview.

Wolfinger, N. H., Mason, M. A., & Goulden, M. (2008). Problems in the pipeline: Gender, marriage, and fertility in the Ivory Tower. *The Journal of Higher Education, 79,* 388–405.

CHAPTER 2

FROM SERVICE FOR MEANING TO MEANINGFUL SERVICE

Maged Senbel

Community-based scholarship is my tether to global responsibility. Teaching and research that are embedded in the expressed concerns of underserved communities bring me a tangible gratification that my work can be of service. In a discipline that is charged with generating practical solutions to intractable urban problems that plague our cities, the opportunity to interface directly with the people suffering most acutely brings respite from the seeming insurmountablility of our burden. Without this respite our work often loses meaning. But moving beyond service as a source of meaning for myself and my students, to service that makes meaningful contributions to people's lives requires ethical reflection and careful action.

The potential for my research to build knowledge that may in some way play a role in advancing environmental and social justice is an important motivator for me as an academic. But these contributions are abstract, ephemeral, and uncertain. Teaching new generations of professional planners often seems a few too many steps removed from making a positive contribution to the lives of those without the privilege of material wealth. These

Finding Meaning in Civically Engaged Scholarship, pages 11–19

words on this page, the job that gives me the time and space to write them, and the discourse that they may generate, all occupy a space of privilege that is wholly foreign to the majority of the earth's inhabitants. The experiential distance between those who benefit from globalization and wealth creation, and those who do not, belies our mutual destiny as co-inhabitants of an intertwined, finite global community. Community-based teaching and research have the capacity to bridge this distance. We learn more about the experience of being without the privileges that we enjoy and in the process our work feels like it may make a difference; it has more meaning.

URBAN PLANNING: A TRADITION OF SERVICE LEARNING

The experience of community-based learning is also consistent with the established learning outcomes of urban planning professional programs (Hardin, 2006; Hoyt, 2006; Schaffer, Paris, & Vogel, 2003). Students connect with segments of society that they must better understand if they are ever to uphold the pluralistic values of their chosen profession (Beamish, 2006). My courses place students in settings where they can practice facilitating the engagement of diverse individuals in neighborhood design, development, and visioning processes. This is a necessary skill that they will need as professional planners working in either the private or public sectors.

Service-learning, of course, is intended to help communities directly benefit from the time, energy, and initiative of young minds applying their new ideas to problems in nearby communities (Forsyth, Lu, & McGirr, 2000). Most often the arena of action is the physical and social space of a partner organization. Students interact with community residents through the services provided by the partner organizations. In planning and architecture service-learning courses, however, students often provide an independent, partial professional service in collaboration with a community partner (Beamish, 2006; Hardin, 2006). The community partner in these cases acts as a facilitator of access into the community and as the body providing continuity from one course to the next (Beamish, 2006; Hoyt, 2006). Students and their faculty supervisors provide a scope of services that their community partners do not have the capacity to undertake. These services range from highly technical design and construction services, exemplified by the Rural Studio in Alabama (Oppenheimer, Dean, & Hursley, 2005), to community design facilitation exemplified by Anne Forsyth's work (Forsyth et al., 2000; Forsyth & Musacchio, 2005). My own work resembles the latter in that I seek to involve diverse groups of community residents in envisioning, articulating, and graphically representing their collective concerns and aspirations. Two ethical dilemmas arise from this position: are we knowingly creating a condition of raised and failed expectations as we implore community residents to join the cause of participatory design; and, is the value of participatory visioning of neighborhood designs imposed on the communities we work in? These questions resonate powerfully for me as impediments to my enthusiastic support of community service-learning. My own story of engagement reveals an epistemology that is sometimes at odds with the application of normative planning trends in community-based scholarship.

A MENTOR BY EXAMPLE

I first became aware of the idea of community-based scholarship through the words of a wise, humble, and perpetually curious professor. He was captivating. He had a presence that mesmerized his students and made them reluctant to interrupt his orations lest they lose their reference point in the territory of thought that he laid before them. His delivery blended intellect and emotion with humility and genuine curiosity. He was completely devoid of the common posturing to appear scholarly, and seemed oblivious to the norm of self-promotion required of promotion-seeking faculty. We recognized him as a rare and precious presence at a top-tier university. So, when he spoke of poverty alleviation we were not concerned with the seeming futility of his efforts. We were fascinated by the power of his convictions. We listened and marveled at how he passionately and compassionately wove together Marxist theory with transportation economics, decision analysis, and social responsibility.

Although he had a successful academic career with prestigious teaching awards and grant funding worth many millions of dollars, he always came across as an antiestablishment maverick. His interests took him from community economic development to Native American development to international poverty alleviation. We knew him as someone who was never concerned with publishing because he saw it as a distraction from his primary focus of helping the disadvantaged. Peer-reviewed publications, we mused, would only serve institutions and peers who are already abundantly privileged, and not the poor people served by his projects. In our youthful idealism we failed to recognize that the peer review process would have allowed his peers to learn from his work and to expand on his efforts in countless other developing countries.

When he characterized the university as a privileged citizen that has failed in its civic responsibilities, we, his students, were enthralled. He characterized the university as an institution that increasingly favors corporate enterprise and profit-generating disciplines over the unfettered pursuit of knowledge. Instead of seeking to aid the underprivileged, universities had chosen to focus on recreating and reaffirming power and privilege in society. His message resonated with what drew me to teaching and to writing in the first place. I had a deep desire to serve. Time and time again I have come to understand that without service my work has no meaning, for me.

Over the years, as I moved on to do a Ph.D. and later to return as a member of the faculty, all at the same school, I came to realize that this professor was far more complex in his work than we had realized. He was far too published and successful in a traditional academic setting to be defined as an academic maverick. Yet the idea outlasted the reality. I remain captivated, intrigued, and inspired by this ethic of serving the marginalized, even when it comes at a personal cost.

MY DISCIPLINARY JOURNEY

Born into a family of architects, I enjoyed countless upper-middle class privileges. Some leave me tethered to a lifestyle that I know to be unjust in its appropriation of more than my share of global resources. Other privileges brought me awareness, through extensive international travel, of my relative prosperity compared to the majority of the world's inhabitants. This is how I came to know myself as a citizen of the world. I now spend my time in this world timidly knowing that I owe a great debt to those upon whom my lifestyle treads.

Yet, somehow, my choice to go to architecture school was born out of complete self-interest. I set out to direct my love of physics, mathematics, art, and literature toward creating memorable, poetic architecture. Architecture was all about refining the congruence of human achievement to create spaces that moved people, that inspired them, that caused them to gaze in awe. That was my dream. I hadn't yet graduated when it started to feel like a vacuous dream. I grew to be repulsed by the thought of dedicating my life to creating monuments to my own ego and the egos of those who already have more than they need. What seemed like a narcissistic pursuit gave way to an awakening consciousness about social and environmental justice. The pursuit of solutions that seek to alleviate the oppression of conspicuous consumption increasingly became the only way I could imagine having a career in architecture.

My path shifted and diverged as I did a Master's in Affordable Housing with research focused on mechanisms for making suburbs less consumptive. I then worked for the only First Nations—Native American—architect in British Columbia at the time. His practice combined community development with architectural services. I came to appreciate the challenges and rewards of working with a committee and, in some cases, the entire community as a client. The capacity of participatory design to express a community's values and aspirations became increasingly clear to me. Years later, I would try to recreate this expression in my service-learning courses.

While there were some minor exceptions left over from 1970 environmentalism, mainstream architectural discourse in the nineties lacked any ecological perspective in the design and construction of buildings. Resource and waste flows were poorly understood and rarely discussed by architects. I therefore chose to migrate to the larger scale, broader scope, and deeper consciousness of urban planning. I sought to reconcile our scientific understanding of finite resources with our seemingly indifferent patterns of urban development. More graduate work and a growing interest in teaching led me to my first academic appointment at the University of Utah and service teaching through the Westside Studio (see Chapter 11, this volume).

The Westside Studio was a lucky break. I didn't seek it out, not intentionally. A couple of months after I was offered the job at Utah, which was also a couple of months before I was to begin my appointment, I attended a faculty retreat at the College of Architecture + Planning. Our Dean had just hired five new faculty and flew us out to the College's annual end-of-year retreat to get us acquainted with the program. Upon mention of the idea of the Westside Studio by the Dean, I simply praised it. I spoke of the great potential it held for bringing together the cultures of architecture and planning. Minutes after the retreat the Dean passed on to me the responsibility of launching, teaching, and administering the Westside Studio. In my newly hired, ABD, wanting-to-prove-myself excitement, I was delighted. It matched my interests and my values, and I saw it as a great opportunity to bring together the two areas of expertise that I had never had the opportunity to combine, architecture and planning. I was to make my mark at the school as a bridge builder and would do so while taking students outside of their comfort zone to work in underprivileged areas.

THE POWER OF ACADEMIC PRIORITIES

What I did not admit to myself at the time was that I, too, would have to step out of my comfort zone. As the following months would prove, I had a lot of learning to do. Only now, after having run the Westside Studio for three years, do I have a sense of what can reasonably be accomplished and how and with whom. Also now, ironically, I have left. I honestly feel that I am the one who benefitted the most from this entire endeavor. I was honored with a Public Service Professorship as a result of this work and my plans for its evolution, and was awarded the Professor of the Year award for 2005–2006 at the College of Architecture + Planning. All of this contributed to my credentials and I was hired back by the institution at which I earned my doctorate. This academic transience, whether through an individual's relocation or through a realignment of institutional priorities, is a significant impediment to building trust and creating mutually beneficial community-university partnerships. Cultivating a long-term relationship with community partners is critical to both the capacity of students to engage in meaningful work, and for community partners to safe in their investment of time and energy (Chapdelaine, Ruiz, Warchal, & Wells, 2005; Forsyth et al., 2000; Hoyt, 2006).

Contrary to the mythical ideal we imagined our noble professor to have upheld, academics need to pay attention to the demands of the academy if they are to retain the privilege of teaching and applying pedagogical resources to community needs. My own priorities have to coincide, to some extent, with those of the director of my school and my dean. I am fortunate in that I have their full support in the teaching and research that I am currently engaged in but this may not last. If it stops, I have to take heed and will necessarily have to withdraw from the community. My position is therefore one of relative detachment. Unlike the constituents with whom I work, I can leave. Even if I don't want to, I can, and would choose to do so if my job demanded it. In the case of my recent move, my position of privilege allowed me to accept a job that took me to another country.

It so happened that the Westside Studio closed shop independently from my leaving. My last task before leaving was to vacate the storefront that we had occupied, but the decision to terminate our tenancy predated my departure. It had more to do with the adequacy and affordability of the space. For a while, the College's commitment to hire someone to replace me who would maintain a presence on the Westside seemed to waver, but that is no longer the case. To my great delight they hired one of the contributing authors to this volume, Dr. Caitlin Cahill, to take the helm of community-based scholarship on the Westside.

IMPOSING PARTICIPATION

Let us now return to the aforementioned ethical dilemmas of building false expectations and imposing a foreign norm of participatory design. One of the most compelling reasons for service-learning in urban planning is the opportunity to practice working with multicultural communities in pluralistic settings. Working with diverse constituents is a necessary skill for today's professional planners (Sandercock, 2000). We teach this value in our classrooms but, without the opportunity to practice it while in school, students will likely revert to old methods of top-down planning once in professional practice (Sandercock, 1998, 2003). Without modeling engagement in service courses we risk relegating participatory planning to the realm of idealistic academic fantasy. Service-learning that combines planning theories of communicative deliberation and participatory design with real communities enables students to practice public engagement in a relatively safe setting (Forsyth et al., 2000). In the Westside Studio we modeled processes that are inclusive of all residents regardless of their ethnicity, gender, culture, profession, income level, literacy level, religion, age, or marital status. Because our projects were deliberately exploratory and designed to bring out community issues, they were manageable processes for students to facilitate. Later, as professionals, the students will have to balance competing interests surrounding contentious decisions involving multiple stakeholders. The stakes will be higher and tempers will be more acute, so practicing their facilitation skills in a service-learning environment is invaluable.

Urban planning prides itself in its pursuit of equity in the allocation of public resources. Within this broad mandate the Westside Studio was physically situated in Salt Lake City's most diverse neighborhood working to help marginalized people. We worked on real issues with passionate and committed students. The stage was set for deep service and the requisite promotional narratives of the University's heroic transformations of deserving underserved communities. Yet it felt somewhat dishonest. We cultivated dreams that we knew we could not follow up on. Not the faculty's dreams, but those of the community residents.

We surveyed the community, we questioned them, and we canvassed aggressively to get them to come out to community design workshops. We asked them to imagine and envision and with them we drew up plans of new improved neighborhoods, but we knew that there was no budget for these plans. Our intent, of course, was not to deliberately deceive, but rather to present an alternative vision of the neighborhood that included resident aspirations. We deliberately created the possibility of change in order to foster participation. Participation was not meaningless. The residents' contributions created a more nuanced understanding of the community and its diverse and varied needs, and eventually perhaps, will lead to improved services and amenities.

As I reflect back, I continue to believe that resident participation in the development of plans is important, but I also think we owe it to the residents to better explain the planning process and the manner in which their ideas may come to affect city policy, if at all. We spent a great deal of time and energy courting them to come out to workshop events. We also carefully crafted the workshop experience with catered dinners and a warm welcoming atmosphere, but we neglected to situate the activity in the larger politics of local government.

BALANCING THE TRADEOFFS

The Westside Studio undoubtedly served my students more than lecture courses would have. They gained facility working with diverse groups in a variety of settings. Every city in North America has become so multicultural that its diversity continuously stretches its planners' capacity to work with difference. Urban planners desperately need skills that enable them to work across different cultures and with different groups. Yet, because the imperative of participation does not come from any community partner's mandate, but from our own canons of progressive planning theory (Forester, 1989, 1999; Healey, 1997; Sandercock, 2003), I wonder if our efforts are but another incarnation of colonial intrusion. Are we imposing our values of participation on communities that would rather focus their energies elsewhere?

The answers to questions of misinformation and imposition are troubling enough to cause us pause in our unrestrained enthusiasm for participatory processes. The manner and method of engaging communities requires deep reflection and honest inquiry. So, while I personally rely on community-based scholarship to give my own work meaning, I am extremely wary of the claim that service-learning for participatory neighborhood design is meaningful for community residents. The benefit has not been mutual, and it certainly should be.

REFERENCES

Beamish, A. (2006). Service-learning in Texas colonias. In M. C. Hardin, R. Eribes, & C. Poster (Eds.), *From the studio to the streets: Service-learning in planning and architecture* (pp. 171–186). Sterling, VA: Stylus Publishing.

Chapdelaine, A., Ruiz, A., Warchal, J., & Wells, C. (2005). *Service-learning code of ethics.* Bolton, MA: Anker Publishing Company, Inc.

Forester, J. (1989). *Planning in the face of power.* Berkeley: University of California Press.

Forester, J. (1999). *The deliberative practitioner: Encouraging participatory planning processes.* Cambridge, MA: The MIT Press.

Forsyth, A., Lu, H., & McGirr, P. (2000). Service-learning in an urban context: Implications for planning and design education. *Journal of Architectural and Planning Research, 17,* 236–259.

Forsyth, A., & Mucacchio, L. R. (2005). *Designing small parks: A manual for addressing social and ecological concerns.* Hoboken, NJ: John Wiley & Sons, Inc.

Hardin, M. C. (2006). Research as ethical practice: When academic goals align with community needs. In M. C. Hardin, R. Eribes, & C. Poster (Eds.), *From the studio to the streets: Service-learning in planning and architecture* (pp. 59–76). Sterling, VA: Stylus Publishing.

Healey, P. (1997). *Collaborative planning: Shaping places in fragmented societies.* Vancouver, BC: UBC Press.

Hoyt, L. M. (2006). A core commitment to service-learning: Bridging planning theory and practice. In M. C. Hardin, R. Eribes, & C. Poster (Eds.), *From the studio to the streets: Service-learning in planning and architecture.* Sterling, VA: Stylus Publishing.

Oppenheimer Dean, A., & Hursley, T. (2005). *Proceed and be bold: Rural studio after Samuel Mockbee.* New York: Princeton Architectural Press.

Sandercock, L. (1998). *Towards cosmopolis.* Chichester: John Wiley and Sons.

Sandercock, L. (2000). When strangers become neighbours: Managing cities of difference. *Planning Theory and Practice, 1,* 13–30.

Sandercock, L. (2003). *Cosmopolis II: Mongrel cities in the 21st century.* London: Continuum.

Schaffer, M. A., Paris, J. W., & Vogel, K. (2003). Ethical relationships in service-learning partnerships. In J. Eyler & S.H. Billig (Eds.) *Deconstructing service-learning : Research exploring context* (pp. 147–166). Greenwich, CT: Information Age Publishing.

CHAPTER 3

THE SEARCH
FOR AUTHENTIC CITIZENSHIP

Luke Garrott

JITTERS ON THE BRIDGE

As I sit down to write, I worry that I've offended one of my community partners in an email last week. I suggested a different course of action to get our community festival project started (this will be its third year in a row), and I haven't heard back from him. No, we shouldn't be deciding the theme of the event this early! I tried to stall him in order to widen the number of partners on board. He seems to have gotten annoyed.

As I saw it, the moment was a crucial fork in the road we were building. Hold it—that's the wrong metaphor, "fork in the road." Because we were making the road as we walked, this moment was a choice of which terrain to travel and how wide to build the road.

At the risk of overdramatizing, this was also a key moment in democracy. While this neighborhood citizen and I shared common characteristics such as gender, class, and ethnicity, the forces separating us were also manifest. Both native-born Americans, we nevertheless came from very different "schools of democracy." This was Alexis de Tocqueville's term for the various settings in which Americans learned their civic skills—professional associations, avocational groups, and, most frequently, religious organizations.

Finding Meaning in Civically Engaged Scholarship, pages 21–27
Copyright © 2009 by Information Age Publishing
21

Here were two citizens, each with his special skills and stocks of social capital, engaged in a common purpose, abruptly stalled over the means to achieve their ends. Had I pushed my participatory ideals too far? Here were two styles of leadership: my laid-back, horizontal, cooperative vibe trying to engage his vertical, patriarchal, traditional authority. I fretted that I had jumped too far, pushed too much.

HOW DID I GET HERE, ANYWAY?

Could I have traveled farther from the comforts of the calm, controlled classroom? Not only that, but I was way out of my area of expertise. As a Ph.D. in political theory, I was determined to share with the world the brilliance of my increasingly rarified sub-discipline. So I had no choice but to risk it "out in the community." After finishing my dissertation, I had entered into a non-traditional role at a "Research 1" institution: a lecturer, with an increased teaching load and no publishing responsibilities. This was a non-tenure track job, of course. I served at the pleasure of my department and field committee chairs, on yearly contracts. What I lost in job security, I convinced myself, I gained in freedom.

I styled myself as a popularizer, trying to make political theory matter to undergraduates. I also wanted more for my students than book learning, regurgitating for exams, and forgetting soon thereafter. If students were going to learn *anything*, it would have to be *from* and *for themselves*. This wasn't a simple capitulation to the individualistic ethos of contemporary American society. Sure, I needed to "know my audience," making my courses appeal to their consumerized preferences. But there was more. All those hours on the receiving end of traditional education taught me that, yes, class readings, lectures, and discussions crucially inform students. However, for the information to impact students' individual journeys, the knowledge would have to be made real. It would have to be largely experiential, a dialectic linking past knowledge and present class content.

It needs to be emphasized: service-learning is not different *in kind* from traditional university pedagogy. Rather, engaged learning (my preferred term) is a natural extension of the classroom. This was the truth I gradually discerned as I thought about improving the quality of my teaching. There may be something inherently virtuous about studying the history of political thought and knowing, say, Rousseau's vision of the social contract or Rawls' principles of justice. But unless understanding these philosophers makes a difference in the student's life, I became convinced, I was failing as a pedagogue.

Like most of us, I came out of graduate school with a professional compass. Mine is a jury-rigged contraption fashioned from the philosophers most important to me: Charles Taylor, John Dewey, Martin Heidegger, and John Stuart Mill. They had helped me make sense of my dissertation question: How can one be true to oneself—authentic—given that one is beholden to ways of being in the world (ideologies) that one does not create? I knew that humans were largely social beings, Aristotle's *zoon politikon*, political animals. It wasn't a large leap to extend my interest in personal authenticity to the political realm. What does it take for a community to be authentic? At the risk of sounding passé to postmodern ears, Dewey (1927) summed it up pretty well in *The Public and Its Problems*: "Democracy is the idea of community life itself."

It was the realization that this normative commitment was at the heart of my academic work that built the bridge to service-learning. I had three goals in creating my course, "Neighborhood Democracy": teach students something about community, about democracy, and about citizenship. Rather than just lecturing and assigning readings on these topics, I would approach their learning through service to the community. To enable a student to access each of these concepts through service-learning is to change the medium of the message. Instead of indoctrinating my students in an ideology of civic engagement, I would lead them in a process of discovery of *authentic citizenship*. In a pluralistic democracy, there is no one correct way to be civically engaged. We are free to choose how to be citizens. Despite the traditional admonishments of democrats to nonparticipants, I understand that there are multiple, even private, ways of contributing to the common weal. Thus, I see my pedagogical task as enabling more informed and reflective citizens, however they may define themselves.

As a service-learning course, Neighborhood Democracy engages 20 students a year (60 total to present) who study in the classroom different facets of democracy—democratic theory, leadership, neighborhood councils, community development and organizing. In the field, they, with community partners, plan and carry out a community-building activity. Notable among the first two years of the class were the Rose Park Community Festival, an inclusive celebration of the northwest neighborhood of Rose Park, and a door-to-door neighborhood survey that gave substantive feedback to multiple community councils about their constituencies. Currently (2008), students are conducting a history project of neighborhood improvement in Salt Lake City, interviewing present and past participants in neighborhood councils and community organizations, collecting documents, adding to public archives, and producing a report of their efforts in print. Students are also helping to produce a documentary film around the themes of leadership and the heyday of the Salt Lake Association of Community Councils (SLACC) in the 1970s and '80s.

How better to teach students about citizenship than to have them not only see it up close, but work together with neighborhood citizens as partners in a community project? Here is politics that is not professionalized, politics where the "mail-order membership" organizations haven't taken over. How else could I have taught students that citizenship is more than check-writing? In Neighborhood Democracy, form and content conspire to offer students the real stuff of democracy—the feel, the smell, the *frisson*—where the challenges of bridging differences with community partners are precisely the work of citizens building democracy.

Despite all the differences that separated my community partner and me, we were committed to an ethic of citizenship. He was a retired Army colonel who returned to professional civilian life as a high school teacher, finishing his career in administration for the State Board of Education. In retirement he has served on the neighborhood council for years, a nearly full-time volunteer. Students work with him and the other members of the neighborhood council to design a project that will benefit the council, while providing students insight into neighborhood democracy.

HOW I GOT HERE: THE ACTIVIST JOURNEY

Born and raised in middle-class suburbia by schoolteachers, I was fortunate enough to be socialized into the practice of voting as civic duty. Catching the political bug at age 17, my undergraduate and graduate schooling was punctuated by progressive political activism. Fieldwork opportunities in Mexico as an undergraduate led to an honors thesis on the mainstreaming of the Mexican communist party and master's studies on the politics of land settlement in the Lacandona rainforest near Guatemala. Then halfway through grad school I discovered political theory.

Party politics in the U.S. had never excited me. In fact, it was the banality of the two-party system that probably drove me to look over the border for something interesting. My parents had never been partisans; registered independents, they modeled political involvement by voting and being active in the teachers' union. I registered to vote when I was away from home, and my first election was the Democratic primary for President in California in 1988. I enthusiastically voted for Jesse Jackson.

Yet electoral politics was disappointing because it offered so little action and so much spectatorship. The action seemed so far away, the dialogue so limited, the real questions never raised. Where was the attention to issues that really mattered to people, like the union politics I saw among Mexican peasants? Digging deeper into academic culture as I focused on my doctorate, I drifted farther away from local political engagement. I remember only speaking once at a City Commission meeting in Gainesville, Florida, the site of my graduate studies, in favor of continuing to allow flyers on city utility poles. As a bass player in a noise band and a frequenter of poetry readings, I knew how important these "poor man's billboards" were to local democratic culture. But my political attention was elsewhere. The only real solutions seemed theoretical and revolutionary.

My move to Salt Lake, marriage, and university employment have mellowed me. In response to a holiday card from my wife Jen and me announcing the purchase of our first home, a dear high school friend wrote, "Congrats on completing your embourgeoisement." Yes, the move to the landed middle class had made a difference. Concurrent with a personal ideology shift from revolutionism to reformism, spending time in any one place made we want to improve it. As I told students who insisted and dreamed on revolution, "Either you start stockpiling weapons or get involved in positive change."

At the last apartment we lived in, I took some steps as a neighborhood citizen, occasionally attending "community council" meetings, getting to know as many of my neighbors as possible, paying a little attention to city politics. Salt Lake had an activist mayor who championed minority causes in conservative Utah and inspired a lot of people like myself. National politics wasn't even that bad in the pre-Bush era. With the barbarism of the war in Iraq, I saw community action on the local level as progress' only chance.

My activist journey was given a great boost when the idea of combining the teaching of democratic theory and service-learning occurred to me. Under the auspices of the Lowell Bennion Community Service Center at the University of Utah, opportunities for service-learning gave me the perfect outlet for my local improvement impulses. At the time I was searching to expand my community activism, Utah made a significant institutional commitment to build bridges to "the community," with a specific focus on the west side of Salt Lake.

The University of Utah resides high up on the east side of the city, and the spatial orientation reflects its socioeconomic and cultural reputation. The west side is known for its working-class ethos and cultural diversity. University Neighborhood Partners (UNP), created in 2002, dramatically increased the opportunities for civically engaged pedagogy, among other important missions, such as increasing the number of westside and minority students who attend the university. I was willingly swept into engaged pedagogy by the confluence of support from both the Bennion Center and UNP.

This development of my professional mission may reflect my suspicion of, and boredom with, ideological electoral politics. The "authentic citizenship" that I seek to instill in students is transcendent of ideology, for it recognizes all sorts of models of citizenship and state-society relations. It is *engagement* that I advocate. It is up to each student to choose his/her unique mode of citizenship. As an instructor I can help them discern the policy options that different ideologies offer their chosen issues of concern. Constantly in the background, however, is the notion that democracy trumps all. My activist, ethical commitment is to the regime that engages the plural voices of the citizenry. In this context, democracy is less of an ideology and more of a regime, an umbrella under which different ideologies interact in a marketplace of ideas that, ideally, advances the public good.

IF THE HAT FITS...

All that said, I recently entered the ideological fray as an elected official. I ran as a Democrat, even though the seat is technically nonpartisan. I'm not sure why I chose to run for City Council to represent downtown Salt Lake, except I saw it as a logical extension of my neighborhood improvement impulses and an opportunity to expand my activism to another realm. I hope I can wear these two hats, the political activist and the engaged pedagogue, with credibility. I already know that by taking office I am sacrificing some important opportunities at school.

Explicitly, politics is a turn away from publishing, one that I made several years ago. With the manifest opportunities for community-based research at the University of Utah, this was a difficult decision. But as a lecturer, my retention isn't predicated on publishing, so the decision to seek public office was relatively low risk. Other complications, somewhat anticipated, are also emerging. Over the choice of routes for a light-rail train in downtown Salt Lake City, I have come into open political conflict with current and former community partners. As I write, our community friendship is under severe strain, and it was my conscious choice to do what I think is best for my district and the city as a whole, in conflict with a position taken by a coalition of westside community councils. I hope that our partnerships can continue despite what might be considered political disloyalty.

This past weekend was the fourth installment of the Rose Park Community Festival, a full year and a half since the anecdote that opened this chapter, and it was a great success. The students were as hard working and enthusiastic as ever, and new community members came forward to participate. There were new co-chairs for the festival, one of whom is a former student of the Neighborhood Democracy class who moved into the neighborhood. There is another veteran of the class who sits on the executive committee of the community council and was on the festival's organizing committee. The festival has real staying power now, and the neighborhood is increasingly taking more ownership of it. Yes, they will still need the students, but local capacity and pride are certainly expanding.

And what about the drama with my community partner so long ago? Obviously, it wasn't as consequential as I thought in the heat of the moment. At this point, I can't even remember how it resolved itself. Better change the introduction, the inner editor tells me. But then I remember why I chose to lead with my anxiety over offending a community partner. If I've learned anything about participatory democracy in my role as an engaged pedagogue, it's the importance of the daily, little disciplines, like following up with a call to a seemingly annoyed community partner. Building bridges means persevering through the disquietude of stepping outside of one's "community comfort zone." Often, it is sincere effort that makes all the difference.

REFERENCES

Dewey, J. (1927). *The public and its problems.* New York: Henry Holt and Company.

CHAPTER 4

THE KNOCK ON THE DOOR

Marshall Welch

It began with a knock on my office door. I could not have imagined that day how this singular moment would change my professional and personal life. The student stood there in the doorway asking me if I had a moment to chat with him and apologized that he had not made an appointment. Looking back, I seem to recall this was a bit of an intrusion and interruption. After all, I was an academician busy creating new knowledge. I had, by all professional benchmarks, "arrived." Over the course of a few years, I had successfully embarked on the quest for tenure and promotion. My course evaluations consistently had high student ratings. I was asked to serve on students' graduate committees. Annually I had anywhere from two to four publications in refereed journals. I had published a textbook and procured more than a million dollars in extramural funding. Not only was I getting presentation proposals accepted for national conferences, I was beginning to be invited to make keynote presentations and serve on discussion panels. My reputation and prominence were emerging within my field as I was courted to serve on this advisory board and that. Eventually, the ultimate accomplishment was becoming department chair. My colleagues would flatter me during their visits to my office encouraging me to "step up" as I was "heir apparent" to this leadership role. Yes, by all indicators, I had succeeded. I had done all the "right things." Yet somehow, I felt like something

Finding Meaning in Civically Engaged Scholarship, pages 29–37
Copyright © 2009 by Information Age Publishing
All rights of reproduction in any form reserved.

was lacking. And now, here was this unknown student at my door, seeking my assistance.

I shook his hand as he introduced himself and I offered him a seat. He said he wanted to do a service-learning project with junior high students who had learning disabilities and that someone had referred him to me since this was my area of scholarship in special education. I replied, "Well then, what's this service-learning thing you're talking about?" And that was how it all started. I had no idea I had entered a teaching and learning moment in which the roles would be reversed. Over the course of the next semester, I would learn more from this student than he would ever learn from me.

TEACHING INSIDE THE BOX

Up to this point, the courses I taught were designed for pre-professionals earning their teaching certificate in special education. Due to a critical teaching shortage in special education, school districts quite literally were hiring people off the streets if they were admitted to and completed a teacher education program. Consequently, the vast majority of my students came into the class viewing it as a "hoop" to jump through to get a paycheck. Additionally, they were teaching full-time in challenging settings with next to no skills. They were tired and frustrated. Because they were in survival mode, their instructional objectives were essentially twofold: (1) what can you teach me that I can use tomorrow in my classroom? and (2) what is going to be on the test so I can pass and earn my teaching certificate? These students' tacit expectation was, "I will pay my tuition for you to take a can opener, open up my head, deposit the information that I need, and I will repeat back to you on an assignment or exam to get an 'A' to complete the course." I used to hold students in contempt for this mindset, but I don't anymore. Rather than blame them, I came to realize that I and the professoriate in general were complicit in this whole agreement of how to teach and learn. We, as faculty, have essentially socialized students to expect this.

Moreover, the state and national accreditation bodies had laid out "competencies" that determined course content. While these external bodies had not dictated *how* to teach the content, the curriculum was essentially set, and students were expected to demonstrate mastery of the skills during field-based education such as student teaching. So the notion of having students "out in the real world" was not necessarily counter to my discipline or new to me. However, rarely did students and their instructors have deep discourse to explore complex issues and matters regarding the educational system. We hardly ever critically examined pedagogical practice. Students struggled with balancing work, school, and family. The real world experience for my students consisted of creating lesson plans that matched competencies. They would be observed in a classroom and then be "signed off." Naturally, they were serving children with special needs but in a very unilateral manner. The real objective was to demonstrate their skill. And while we had "partnerships" with the cooperating school districts, I can't ever recall sitting down with administrators or teachers asking them for their input on what was taught, how it was taught, who and when pre-professionals would be "placed" in *their* classrooms let alone what might be pressing issues or needs they had.

This was the extent of my classroom experience and authentic experiential education role. It was essentially a knowledge factory; information going in and going out of students checking off competencies as they went along. Needless to say, the teaching was not necessarily fulfilling. This is not to place blame on the students. After all, they were in survival mode.

But I had gone into higher education with the hope of mentoring young people and shaping them personally and professionally as my professors had done with me back in the '70s. I had looked forward to having lively discourse in the classroom and during one-on-one sessions in my office. It just didn't happen. Further, it just didn't seem to matter in the larger scheme of things. What did matter was my research track record and the fact my efforts appeased and served the personnel needs of school districts.

TEACHING OUTSIDE THE BOX

Given this background, I was interested to hear what this student at my door had to say. He explained to me he wanted to use service-learning to help teenagers with learning disabilities. He said he wanted to ask them what mattered to them, to identify an issue or concern, then use it as a catalyst for teaching and learning. The idea was to use a cross-curriculum approach incorporating writing, research skills, reading, science, and math to become informed on the issue then develop their own textbook. Further, the young man said he was going to ask the students to consider what their role and responsibility were in addressing the issue they had identified and studied. I was both impressed and skeptical. Nevertheless, I said I would help and contacted a doctoral student of mine who coordinated special education classes in a junior high school in a diverse and lower socioeconomic area of the community.

Lo and behold, this student, who was not majoring in education, accomplished what he set out to do. I watched and learned in amazement as he and the students collectively identified the exploitation and depletion of the rain forests as their issue. It immediately became apparent to the students in the classroom and to me that no one had ever bothered to ask them what "mattered" to them. Schoolwork was always just something assigned to them. Because they now had a personal and vested interest, as well as a role in their learning, the students eagerly began researching the topic. They integrated their science and math to learn about average rainfall and temperatures. The information was culled and reported in written documents. Keep in mind these teenagers had a history of frustration and failure in school. Yet they had thrown themselves into this academic work in a way I had never seen before. But that was not all.

This young man who knocked on my door then did something else I had never seen. He sat with the students and said that, now that they had learned about the rain forest, it was time to reflect on what they could do to help. He told them they were global citizens and had a responsibility to make a difference, even if the rain forests were a world apart from their surroundings. Over the course of the discussion, one student reminded the class that an international conservation group had a program in which portions of rain forest could be "adopted" and then protected. It would require obtaining and donating funds. Then and there, the class decided to begin a fundraising campaign. As a teacher-educator concerned with the functional life skills of individuals with disabilities, I saw and experienced an amazing teaching and learning moment.

These students were now learning how to problem solve, work together, organize, coordinate, and communicate effectively, both orally and in writing, to articulate their mission. These were the life skills that would empower these students to be successful in relationships and careers. It dawned on me that this "hidden curriculum" was probably much more important than learning the state-mandated curriculum on the three branches of government. The end result was that the students did, in fact, raise a small amount of money; they received and proudly displayed their certificate thanking them for adopting and protecting a small parcel of rain forest.

QUESTIONING THE TRIED-AND-TRUE

As amazing as all of this was, the true revelation was beginning to unfold. Here I was, an "expert" in teacher education, and yet I had not known about or ever seen this way of teaching and learning. These were disenfranchised students meaningfully engaged in academic lessons—something teacher education attempts to promote. They were actively involved in making a difference and learning their role and place in the world as citizens. Perhaps for the first time, these students were getting a sense of who they were, transcending their own adolescent needs to be actively engaged in something bigger than themselves. They were gaining a sense of social responsibility while simultaneously integrating their formal curriculum. I began to ponder if my *own* students were meaningfully engaged, developing life skills and learning how to be good citizens.

The experience forced me to reflect upon my own knowledge and practice. It was a profound awakening to what I thought I knew and what I didn't know—of what I did and didn't do as a teacher. Clearly, despite "arriving" as a tenured full professor, I was ignorant of this thing called service-learning. Furthermore, I began to grapple with all I had accomplished. I questioned the meaning and value of my publications, wondering if they were truly making a difference or merely gathering dust on library shelves. It didn't seem to really matter whether that knowledge was used, as long as it was imparted and listed on a curriculum vitae. Likewise, observing this pedagogy made me question the didactic, expert model of teaching I was using in my own classroom. In some sense, my teacher candidates were as disenfranchised in their learning as the junior high school students. The only evidence of impact I had was a final grade and check marks for observations of student teaching.

It was both exciting and humbling. I had come to recognize my role and position within the ivory tower. I was a detached imparter of information. It also became a question and matter of values and rewards. Naturally, I wanted to be recognized for my scholarship. I certainly wanted tenure as well. But I soon began to discover and question the value and true impact of what I was doing. Research was important and exciting to me. At the same time, I longed to see tangible impact of that work beyond a list of publications on my vita. I wanted and needed to know if it was making a difference. Moreover, I wanted the learning experience in my classroom to be different. I wanted it to matter for both students and me.

The role of teacher and student was turned on its head with that knock on the door. From that experience I realized I needed to learn right along with my students and co-create not just new knowledge, but an understanding of underlying and complex issues that were associated with or contributing to the role of being a teacher of students with special needs. Up to now, the system and approach I had been socialized to incorporate had not done that. I was simply "informing" (as opposed to transforming) students with discrete facts and skills for them to demonstrate and receive licensure. Upon discovering this new pedagogy, I also realized there was room to integrate this form of teaching and learning at the post-secondary level with my research. I decided to study and write and study about service-learning. But how would I go about learning to do all of this?

LEARNING THE SERVICE-LEARNING ROPES

I began seeking information about service-learning from the Lowell Bennion Community Service Center on my campus. The director, Irene Fisher, suggested I attend a brown bag gathering to hear other faculty and their students talk about their courses. I was amazed to hear their stories, especially the students' perspective. These students certainly did not talk or behave the way my students did. Clearly, this was a much more meaningful experience for them. I didn't need any more convincing.

I decided to embark on this new pedagogical path by creating, not one, but two service-learning courses: one for *non*-education majors on issues related to children in school who are placed at risk by factors such as poor health and disability, socioeconomic status, and race; the other a graduate-level, interdisciplinary course for students in the College of Education. The former course did not view "risk" as an innate or pathological condition; rather, I wanted my students to examine social and cultural factors that seem to unfairly "place" students at risk. We explored our roles as citizens and professionals in a variety of fields to address these critical issues.

The latter graduate-level course was tied to a federal grant I had with a colleague in which students from general education, special education, educational psychology, and educational administration programs were put into interdisciplinary teams to work with schools to identify a critical issue related to serving students placed at risk and then create a pilot program to address those needs. Even with technical assistance, I stumbled my way through the course, making mistakes and learning from my students along the way. What amazed and fulfilled me was how receptive and committed the students were. This was such a profound difference from my other classes.

Consequently, I began reflecting on my teaching and pondered ways I could transfer techniques I used in my new service-learning classes to my traditional teacher education courses. This process took me back to what I observed with the student who knocked on my door. I suddenly became aware that my students, like those this young man worked with, had to have a role in constructing their learning experience to gain meaning, rather than having me impart the knowledge. While my teacher education classes had a field component such as a practicum, there was little time to reflect and discuss what students saw and learned. Furthermore, any debriefing that did occur was often nothing more than perfunctory reporting out and "checking off" skill sets. What was missing was exploration of deeper issues and contexts that seemed to underlie our purpose and mission as educators. I began to include discussion and assignments related to family ecology and cultural values. Similarly, I put my students into teams to learn those important skills from the hidden curriculum that would empower them later. Finally, I knew the basic objectives of my class were theoretically grounded, but I reframed how to achieve those instructional goals by asking the teams to consult with teachers, administrators, and even parents to get their perspectives and an understanding of their needs. This, in turn, led my student teams to a focused goal of creating a product or program that could actually be incorporated by schools. It gave my students an opportunity to test and validate the theory and apply the skills while attempting to make a meaningful difference.

The response was astounding. Not only did some of the participating schools adopt what my student teams created, they actually contracted some of my students to coordinate the programs. This turn of events seemed to reflect what transpired during the service-learning project that was conducted by the student who came to my door. My students were more engaged while applying their skills in a manner that truly met the needs of the schools, teachers, and children with whom they were working. Perhaps equally important and self-serving was the fact I drew personal and professional satisfaction from the process. I took pride in my students' accomplishments. I could readily see the impact of my efforts as a scholar in a way that was much more tangible and meaningful than citations on my curriculum vitae.

But I wasn't naïve, either. Realizing the importance of integrating my research and teaching, I began writing about what I was doing with service-learning. Since the knock on my door, I have taught many different service-learning courses over several years, all incorporating activities that promote the hidden curriculum, or what is sometimes called the "pedagogy of engagement." Beyond learning specific skills and content related to the disciplinary topic, my students are learning how to problem solve and communicate their ideas in various ways. This not only prepares them to be competent professionals, but to be good citizens as well, gaining insight into their roles and place in the world. I use what I observed from the junior high students trying to save the rain forest as a benchmark or rubric for what I do at the University. Consequently, I see my students transformed and not merely in-formed. Their experience changes them. In some cases, the transformation has been extremely powerful as they continue their initial work even after the course has ended. Thus, the learning transcends their sense of self and own needs. To me, this is the essence of what Carnegie Scholar Ernest Boyer (1990) talks about when he refers to the academy "as" citizen.

GOING THERE WITH COURAGE

So yes, it appeared that nearly 10 years ago I had "arrived," but I seemed to be at the wrong place. The humbling conclusions I reached were that an unassuming undergraduate student who wasn't even an education major knew more about effective pedagogy and essentially taught me. This made me question my own role as teacher and scholar, as well as to what extent the ivory tower truly does have the ability to impart knowledge in a way that truly made a difference. Certainly, I had the background and skills. My advanced degree was not worthless. I have an expertise and something to offer my students and discipline. Yet I also discovered that students, parents, and community partners could take an active role in co-creating knowledge and understanding—not just for them, but for me as well. This process reflects a marvelous quote by Vincent Donovan (2003), who cautioned that when working with people: "do not try to call them back to where they were, and do not try to call them to where you are, beautiful as that place may seem to you. You must have the courage to go with them to a place that neither you nor they have been before." (p. xi). I think the key word in this quote is courage. This type of pedagogy is a scary enterprise. It makes one vulnerable. Such an approach is counter to academic culture. Ultimately, I think my students and the community partners we work with come to recognize and respect this willingness to be partners in the learning process.

As I revisit this quote, I am reminded of a question posed to me by a colleague serving on a curriculum committee charged with "approving" my first service-learning course. As I described the proposed course, he asked, "But how will you control what your students learn if they're out in the community?" I was floored by the question yet able to respond. I said, "I don't think I ever have, or ever will be able to, 'control' what my students learn . . . that's up to them. I can 'control' what I teach in terms of framing assignments and activities but the rest is up to them." His question clearly illustrated the existing and traditional paradigm of a didactic instructional approach. I'm not saying this approach is wrong or inappropriate. Lecturing and discussing reading assignments are an extremely efficient way of imparting facts. In truth, I continue to incorporate those methods in my own classes, including my service-learning courses. It is not, however, the only way to teach and it certainly does not "control" what students learn. What frustrates me today after teaching service-learning for more than a decade is that it is often not valued or respected by my colleagues. This is largely due to the myths and misunderstanding of what service-learning is and isn't, especially when these appear to conflict with the pedagogical status quo of talking *at* students in a classroom. We merely assume learning has taken place when students rehash what we tell them.

A curious postscript to this journey is the crossing of paths that has occurred. The student who knocked on my door eventually changed his major and career goals and went into special education, largely due to experiences I helped facilitate. Meanwhile, I left my field of special education to devote my energies to service-learning and promote civic engagement as the new full-time director of the Bennion Center. Who could have predicted such a turn of events?

REFERENCES

Boyer, E. L. (1990). *Scholarship reconsidered: Priorities of the professoriate.* Princeton, NJ: The Carnegie Foundation for the Advancement of Teaching.

Donovan, V. (2003). Preface to *Christianity rediscovered* (2nd ed.). Chicago: Maryknoll, NY: Orbis Books.

CHAPTER 5

EXPANDING HORIZONS THROUGH SERVICE AND SERVICE-LEARNING

Gina Maria Musolino

FORMATIVE YEARS

My journey in service-learning began before gathering with the University of Utah Civically Engaged Scholar Cohort (CESC), and dare I say when I was a youngster. During my formative years, I was blessed with the opportunity to "shadow/assist" my father, who was a Doctor of Veterinary Medicine. Beginning at four years of age, I watched him work with swine and cattle, cats and dogs, skunks and horses, and was fascinated not only with his skill at interacting with those who had no human voice, but also his savvy communicating with a wide range of animal owners. I never hesitated to jump in the truck to go on a country call with him. Needless to say, there was many an interesting owner—with an even more interesting tale of how their animal "arrived" in its current state of "emergency."

My father taught me how to serve the underserved by being aware of the fact that many did not have the ability to pay—he always worked out something—and for those who insisted on full payment, due to the pride factor, bartering was always in order. Ah—the Midwest was a wonderful

Finding Meaning in Civically Engaged Scholarship, pages 39–45
Copyright © 2009 by Information Age Publishing
All rights of reproduction in any form reserved.

place to grow up. I also admired my father's ability to volunteer his time not only to serve animals, but also to engage young minds who were potentially interested in veterinary medicine. I began to serve under his tutelage, during my formative years, volunteering my time with his practice. With my six siblings in our many activities (Mom always said "service begins at home!") and through numerous volunteer civic projects at St. Peter's Patriots grade school, service to the community was ever at the forefront of a Catholic school education in the rural Midwest.

Along the way, as a high school student and during my college years, I was introduced to the more formalized concepts of service and service-learning. I participated in fund-raising efforts for needy organizations, volunteered time with community events and those with special needs, and in my pre-physical therapy preparations volunteered with those with physical and mental disabilities. Through my efforts with the physically challenged, I gained powerful insights from the participants. Through this service, I realized my own personal career goals. Upon entering physical therapy school, I was provided ample opportunities to put to use our emerging skills with many willing participants. I always gained more from the service experiences than I thought possible, not realizing at the time that community service was already embedded deep within my soul. Honestly, I thought all communities were civically engaged. Ah—the sheltered youth.

LEADERS AND GUIDES

More recently, as a College of Health faculty member in physical therapy, I continued these efforts side-by-side with my students and interns. However, it was not until I arrived at Florida Gulf Coast University (FGCU), Florida's tenth state institution and a brand-new university with service-learning in its vision and mission, that I discovered the powerful influence an institution's overarching principles can have on the ability to fully and meaningfully integrate service-learning into a curriculum. Never before had I found a university where service-learning was so genuinely ingrained within the institution.

During my early days at FGCU, my dear friend and colleague, Pamala Feehan, PT, MS and I, were able to design, develop, and evaluate a three-semester sequence course with service-learning mentoring projects as a primary component. This course was designed to progress students from being protégés to becoming mentors within communities of need. In the first semester, students were provided with clinical community mentorship. In the second semester, groups of students identified, with their mentors, communities of need and, with their clinical community mentors, proposed a community-based service-learning project. The proposals included a planned needs assessment, program plan, and plan for evaluation. Students, with mentors, then implemented the planned service-learning activities in the third semester of the course sequence and provided evaluative presentations to community partners.

As a result of this work, Pamala and I coauthored a manuscript that was published and later recognized by the *Journal of Physical Therapy Education,* American Physical Therapy Association (APTA) Education Section, with the inaugural Feitelberg Journal Founders Awards in 2005. The Feitelberg Journal Founders Award acknowledges excellence in publication by a first-time author in the *Journal of Physical Therapy Education* for the calendar year. This method/model presentation article (Musolino & Feehan, 2004), described the development and implementation of an innovative approach to education used in physical therapy. We examined the learning outcomes of the community-based, service-learning projects while providing a framework to implement the service-learning teaching methods within a physical therapy curriculum. Learning outcomes were examined from the perspectives of students and participants in communities served, and the evaluative insights of the community-based partners were also gathered. Further, we provided linkages to both accreditation standards (university and professional) and ethical/legal issues. Finally, we discovered that students become leaders while serving and faculty become "guides on the side" while teaching others to serve, and communities benefit beyond the expected outcomes.

As faculty, we were honored for our work, and the inaugural class of 12 physical therapy students received the Student Outreach for Cultural Diversity and Awareness Award from the American Physical Therapy Association (APTA), Student Assembly. Students were honored particularly for their projects in two communities: (1) a hands-on museum attracting diverse K–6 students from six counties, including those who are deaf or hard of hearing and the children of migrant farm workers of Hispanic descent and (2) an after-school program for African-American children from low-income families. Evaluative data from these projects determined that the effectiveness of mentoring interventions and experiences aligned with service-learning course objectives. These data were summarized and submitted to the APTA Student Assembly for the competitive award selection.

The teaching experience at FGCU, with its shared learning outcomes, was rewarding not only for all internal stakeholders (community, student, faculty, institution), but also for our external stakeholders (patients/clients served, community-at-large). As we researched the "drawbacks" of service-learning, it was difficult for us to imagine these hurdles as insurmountable, based upon our incredibly rewarding experience. That is not to say we did not proceed with trepidation—as we "gave up" the learning to the learners and the communities—yet we were there to guide and intervene, as needed, along the way. Facilitating both the content and process for service-learning, while challenging, enriched our teaching experience by providing an interactive learning opportunity. We received support from all levels of FGCU's administration and celebrated our accomplishments at a public reception with College of Health students and faculty, community partners, and the University's President. In the end, our work had solidified linkages with FGCU's vision and mission and established a strong foundation for further service-learning efforts within the College of Health.

FINDING A SERVICE-LEARNING "FAMILY"

Upon arriving at the University of Utah, eight years ago, I was delighted to discover the Lowell Bennion Community Service Center. Although it was not what brought me to the University of Utah, in the everlasting Wasatch mountains, it certainly remains a sustaining factor. After getting my feet on the ground, I followed up on an email communication from the Bennion Center's then Service-Learning Manager, Joani Shaver, touting the opportunity to designate appropriate courses as "service-learning." This was exciting for me, as I brought along the service-learning model we designed and developed at FGCU and adapted this model and implemented a two-semester, Teaching & Learning I & II course sequence, within the College of Health's Department (then Division) of Physical Therapy curriculum.

After meeting with Joani and sharing the course intent and philosophy, we reviewed the criteria for service-learning designation and realized it was a likely match. The next step was to present the class to the Bennion Center's Service-Learning Class Committee for formal approval. To prepare, I revisited the course syllabus, objectives, assignments, and self- and peer-assessments—an exercise that was both reflective and enlightening. I determined that the course did indeed match the service-learning designation criteria, and, with the blessing of my Department Chair and Dean of the College of Health, arranged to present at the next meeting of the Service-Learning Class Committee.

Walking across campus to that meeting, I wondered what I had gotten myself into—why should I "want" to have these courses designated as service-learning—what was to be gained? I would still teach them anyway—why was I putting myself through this peer review and extra effort? Just before I entered the building where the committee was meeting, I saw Joani approaching and gave her a big wave. She waved back—she remembered me!—and we connected in this big new world that is the University of Utah. Then it dawned on me: I was likely about to meet other colleagues who were also highly interested in service-learning. This remains highly important to me in our clinically focused arena of health care education. I was not disappointed; for one hour I was "grilled" about my courses by thoughtful and responsible colleagues serving on the committee. They wanted to know how we did things, why we did things, how and when we integrated the reflective piece, how the needs assessments fit, where in the curriculum the courses fell, why physical therapy students would be interested, what the bigger picture was for the students and communities.

Although it was a friendly exchange, at times it felt like I was revisiting my doctoral defense. Yet in the end, it was clear that the reason for all their questions was their interest in the course and the service-learning models presented. These folks not only believed in service-learning, they wanted to continue to improve how they did it! When does *real* curriculum review ever happen outside the formal reviews and accreditation processes? How often do collegiate faculties really discuss teaching and learning curricula? How often do we really take the time to have spirited and thoughtful exchanges about our teaching and learning? Afterward, I was both exhausted and exhilarated. It felt good to share something that was so meaningful and rewarding, yet also be challenged to take it to the next level. I had indeed met my service-learning colleagues. I felt strongly that Brookfield's ideals (1995) of "critically reflective teaching" were being implemented through service-learning courses at the University of Utah.

EXPANDED HORIZONS

From there, whenever possible, I became involved in Bennion Center and Utah Campus Compact activities. I applied for and received Bennion Center funding to advance the service-learning agenda within the Department of Physical Therapy. Many of my non-University of Utah colleagues appreciate the support we have through the Bennion Center. Each time I participate in these civically-engaged activities, I am reminded that we are heading in the right direction, that we can continue to improve the world and those we serve in small ways that make a difference, while at the same time meeting educational learning outcomes. I have been inspired to apply for external service-learning grant funding and have received a State Farm/Good Neighbor service-learning grant to fund our student-led service-learning projects for 2008–2009.

Without networking with my interdisciplinary colleagues in service-learning, I would not have been apprised of these many opportunities for personal growth, development, and assessment of service-learning. In fact, an undergraduate service-learning student who is a McNair pre-physical therapy scholar brought the State Farm opportunity to my attention. I have also been blessed to have a profession, physical therapy, that continues to embrace the concepts and applications of service-learning. We have enjoyed themed service-learning programming at our national conferences and have scholarly publications dedicated to service-learning topics. For example, the *Journal of Physical Therapy Education* devoted an entire issue to "Service Learning and Community-Engaged Scholarship" (Winter, 2006) and continues to seek manuscripts exploring this teaching strategy to enhance learning and promote civic engagement and community-based research.

In 2007, the American Physical Therapy Association, from peer-reviewed educational proposal submissions for its annual conference in Denver, devoted 15 hours of educational themed-programming on the topic, "Scholarship of Teaching and Service-Learning." My colleague Alecia Thiele, MS, PT, DPT ATC/L, ACCE, Academic Coordinator of Clinical Education at Cark College, Iowa, and I co-presented our works during a three-hour, educational session entitled, "The Value of Integrating Service-Learning for your Practice: Academic and Clinical Perspectives through Community Partnerships."

Additionally, we asked a former University of Utah student, Stephanie Rock, DPT, to share and present her service-learning team project on behalf of her peers. This project had culminated earlier in the year at the "Expanding your Horizons Career Conference" in Orem, Utah. Targeting middle and high school girls in rural areas of the state who might not otherwise be interested in pursuing math or science careers, the project received the "Best Booth" award at the Orem conference as the most interactive and informative, by vote of conference participants.

At the APTA conference in Denver, Dr. Rock presented all three phases of the service-learning project, from proposal to planning through evaluation, and provided the learning outcomes for both her peers and the students served. Dr. Rock, Dr. Thiele, and I shared qualitative and quantitative evaluative data, as well as videotape vignettes and photographic images of our experiences, to demonstrate our teaching and learning methods, then conducted a panel discussion and question-and-answer session. As a result of this session, we discovered that many of our colleagues continue to be interested in learning about methods and means of implementing and evaluating service-learning within Doctor of Physical Therapy (DPT) and Physical Therapist Assistant curricula.

CONCLUSION

Service-learning is truly an amalgam of everything I love—service, variety, diversity, caring, meeting others' needs while fulfilling goals, and being appreciated for what you can offer the world while influencing others' lives. Service-learning is not the instructional strategy of choice in every course, but it is the preferred method in many of my course offerings. Service-learning has provided not only a teaching venue, but a scholarship opportunity. Additionally, service-learning has provided, for me, a networking of like-minded scholars in service. When Ernest Boyer (1990) suggested that institutions, students, and communities must "embrace each other," I was certain that service-learning was an avenue I would continue to pursue, to assure civic engagement in my communities of service. I have a passion for my profession, and service and service-learning will only continue to expand my horizon of influence. It is exciting to consider where my service-learning journey will lead to next.

REFERENCES

Boyer, E. (1990). *Scholarship reconsidered: Priorities of the professorate.* Princeton, NJ: The Carnegie Foundation for the Advancement of Teaching.

Brookfield, S. D. (1995). *Becoming a critically reflective teacher.* San Francisco: Jossey-Bass.

Musolino, G., & Feehan, P. (2004). Enhancing diversity through mentorship: The nurturing potential of service-learning. *Journal of Physical Therapy Education, 18*(1), 29–42.

CHAPTER 6

BEYOND "US" AND "THEM"

Community-Based Research as a Politics of Engagement

Caitlin Cahill

Communities, particularly communities of color, have too often been used as laboratories by outsiders, and have rarely benefitted from the results of research. Community-based engaged scholarship is a response to the exploitative practice of outsiders. As indigenous scholar Linda Tuhiwai Smith (2007) explains: "Research, like schooling, once the tool for colonization and oppression is very gradually coming to be seen as a potential means to reclaim languages, histories and knowledge, to find solutions to the negative impacts of colonialism and to give voice to an alternative way of knowing and of being" (p. 10).

But what does this type of scholarship look like in practice? How can engaged scholarship contribute to decolonization and be accountable to the communities with whom we work? How does research change when it is explicitly developed to be used by the community for their own purposes? How might research contribute to social change movements? In this chapter I share my personal experiences doing community-based participatory action

Finding Meaning in Civically Engaged Scholarship, pages 47–57
Copyright © 2009 by Information Age Publishing
All rights of reproduction in any form reserved.

research in Salt Lake City, Utah with a team of high school youth researchers who developed a participatory action research documentary project entitled "Red Flags: Stereotyping & Racism in the Schools" (2006–8). Teasing out the critical issues that engaged scholarship raises, I reflect upon my commitments to community-based participatory action research (PAR).

An example of community-based PAR is the "Red Flags" project. Red Flags is a collaborative research project that involved a small group of high school students of Latino, African, and African-American backgrounds who were interested in understanding how stereotyping and racism affect teens in schools. The youth research team decided to develop a documentary research project because they wanted to interrupt the silence about racism and stereotyping within their schools and reach a large public. For our research, we conducted and filmed interviews and focus groups with students of diverse ethnic and racial backgrounds. The three themes the youth research team identified are (1) feeling unwelcome in school; (2) institutional racism; and (3) losing motivation.

As part of the documentary, the youth researchers also decided to perform their own experiences of everyday racism in order to visually express the themes raised by their research. In one of the "scenes," I was drafted to perform the role of a white guidance counselor in a situation where one of the youth researchers, an African-American young woman named Jasmine, is aggressively interrogated by the principal of her school. He accuses her of carrying a blade and asks her to prove that she isn't by taking off her shoes, emptying her pockets, and taking down her hair. For Jasmine, this humiliating experience epitomizes the institutionalized racism she deals with in her school on a daily basis. Not only was it challenging to reenact this traumatic event, it was also a painful scene to watch.

My role as the guidance counselor in the scene is to witness the humiliation. I just sit there in the background and watch the principal chastise Jasmine. I do nothing. I am complicit. In the scene, the guidance counselor makes the personal choice to not interrupt the principal. And as such, she represents part of the power structure—the institutional racism of a school structure where young people of color are regularly targeted, humiliated, and ignored as part of the policies, institutional practices, and cultural representations of the school. Students' everyday experiences of institutional racism were one of the central findings of our research. What, we might wonder, would have happened if the counselor had challenged the principal and stepped forward to support Jasmine? Or what would have happened if she had smiled at Jasmine or given her a hug afterwards to let her know that she cared? But she did neither of these.

This reenactment makes me pause and reflect upon moments in my life when I did the same, when I remained silent in the face of social injustice, either consciously or unconsciously. One only has to consider what it means to be an American at this historical moment, in the face of U.S. imperialism, ongoing war, Guantanamo Bay, the prison industrial complex, structural racism, and the multiple intersecting asymmetries of our world, our country, our cities, and our neighborhoods. The question of our own roles and responsibilities is overwhelming. In my everyday life, I consider other moments when I have done nothing. For example, I think of how, on a daily basis growing up in New York City, I stepped around the bodies of homeless people who slept in the subways or in my doorway. I think of how I have benefitted from public practices and institutional policies that reproduce structural racial inequities. I reflect upon the advantages of my unearned privileges of being born white in America. This awareness informs my approach to working collaboratively with communities of color, and my sense of purposefulness as a researcher. Self-reflexivity, my conscious reflection upon my positionality, is central to my praxis. I consciously shift from the "objective," dispassionate observer (if this type of observer is even possible) and engage a sense of responsibility and solidarity for the situations I study.

COMMUNITY-BASED PARTICIPATORY ACTION RESEARCH AS A POLITICS OF ENGAGEMENT

"If you are neutral in situations of injustice, you have chosen the side of the oppressor. If an elephant has its foot on the tail of a mouse and you say that you are neutral, the mouse will not appreciate your neutrality." In this quote, Bishop Desmond Tutu speaks to the responsibility to challenge the South African apartheid and, more broadly, to interrupt abuses of power, hegemony, and structural inequalities. Tutu's comments are relevant also to the academy. As Delgado-Bernal and Villalpando (2002) have argued, there is an "apartheid of knowledge" in the academy as the scholarship, epistemologies, and cultural resources of communities of color are consistently devalued and marginalized within the context of institutional racism. The so-called "ivory tower" not only embodies, but also reproduces, class, raced, and gendered hierarchies (Marable, 2000). In the academy, too, to do nothing, to not actively work to challenge the hegemony of knowledge production, especially as a white researcher, is to be complicit. How can we strategically engage in the project of "contesting research," in which critical research is designed to challenge hegemonic practices and discourses, and rearticulate our understanding of on-the-ground realities (Fine, 2006)? And, if we recognize our research as a site of contestation in itself, what then are our roles and responsibilities as researchers?

These questions, of positionality, privilege, and responsibility, are central to my praxis doing collaborative research with diverse collectives of young (and old) people. My engagement with community-based PAR is inspired by a vision for "what could be" (Torre et al., 2001) and the possibility of addressing asymmetries of power, privilege, and knowledge production. I am motivated by the words of the radical educator and philosopher Paulo Freire (2001): "When I speak of intervention, I refer both to the aspiration for radical changes in society in such areas as economic, human relations, property, the right to employment, to land, to education, and to health, and to the reactionary position whose aim is to immobilize history and maintain an unjust socioeconomic and cultural order" (p. 6).

Community-based PAR might be re-imagined as an intervention, a stance against neutrality, and an "existential commitment to an ethical ideal rather than to historical inevitability" (Aronowitz, 2001, p. 7). Community-based PAR builds upon long-standing traditions of grassroots social movements, activism, critical race and feminist research, and the work of social justice advocates who strive to address unequal power relations, provide new spaces for decolonized knowledge production, and challenge the dominant hegemonic paradigm (Kelley, 1998; Kretzmann & McKnight, 1997; Smith, 2007). Starting with social concerns and personal experiences, PAR values the knowledge produced through collaboration and in action, places emphasis upon the research process, and reconsiders the value of research as a vehicle for social change (Cahill, Sultana, & Pain, 2007).

That said, critical scholarship has pointed to the ways broad applications of the term "participation" may mask tokenism and provide an illusion of consultation (Cooke & Kothari, 2001; Mohan, 2001). When participatory research is presented as a set of techniques rather than as a commitment to working *with* communities, it may result in the reproduction, rather than the challenging, of social inequities (Kesby, 2005; Kothari, 2001). As ironic examples, the International Monetary Fund and World Bank, two notorious bastions of multinational capitalism and global restructuring, use participatory research practices in "developing" countries (Cooke & Kothari, 2001), raising the question of how uneven power relations are addressed. Here, however, I speak to the promises and potential of PAR as a transformative social justice project—an ethical praxis of care in which relationships and the responsibilities involved in working *with* communities are primary (Cahill, 2007a; Gilligan, 1982; Kindon, Pain, & Kesby, 2007). As a practice of engaged scholarship aimed toward social change, PAR explicitly challenges the understanding of the social researcher as a detached, neutral, distant observer. Instead, as an explicit politics of engagement, community-based participatory researchers are involved with and accountable to the people, collaborators who have agreed to work together to solve a particular issue. PAR is a commitment to collaboration in its most profound sense (Ayala

& Torre, in press; Torre, in press). PAR is, therefore, not only a politics of engagement but of solidarity. What then does this look like in practice in terms of antiracist commitments? And how does this shift the way that we do research?

As both a process and a theoretical stance, I have found Guiner and Torres' (2002) conceptualization of political race to be a useful framework for understanding the political potential of community-based PAR as an antiracist practice. "It is a political project that does not ask who you married or who your daddy was. At its core it does not ask you what you call yourself, but with whom you link your fate. It is a fundamentally creative, political project that begins from the ground up, starting with race and all its complexity, and then builds cross-racial relationships through race and with race to issues of class and gender in order to make democracy real" (pp. 9–10).

With whom do you link your fate? Guinier and Torres (2002) suggest that progressives need to interrogate their relationship to power and privilege and yoke their fate to those with a long history struggling for justice. For participatory antiracist researchers, this means consciously decentering the privileges associated with whiteness. Community-based PAR involves an articulated positionality and an ethical obligation to foregrounding the concerns, questions, and perspectives of those who have been excluded or whose contributions to knowledge production have been otherwise marginalized, distorted, or invalidated.

Guinier and Torres (2002) offer the metaphor of the miner's canary as a diagnostic tool and a point of mobilization for participatory antiracist researchers. The miner's canary is a relevant metaphor in Utah, home to a significant mining industry where last year nine people died in a collapsed mine. The purpose of the canary is to alert the miners to poison in the air; the canary's distress is the first sign of a danger. The canary suggests both the need for systemic critique and also points toward the possibility of social change. What then can we learn from young people of color about stereotyping and racism in the schools? Even though in a cage, the canaries continue to have agency and voice, and, similarly, even within the confines of a high school riddled with racism, the students find their voices and speak back. Significantly, at the same time that we were conducting our research, the Jena 6 case brought national attention to the ongoing racism in U.S. schools and rallied people from across the country to speak out against discrimination. This event informed the youth researchers' sense of purpose as they understood the significance of the "Red Flags" research within a national context.

THE "RED FLAGS" RESEARCH PROJECT

Our research project began with the personal concerns and experiences of the youth research team: Why are my friends dropping out of high school? Why am I ignored by my teacher when I ask for help? How come I feel unwelcome in school? Is it only me? Framed as a political race project, PAR starts with the belief that our analyses are most powerful when we follow the lead of the canary. Exploring the contradictions of our experiences in school, the pressure to do well in school as the key to success, and the everyday ways that school is experienced as a hostile environment for young people of color, becomes a basis for developing social theory. Questioning the high dropout rates of youth of color, the Red Flags youth research team explores why and how this happens in the everyday lives of young people at school (Alémán & Rorrer, 2006). Their research examines how stereotyping and racism affect teens in school. The miner's canary suggests the experiences and concerns of young people of color expose fractures in our society. We need to examine what these fractures mean for our public education system and how young people of color are denied access to opportunities more broadly.

Doing community-based PAR significantly shifts the role of the researcher. Instead of framing the project based on the literature or my own concerns about young people, the research is co-constructed collaboratively by the research team. Their questions and concerns drive the project. When underrepresented perspectives (for example, those of young people, of women, of people of color) enter the academy and participate in the production of "official" knowledges, not only might they transform themselves, but they might also transform the academy (see Collins, [1990] 2000; Kelley, 1998; Kindon et al., 2007). This is the ground upon which new knowledge can take root, push scholarship in new directions, ask new questions, challenge assumptions, "think outside the box" and move beyond the privileged perspectives of the ivory tower (Cahill, 2007b). PAR creates an opportunity for the production of new knowledge and has profound implications for challenging what Foucault (1980) identified as the "subjectifying social sciences." The Red Flags documentary video project illustrates one of PAR's critical contributions, the opportunity to represent oneself and speak back to reductive mischaracterizations. In fact, one of the primary objectives of the PAR project was to challenge deficit representations of young people that stereotype them as dropouts, lazy, or disinterested in school.

Working within a political race framework, a PAR project like Red Flags involves an excavation of power and privilege both within the research process itself and in a consideration of its intended outcomes (Torre & Fine, 2006). As Torre (in press) suggests, the question of positionality, our relationships to power, and the vulnerabilities of participating are highlighted in "the privilege of silence (and the silence of privilege)" (Torre, in press). For antiracist researchers, it is important to explicitly address whiteness and interrupt performances of privilege. This is especially important in Utah, which the research team half-jokingly refers to in their documentary as "A Big White State," as nearly 90% of the population is white. The demographics of Utah are changing, however. Between 2000–2004, 41% of Utah's population growth consisted of people of color, predominantly of Latino background. During the same time period, 75% of the enrollment increase in Utah's public school system were students of color (Perlich, 2006). The Red Flags research team resides on Salt Lake City's west side, in the most diverse zipcode in the state, where almost 40% of the residents are ethnic minorities. Although the students' neighborhoods and schools are diverse, the Red Flags research demonstrates their sensitivity to the whiteness of the state. The structural racism students negotiate on a daily basis in their schools deeply affects their sense of belonging, efficacy, and esteem.

Calling attention to white privilege is a way to begin a discussion of power and responsibility, collectively thinking through the connections between structural advantages and disadvantages as part of a politics of solidarity. For example, Mario, a Red Flags youth researcher who is Latino but often passes as white, notices how he is never questioned in the hallway about his whereabouts and intentions, whereas Jasmine, who is African-American, is always asked to present her hall pass and is regarded with suspicion by teachers and security. In "Red Flags," the students and I reflect together on the space between Mario and Jasmine's experiences as well as the connections. Although Mario didn't recognize the special treatment he was granted based on his lighter skin until Jasmine shared the ways she felt at school, once he did, he started to see white privilege everywhere. For Jasmine, being involved in research with other students of color who shared similar experiences made her feel less alone; furthermore, she began to see racism not just as a personal insult but as an institutional problem.

Addressing race, and white privilege in particular, is a critical pedagogical approach, what Twine (2004) identifies as a racial literacy project, a strategic enterprise where we examine everyday experiences of racism as part of our ongoing work, introducing new frames for understanding and interpreting our experiences and research (Chavez & Soep, 2005). For example, when one youth researcher described her teacher not being "nice" that day in school (a code word for racism—see Low, 2003), we could collectively situate her experience within the framework of institutional racism and privilege, terms that were new to the youth research team.

Engaged participatory action research reflects what Chavez and Soep (2005) identify as a "pedagogy of collegiality"—"a context in which young people and adults mutually depend on one another's skills, perspectives, and collaborative efforts to generate original, multitextual, professional quality work for outside audiences" (Chavez & Soep, 2005, p. 3). While Chavez and Soep are specifically addressing youth-adult partnerships, the same approach is relevant for community-based participatory researchers more broadly.

Although the "Red Flags" project was driven by youth perspectives and concerns, I (along with the other adult mentors involved) provided training in research skills and critical perspectives on the research itself. In our project, my role involved working closely with the youth researchers to frame questions, collaborate on editorial decisions, and strategize how to represent their concerns most effectively to diverse audiences. Our process was characterized by collective negotiation. The process of exchange challenged all of us, young and old, White, Latino, African-American, to rethink both our everyday experiences and our research findings. We all have a stake in the integrity of the research, the personal and political implications of our research, the production of knowledge, and the potential impacts on each other and our communities.

As explicitly political, engaged, and collectively negotiated, community-based PAR's alternative epistemological approach has profound implications for moving beyond the critical problem of academic research being a conversation of "us" with "us" about "them" (Cahill, 2004). Here I have reflected upon how a collaborative antiracist PAR process shifts the research process, the role of the researcher, and the potential outcomes. If community-based PAR is to make a meaningful contribution to social change, beyond an "armchair revolution" (Freire, 1997), the impact of our research—*action!*—is of critical concern. PAR introduces new questions about representation, audience, and product that compel us to rethink the impact of research. Concluding questions we grappled with, and that are of relevance for all engaged scholars, include: Who has the "authority" to represent a community's point of view? Is there a "we" within the community being represented? What kinds of research products speak to what kinds of audiences? What is the research asking audiences to do? And finally, how can we effectively provoke action by developing research that engages, that reframes social issues theoretically, and motivates audiences to change both the way they think and how they act in the world (Cahill & Torre, 2007)?

ACKNOWLEDGMENTS

What a privilege to work with the Red Flags youth research team in developing this project. Special thanks to my warm and wonderful colleagues on the Growing Up in Salt Lake City project: the amazing youth researchers and my incredible colleagues/co-collaborators with whom I was privileged to work: Matt Bradley, Denise Castañeda, Ariana Prazen, Angela Romero, and Roberta Targino. We are grateful for the opportunity to collaborate with the University of Utah's University Neighborhood Partners. This research is supported by a community-based research grant from the Bennion Center of the University of Utah and a research grant from the American Association of Geographers.

I am especially grateful to María Elena Torre, Janet Kaufman, and Marissa Diener for their constructive critical feedback. Thanks also to the Civically Engaged Scholars Cohort for their support and comments on an earlier draft. I am appreciative of Marissa Diener's patience and persistence.

REFERENCES

Alemán, E., & Rorrer, A. K. (2006). *Closing educational gaps for Latino/a students in Utah: Initiating a policy discourse and framework.* Salt Lake City: Utah Education Policy Center.

Aronowitz, S. (2001). Introduction. In P. Freire, *Pedagogy of freedom: Ethics, democracy and civic courage.* Lanham, MD: Rowman and Little.

Ayala, J., & Torre, M. E. (In press). In search of *nos* and *otras* in the *entremundos* of PAR. Special Issue of *Feminism & Psychology.*

Cahill, C. (2004). Defying gravity: Raising consciousness through collective research. *Children's Geographies, 2,* 2.

Cahill, C. (2007a). Repositioning ethical commitments: Participatory action research as a relational praxis of social change. *ACME: An International E-Journal for Critical Geographies, 6,* 360–373.

Cahill, C. (2007b). Including excluded perspectives in participatory action research. *Design Studies, 28,* 325–340.

Cahill, C., Sultana, F., & Pain, R. (2007). Participatory ethics: Policies, practices & institutions. *ACME: An International E-Journal for Critical Geographies, 6,* 304–318.

Cahill, C., & Torre, M. E. (2007). Beyond the journal article: Representations, audience, and the presentation of participatory research. In S. Kindon, R. Pain, & M. Kesby (Eds.), *Connecting people, participation and place: Participatory action research approaches and methods* (pp. 196–205). London: Routledge.

Chavez, V., & Soep, E (2005). Youth radio and the pedagogy of collegiality. *Harvard Educational Review, 75,* 1–23.

Collins, P. H. (1990). *Black feminist thought: Knowledge, consciousness, and the politics of empowerment.* New York: Routledge.

Cooke, B., & Kothari U. (2001). *Participation: The new tyranny?* London: Zed Books.

Delgado-Bernal, D., & Villalpando, O. (2002). An apartheid of knowledge in the academy: The struggle over "legitimate" knowledge for faculty of color. *Equity and Excellence in Education, 35,* 169–180.

Fine, M. (2006). Contesting research: Rearticulation and 'thick democracy' as political projects of method. In L. Weis, C. McCarthy & G. Dimitriadis (Eds.), *Ide-*

ology, curriculum, and the new sociology of education: Revisiting the work of Michael Apple (pp. 145–166). New York: Routledge.

Foucault, M. (1980). *Power/knowledge: Selected interviews & other writings 1972–1977.* Colin Gordon (Ed./Trans.) New York: Pantheon Books.

Friere, P. (1997). *Pedagogy of the oppressed.* Harmandsworth, Middlesex: Penguin Books.

Freire, P. (2001). *Pedagogy of freedom: Ethics, democracy, and civic courage.* New York: Rowman and Littlefield.

Gilligan, C. (1982). *In a different voice: Psychological theory and women's development.* Cambridge, MA: Harvard University Press.

Guinier, L., & Torres, G. (2002). *The miner's canary: Enlisting race, resisting power, transforming democracy.* Boston, MA: Harvard University Press.

Kelley, R. D. G. (1998). Check the technique: black urban culture and the predicament of social science. In N. B. Dirk (Ed.), *In near ruins: Cultural theory at the end of the century* (pp. 145–166). Minneapolis: University of Minnesota Press.

Kesby, M. (2005). Retheorizing empowerment-through-participation as a performance in space: beyond tyranny to transformation. *Signs: Journal of Women in Culture and Society, 30,* 2037–2065.

Kindon, S., Pain, R., & Kesby, M. (Eds.). (2007). *Participatory action research approaches and methods: Connecting people, participation and place.* New York: Routledge.

Kothari, U. (2001). Power, knowledge, and social control in participatory development. In B. Cooke & U. Kothari (Eds.), *Participation: The new tyranny?* (pp. 139–152). London: Zed Books.

Kretzmann, J., & McKnight, J. L. (1997). *Building communities from the inside out: A path toward finding and mobilizing a community's assets.* Evanston, IL: Institute for Policy Research, Northwestern University.

Low, S. (2003). *Behind the gates: Life, security and the pursuit of happiness in fortress America.* New York: Routledge.

Marable, M. (2000). *Dispatches from the ebony tower: Intellectuals confront the African American experience.* New York: Columbia University Press.

Mohan, G. (2001). Beyond participation: Strategies for deeper empowerment. In B. Cooke & U. Kothari (Eds.), *Participation: The new tyranny?* (pp. 153–167). London: Zed Books.

Perlich, P. (2006, May). *Long term demographic trends impacting higher education in Utah.* Prepared for the Board of Regents, Salt Lake City, UT.

Smith, L. T. (2007). On tricky ground: Researching the native in an age of uncertainty. In N. Denzin & Y. Lincoln (Eds.), *Handbook of qualitative research* (pp. 85–108). Beverly Hills, CA: Sage.

Smith, L. T. (1999). *Decolonizing methodologies: Research and indigenous peoples.* London: Zed Books.

Torre, M. E. (in press). Participatory action research and critical race theory: Fueling spaces for nos-otras to research. *Urban Review.*

Torre, M. E., & Fine, M. (2006). Participatory action research (PAR) by youth. In L. Sherrod (Ed.), *Youth activism: An international encyclopedia* (pp. 456–462). Westport, CT: Greenwood Publishing Group.

Torre, M. E., Fine, M., Boudin, K., Bowen, I., Clark, J., Hylton, D., Martinez, M., Roberts, R.A., Rivera, M., Smart, P., & Upegui, D. (2001). A space for co-

constructing counter stories under surveillance. *International Journal of Critical Psychology, 4,* 149–166.

Twine, F. W. (2004). White anti-racism in multiracial families. In M. Fine, L. Weis, L. P. Pruitt, & A. Burns (Eds.), *Off white: Readings on power, privilege and resistance* (pp. 395–410). New York: Routledge.

CHAPTER 7

TEACHING ENGLISH, READING POETRY, LIVING IN THE WORLD

Janet Kaufman

"I realize the site director is doing her best, trying to find a placement to fit with my impossible schedule . . . but a *ceramics* class after school?" "Sounds odd, I realize," I say, putting faith in the director of the Family Literacy Center and trying to reassure my new student who is doubting the tuition he paid for the service-learning portion of my class. "But if you're going to be an English teacher," I continue, "you'll be in English classes for your whole career. The kids in the ceramics class are on the verge of dropping out. The principal created it as part of a last-ditch-effort-program to get the students curious about school again. Consider what you could learn in ceramics . . . What could you learn about the students? What could you learn about you? What could you learn that would make you a stronger English teacher?"

I have been involved in civically engaged scholarship (CES) because I want my work and the study of the humanities to matter in my life, my students' lives, and the world. With CES, I think, ask, read, and write about the work I do as a scholar and a teacher of teachers, to apply my learning and participate in my community, and to create a reality check that my universi-

Finding Meaning in Civically Engaged Scholarship, pages 59–68
Copyright © 2009 by Information Age Publishing

ty work indeed matters beyond the university. Would my student's service in the ceramics class matter in the way I thought possible? Would he discover what I trusted he could? Would his reflections on his experience forward the learning of other students in my class? It became my task and challenge as a teacher to help this kind of learning unfold, and to keep finding and making links between Justin's experience in ceramics, his academic work to becoming an English teacher, and his—and our—roles as contributing members of a democratic society.

CES involves imparting and creating disciplinary knowledge, while remaining curious about how that knowledge could affect one's place in community. It helps me see my work in a range of concentric circles: my university students; their high school students; the schools and organizations I partner with through service-learning; the kids and families in those schools' neighborhoods; Salt Lake City itself; the state of Utah; the U.S.; the world. Civic engagement gives me a formal, academic way of thinking about questions I've always asked about the connection between literary work and our lives. The poet Muriel Rukeyser (1974) once said, "It's not that we bring things in life together. It's that we refuse to allow them to be torn apart." What is the link between literature and ceramics? Life during school and life after school? CES affirms that those questions have a place in the academy.

THE PERSONAL JOURNEY

As I think about my involvement with CES and what I hope my students and I gain from it, I know that my answers are personal. Inquiry of the self in teaching is crucial, and I have found the writing of Parker Palmer (1998) helpful in contemplating this. Discussing the possibilities for including the subjective and personal in teaching, Palmer embarks on a discussion of objectivism:

> The mode of knowing that dominates education creates disconnections between teachers, their subjects, and their students because it is rooted in fear. This mode, called *objectivism,* portrays truth as something we can achieve only by disconnecting ourselves, physically and emotionally, from the thing we want to know. (p. 51)

Being involved in service-learning, seeing the impact of acknowledging and integrating the lived experience of my students in literature and teaching classes, working in partnership with community members, grappling with the complexities of sustaining partnership, working with our Civically Engaged Scholar Cohort, and now writing this essay, I find the chance to voice the significance of the personal in my professional work. Palmer believes that fear keeps us from honoring the subjective in our work, and thus it takes some courage to do so. Yet CES, by connecting classroom learning to our learning in the world, inherently welcomes the subjective and offers a structure for recognizing its crucial place in learning. I engage in CES because it feels like the right thing to do. When I began working with CES, I was doubtful. I had a colleague who knew about service-learning and wanted to try it in the classes that we both taught, so I hesitantly agreed to investigate the possibilities while remaining wary of the kinds of things faculty are always wary about in the beginning—especially the time that service-learning would take and the distraction it would create from our conventional course materials. I didn't know how we would meet the multiple needs that genuine service-learning demanded—my needs, my students' needs, the community partner's needs. But I ended up getting involved in service-learning more deeply and quickly than I had anticipated, and soon saw that it was a good way to go: my students were getting genuine experience in the field related to English/Language Arts teaching; and I was getting to know and work with teachers, administrators, and students in the large urban high school where we were establishing the Family Literacy Center. This helped me feel grounded in my field—English teaching. Creating a link between my academic department and the community felt important, as I always believed that English studies, literature, and writing ultimately could make a difference beyond academy walls. As significant was my personal satisfaction—I *enjoyed* the hands-on work with students and community partners and the feeling that I was doing something that could make a difference in the city I lived in and liked so much.

But to answer why I do this work I can go farther back. As a child, I was always sensitive to injustice and, for as long as I can remember, wanted to grow up to do something that would matter. I remember in second grade when a boy in the lunch line called out, "You're a Jew!", and I knew something was terribly wrong about the way he said it. I remember reading my first Holocaust narrative at age 10, sitting in my fifth grade classroom reading Gerda Weissman Klein's (1957, 1995) *All But My Life*, while I surely was supposed to be doing something else. And though my religious education was sparse, I took in the idea that *tikkun olam*, repairing the world, was something I was obligated to do. It appealed to me, struck me as accurate, that one could feel one's spirit come alive when doing something to strengthen the world. I have been driven by my own inexplicable desire to feel my spirit alive in this way, and also by my religious tradition, from which I learned to imagine that I was the stranger and thus knew what it felt like to be oppressed. This, coupled with my understanding of myself as a girl who was able to emerge as a woman through the ideas and developments of the feminist movement, has made me want to find ways to work against silencing and oppression and toward social justice.

Reading and writing, using and interpreting language, are the two great acts that comprise my discipline. Growing up, with too many silences around me, I looked to poetry to find my voice. As a young adult reading Rukeyser's (2005) "Effort at Speech Between Two People," where she writes the refrain, "Speak to me. What are you now?" I felt invited and obligated to reply—to her, to myself, to those I loved. It wasn't enough to have words on the page. Moving forward in my life, I have continued learning to use language in new ways with family, friends, and students, hoping my classes are meaningful to their lives as well as their intellects. I strive to understand where language fails us and where we fail it, and how we can use it to create possibilities. As I reflect on my choice as a graduate student to write a dissertation about Rukeyser, I know it is in some large part due to her belief that poetry is something "to be used." She wrote that the experience of art "will apply to your life; and it is more than likely to lead you to thought or action, that is, you are likely to want to go further into the world, further into yourself, toward further experience" (1996, p. 26). I return to these words again and again, and to her idea that the reader and writer are a witness not only to art but to experience. A poem doesn't become real or even really exist in the world unless it has an audience that makes it meaningful; the poem exists through the dynamic relationship of the poet, the poem, and the reader. When my students can read poetry not only for aesthetic and critical meaning, but also for inspiration, for taking it into the world and sharing it with younger students, for seeing something new, then I feel that I am honoring my discipline.

Academic learning has given me tools to investigate my life, and the sacred parts of my life have compelled me in my professional work. Through academic work, I am able to teach and carry out a project like the Family Literacy Center (see Chapter 16, this volume), which enables me to support the reading and writing of poetry in school and sometimes to mentor, through my students, adolescents who desperately need tools to communicate. As a teacher of English/Language Arts teachers, I tell my students that our job, ultimately, is to keep learning the art of language and enable our students to use language artfully in and for their lives. Thus service-learning allows us to keep learning while it presents an opportunity to help young people and families find and use empowering language. I always love Joseph Brodsky's (1991) quote from the speech he gave as Poet Laureate: "What concerns me is that man, unable to articulate, to express himself adequately, reverts to action. Since the vocabulary of action is limited, as it were, to his body, he is bound to act violently, extending his vocabulary with a weapon where there should have been an adjective." (p. 34). Would that we all could speak up for what we need, for what is needed, against injustice and for all that allows us to thrive.

Being a parent of young children intensifies my feelings about needing to act in the world, even though the daily challenges of parenting have limited my ability to participate in both work and community projects as much as I want. Yet I hope that I will, through my work, be able to show my children the need and obligation for individuals to contribute, and the capacity an individual has to effect the world around her. And I hope they will discover the pleasure and richness that comes from knowing and working with people from different backgrounds; from knowing you have something to give; from working in a community deeply so that you feel it's yours, that you belong to it and it belongs to you; and from the deep joy of knowing there are many good people doing good work in the world.

THE PERSONAL ACADEMIC JOURNEY

When I consider what it would be like not to do this work—which I do consider, because sometimes the demands of it feel too heavy—I imagine I'd feel lonelier and more limited. And without service-learning and CES, the university would be limited. Conventional ideas about what makes a person an academic—teaching, service, and scholarship—narrow us. About 10 years ago, as the Lowell Bennion Community Service Center at the University of Utah began to focus on the relationship between service-learning, ABCS (Academically Based Community Scholarship), and CES, I became part of the Civically Engaged Scholars Think Tank on campus, perhaps our campus' first such interdisciplinary effort to understand the possibilities of broadening CES across campus. At one meeting, the university president had been invited to talk with us and, when I raised my hand to ask a question about institutional support on RPT for junior faculty working in civic engagement, he looked straight at me, acknowledged that he knew about my Family Literacy Center project and admired it, and then said only, "Be careful." While service and community involvement certainly were lauded, explicitly and implicitly the message conveyed was that publication counted most. I took the president's warning to heart and focused on developing scholarship about the project.

Subsequently, for my tenure file, I prepared not only a personal statement about my teaching, research, and service, but also an additional statement about the Family Literacy Center and its significance to those three areas of evaluation. As a professor of English Education in a mainstream English department, it became important to help my departmental colleagues understand the place of service-learning work in the broader context of both my discipline and the CES movement. Below I excerpt a few paragraphs from that statement, hoping they might be helpful to readers now facing similar challenges.

THE INTRODUCTION

As my academic career evolves, the Family Literacy Center project that I began developing in 1998...has become more central to my work. Thus, I discuss it separately because of the way it integrates my research, teaching, and service. The project continues to evolve in new directions, with a focus that I anticipate will drive much of my research and scholarship in the next few years, bringing new discussion about teacher training to the field of English Education. Here I will discuss: (1) the history and ongoing development of the project in terms of teaching, research, and service; and (2) the impact of the project on the English Education program at the University of Utah.

An excerpt from the section on teaching:

> As coordinator of the English Education program, my role in the English department is to provide unique opportunities for my students to prepare themselves to teach secondary English. When I took on this role in 1998, my goal was to offer students field work experience in the most urban, diverse public high school in Salt Lake City while they were still completing coursework, before beginning their student-teaching experience. Service-learning seemed an ideal way to achieve this. The term "service-learning" (S-L) is used to describe pedagogy that integrates community work with course content in order to strengthen the academic learning of the course and to set academic learning in the context of civic participation. It puts the university in direct relation to the "university civic responsibility movement," a national movement designed to construct "a democratic schooling system and advance American democracy." (Benson & Harkavy, 2000, p. 193)

The University of Utah Bennion Center's has developed its own definition of service-learning:

> An experience-based form of pedagogy in which students, faculty, and community partners work together to integrate and apply empirically-grounded knowledge in authentic settings to address the needs of the community and meet instructional objectives using action and critical reflection to prepare students to become meaningful members of a just and democratic society.

This definition is important to me as it emphasizes the work of meeting instructional objectives by/while meeting community needs, as well as the importance of experience and critical reflection in the learning process.

In a section on "Scholarly Research: Ongoing and Future," I detailed a record of numerous conferences at which I'd presented, grants I'd been awarded to sustain and develop the Family Literacy Center (at that time, $160,000), and a couple articles that I had published. Then I concluded:

In many ways...the project has just begun to coalesce. It is unusual to find a project like the Family Literacy Center among service-learning projects: a project in which a new institution is created through a university-community partnership to serve needs of both university and community. Therefore, my scholarship thus far has focused primarily on questions related to campus-community partnerships: how they work, what makes them successful and sustainable. Writing about this will make a valuable contribution to the literature on service-learning.

In a traditional sense, the Family Literacy Center could be perceived as a laboratory for my research. However, looking from within a new paradigm, the project reflects basic tenets of Academically Based Community Scholarship (ABCS) (Lawson, 1998) where the generation of new knowledge takes place in, through, and from direct engagement with questions and problems emerging from a university-community partnership. ABCS is *academically* based "because it requires the knowledge-related skills and abilities of faculty scholars as well as students, especially their abilities to generate, interpret, criticize, organize, disseminate, and use various kinds of formal knowledge" (Lawson, 1998, p. 210). At the same time, it is *community scholarship* because faculty expertise and leadership offer "documented, beneficial effects on the problems of community and society" (Lawson, 1998, p. 211). Metzler (1994) has called this the "the scholarship of engagement." ABCS is recognized as occurring in the community and being both collaborative and participatory.

While both S-L and ABCS can be seen as primarily meeting the teaching and service missions of the university and individual faculty members, the term Civically Engaged Scholarship (CES) is used to describe work that is linked to research, scholarship, and the mission of the university. E.L. Boyer, president of the Carnegie Foundation for the Advancement of Teaching from 1979–95, published a report in 1990, *Scholarship Reconsidered,* that has become a focal point for faculty discussions across the nation about the roles of scholarship in the university as it moves away from a restrictive, Cold War, model. Such a model, he argues, moves linearly and hierarchically from research to publication to application in the classroom or further research; the new model he describes creates and seeks commonalities among the disciplines, and sets itself in relation to the construction of democratic schooling and the development of a fully democratic society. To quote Boyer (1990):

Specifically, we conclude that the work of the professoriate might be thought of as having four separate, yet overlapping, functions. These are: the scholarship of *discovery*; the scholarship of *integration*; the scholarship of *application*; and the scholarship of *teaching* (p. 16).

I see my work as integrally involved in each of these four functions. Even more recently, carrying forward Boyer's efforts to conceive and design a new model for the understanding and evaluation of scholarship, the Imagining America Tenure Team Initiative (TTI) has sought ways to remove obstacles for faculty carrying out collaborative and publicly engaged academic work, proposing that such work "carried out for and/or with the public should have full standing as scholarship, research, or artistic creation." It declares that beyond procedural and policy changes, enlarging the conception of peer evaluation and scholarship "is part of something bigger: the democratization of knowledge on and off campus" (iv). The TTI document, with numerous universities supporting it, clarifies the developing significance of publicly engaged academic work to institutions of higher education.

At the time, the struggle to situate my work in personal, community, and academic contexts was a valuable one, full as it was, at the time, of the fear of being misunderstood. Thus to find, through the Lowell Bennion Community Service Center, a community of people also doing this work and then to feel a sense of kinship among them has been a tremendous gift. The university, to be strong at its core, must accept and embrace multiple ways of being intellectuals and teachers. Without this work, we would be giving up on parts of ourselves and on a vision for higher education that includes acknowledging the connections among our intellectual lives, our personal lives, and our lives in community.

CES changes my scholarship as it encourages and affirms the need to write in language that can be understood by, and appeals to, an audience beyond the academy; it also requires and invites a range of writing beyond the genres of conventional scholarship in my field, including letters, grant proposals, and collaborative projects such as this book. To succeed in this work, I seek partnership with members of the community, individuals in my field of English/Language Arts, and individuals from other disciplines. Leading me to venture into realms of learning beyond my formal training, CES takes me to places like social work and political science, which takes time and energy and can make my work look slow. But going to new places means that I am constantly learning about what it means to be a citizen, or simply a contributing person (Irene Fisher—who pioneered and was the first director of the Bennion Center, made me realize that sometimes we need another word to include those who politically don't have a safe relationship to the word "citizen"). Seeking language with my students to understand the connections between English/Language Arts teaching and our place in the world helps me constantly develop new questions, and thus my writing, teaching, and work in the community are integrally linked.

CONCLUSION

My student who spent a semester doing service-learning in the ceramics class described, in his final written reflection, a rambunctious, distracting moment in the class when, against the directions of the teacher, one of the high school students plugged her iPod into her ears and cranked the volume. Justin started to sing along and, struck by disbelief that "anyone who would want to be a teacher would listen to the same music I do," the high school student and others in the class "started to open up and talk" with him. He wrote, "After this we had fewer discipline problems, fewer motivation problems (the students no longer wanted me to do their assignments for them, they wanted me to show them how to do them), and more work was done." Justin ended his reflection with a discussion about the idea of "connecting": "the creation of a new idea, relationship, or individual by fusing together two parts to create a new whole. E.M. Forster had it right all along . . . 'Only connect!'" Here Justin made a link—implicit and explicit—between ceramics and English/Language Arts: the language of literature helped him interpret and make life-giving meaning of a moment far removed from the confines of an English class or a private experience of reading; the moment with the teens helped him understand Forster better and carried him to the heart of his discipline. And there he saw anew his place as a teacher, mentor, adult.

In *Education for a Caring Society,* D. Kay Johnston (2006) writes about the "relationship landscape of classrooms," saying that "learning is embedded in relationship" and that "classroom relationships are the ground on which students think and act" (p. 16). In his experience, Justin discovered just that; he wrote: "[s]ervice-learning has taught me in a very empirical way that connections must be made for learning to occur—more specifically between the student and the teacher and between the student and the subject. And the more square, complete, and true the connection is, the greater the learning that occurs." As scholars, we continue to learn, wrestle with new questions and knowledge, doubt, and risk. Our learning is embedded in relationships with students, colleagues, our disciplines, and our personal lives. For this reason, it has been a joy and a necessity to feel connected to the group of individuals involved with this book. I have found among them people in whom I trust to share my work, people I learn from, who value my work and whose work I value, and with whom I can collaborate. It is a great privilege to connect across the university, to be inspired and challenged in my life and work, and feel strengthened to give back in turn.

NOTE

Names of students in this article have been changed to protect anonymity.

REFERENCES

Benson, L., & Harkavy, I. (2000). Integrating the American system of higher, secondary, and primary education to develop civic responsibility. In T. Erlich, *Civic responsibility and higher education* (pp. 174–196). Phoenix, AZ: American Council on Education and Oryx Press.

Boyer, E. (1990). *Scholarship reconsidered: Priorities of the professoriate.* San Francisco: Jossey-Bass.

Brodsky, J. (1991). An immodest proposal. *The New Republic, Nov. 11*, 31–36.

Ellison, J., & Eatman, T. K. (2008). Scholarship in public: Knowledge creation and tenure policy in the engaged university. *Imagining America: Artists and scholars in public life, Tenure team on public scholarship.* Available at, http://www.imaginingamerica.org/TTI/TTI_FINAL.pdf

Johnston, D. K. (2006). *Education for a caring society: Classroom relationships and moral action.* New York: Teachers College Press.

Klein, G. W. (1957, 1995). *All but my life.* New York: Hill and Wang.

Lawson, H. A. (1998). Academically based community scholarship, consultation as collaborative problem-solving, and a collective-responsibility model for the helping fields. *Journal of Educational and Psychological Consultation, 9*, 195–232.

Metzler, M. (1994). Scholarship reconsidered for the professorate of 2010. *Quest, 46*, 440–455.

Palmer, P. (1998). *The courage to teach: Exploring the inner landscape of a teacher's life.*

Rukeyser, M. (1949/1996). *The life of poetry.* Ashfield, MA: Paris Press.

Rukeyser, M. (1974). Craft interview with Muriel Rukeyser. In W. Packard (Ed.), *The craft of poetry* (pp. 153–176). Garden City, NY: Doubleday.

Rukeyser, M. (2005). *Collected poems of Muriel Rukeyser.* J. Kaufman & A. Herzog (Eds.). Pittsburgh, PA: University of Pittsburgh Press.

CHAPTER 8

A JOURNEY
OF VOLUNTARISM

Nancy Winemiller Basinger

Despite Putnam's (2000) claim that more and more often we are "bowling alone," I remain unconvinced that lower membership in some civic organizations, such as bowling leagues, necessarily marks a decline in social capital (2000). In stark contrast to Putnam's findings, the size of the charitable sector grew 39% nationally from 1992 to 1998 (Weitzman, Jalandoni, Lampkin, & Pollak, 2002). Opportunities to learn and to serve through civic engagement are growing with the sector. DeToqueville's observation that America was a nation of joiners is perhaps too often cited. His remark, nonetheless, seems to aptly describe my view of civic engagement. Intellectually, I understand that civic engagement is more than just joining a nonprofit organization in my community.

As a political scientist, I cannot discount the value of political involvement. I have regularly cast my vote, displayed candidate signs in my yard, and signed petitions. I feel I have a responsibility to participate in the democracy through regular government channels. These things I do out of a sense of duty or obligation. I do them because I think I should—not necessarily because I want to or because they make me feel good. I see this motivation as distinct from my motivation for civic participation through

Finding Meaning in Civically Engaged Scholarship, pages 69–75

nonprofits. My civic engagement is about participating with nonprofits in work that promotes their missions on a day-to-day basis. It is about doing something good. It is about making the world a better place, about thinking globally while acting locally.

THE ROLE OF NONPROFITS IN CIVIC ENGAGEMENT

Many nonprofit scholars divide society and the interactions between individuals and organizations into three sectors. The private sector includes those businesses that serve our private needs—the grocery store, the airlines, the computer software developer. These organizations interact with individuals and other corporations as consumers and suppliers and their existence and behavior are well understood through economic models. The public sector is composed of government entities who serve the broad public interest. The third or voluntary sector includes nonprofit organizations that serve the public good through a specific mission. For me, civic engagement is about participation in this third sector. It is about joining forces with others through organizations that improve society.

The third sector performs many important roles in our society. The businesses in the private sector supply goods and services to those who are willing and able to pay for them. The governments in the public sector must serve the common good. They seek to serve all citizens by remaining mindful of equity among citizens as well as the preferences of voters. Charities can, and indeed are best suited to, improve society by tending to narrow and specific needs. The third sector exists, in part, to fill this gap between the needs of society and what businesses and governments choose to provide (Douglas, 2001; Young, 2001). Charities have three roles in their interactions with government: supplementary, complementary, and adversarial. I believe that each of these third sector roles is vital to the health and welfare of our society. Charities provide so much to society; they provide things that otherwise would not exist, ranging from the symphony to the food bank and everything in-between.

By providing opportunities for civic engagement through volunteering, donating, and advocating for policy change, nonprofits improve society. Not all civic engagement will occur in this third sector. But this is the civic engagement that means the most to me. My research and teaching both focus on the role of nonprofits in democracy because I believe this is how the nonprofit sector can and should make a difference. It is hard for me to imagine a world with only businesses and governments—a world without the Salvation Army, Big Brothers/Big Sisters, the local symphony and art museum, and the ARC. In such a world we would not have organizations that worked to legislatively define civil rights for people with disabilities through passage of the Americans with Disabilities Act and to ensure implementation of the act through the courts. Without nonprofits, the world would be a different place. That would affect each of us in different ways.

THE ROLE OF PERSONAL EXPERIENCES IN CIVIC ENGAGEMENT

It is for this reason that I challenge my students to think in a personal way about the important roles charities fulfill in society. I often begin a new semester teaching a nonprofit class by challenging students to respond to the following question, "What have nonprofits done to or for you in your lifetime?" Many students are at a loss. Most are unaware what a nonprofit is or how to distinguish it from other organizations that have touched their lives. The conversation often starts with a discussion of membership at the University credit union, or giving blood at the recent Red Cross blood drive. Generally at least one cynical student will say that a nonprofit is competing unfairly against their place of employment or point to a "special interest" like the National Rifle Association unfairly influencing public policies.

I give them time to write a list of their own and then I model my response for the class. I brainstorm a new list each time I teach, and each time I come up with new ways that nonprofits have affected my life. The list began with only my own experiences and grew to include how nonprofits have affected me through my family as well. I read my list and then I ask my students to share theirs with the group. I realized the last time I read my list for the class just how significant nonprofits have been in my life when I began to weep a bit as I read the part about the nonprofits in my son's life. This is my current list:

- I was an Indian Princess, a Blue Bird, and a Girl Scout.
- I went to three nonprofit schools for preschool, elementary, and secondary education.
- As a child, I loved going to the Indianapolis Children's Museum, the Indianapolis Zoo, and a living history museum called Conner Prairie (and I still do!).
- As a teen, I loved the symphony and went to performances as often as I could.
- A frequent volunteer, I loved giving historic house tours and leading social activities for patients in a local nursing home.
- I was a Job's daughter.
- In college, I gave campus tours to prospective students.

- I went to work for a nonprofit. I worked countless hours and then volunteered to help throw Halloween and Christmas parties for our clients—people with developmental disabilities.
- I was a Girl Scout leader and a Big Sister.
- In graduate school I studied boards and trained many how to function more effectively. I studied nonprofit advocacy and trained nonprofits how to influence public policies.
- Today, I serve on several boards and board committees.
- I belong to a church with an active mission outreach and participate in it.
- As a mother, I am grateful for the nonprofit school my child attends, the Jewish Community Center where he attends summer camp, and the natural history and art museums he loves to visit. I am grateful for the nonprofit ballet company that taught him to love The Nutcracker.
- Last year I was my son's Cub Scout leader.
- I am also grateful that my son thinks it is important for us to help our church make sandwiches one Sunday each month to serve at the homeless shelter. It is not only important for me to be a volunteer but to raise one.
- I am grateful to nonprofits for how they have helped my extended family as well. In rural southern Indiana near my family homestead, the only hospital is a small nonprofit. They have saved many a Winemiller over the years. Recently, my cousin died at age 47 only two weeks after being diagnosed with lung cancer. I am grateful that I am able to make a difference for others by donating to the American Lung Association.

I can chronicle my life through interactions with these nonprofits. They have been important organizations in all stages of my life. I created this exercise in order to help my students make this connection to the topic they would be studying for themselves. I then ask my students to share parts of their lists if they feel comfortable doing so. What I have learned from and about my students through this activity is amazing. After the most recent semester I received a note from a student discussing this activity:

> ...I wanted to say how much I enjoyed the exercise in our class...descanting what nonprofits we have been involved with or have affected our lives....I gained new and humbling insights on the character of my classmates. I learned far more about them as people than their professional titles or contributions in class reveal. (excerpted with permission, Private Communication, 2008)

I appreciated this insight greatly. I never realized, until they taught me, that the ways in which nonprofits affect people's lives are intimate reflections of many of their life experiences. Civic involvement is bigger than a campaign sign. I am giving to the American Lung Association because of a disease that has affected a loved one. Civic involvement may be as a result of the loss of a child or a love of wilderness or a fascination with the oboe. All of these are opportunities to be involved in society in a way that is beyond work, outside the bounds of family, and not required by basis of citizenship. This third sector allows us all to participate in improving society in ways that are important to us as individuals by joining groups. It is a fascinating phenomenon.

THE MOTIVATIONS TO ENGAGE FOR SCHOLARS AND STUDENTS

As a scholar/teacher it is important to me that my students also understand the importance of service in the third sector to help nonprofits achieve their missions. When people volunteer, they are nearly always motivated *both* by altruism and by egoism (Mount, 1996; Wolfe, 1998). For me, this is definitely true. I want to feel a part of groups as they work to accomplish their goals. I get a sense of satisfaction from contributing to a desirable outcome. These solidarity benefits (Clark & Wilson, 1961) are perhaps the most rewarding to me personally. I spent the first year in my new community looking for groups to join. I knew this solidarity would make me feel a part of my new community.

My journey, then, is not a journey *to* civic engagement. I have always been civically engaged. I am a volunteer. I am a joiner. It is who I am and it is how I think. Clearly this was part of my socialization. I don't know how to be a part of the world without being engaged in my community through working with nonprofits. I am literally unsure what that would look like. As I ventured into the world of the academy, I remained an instigator, a joiner, and a builder. I am still learning how to blend this world view with the realities of academe.

When teaching my first graduate class, I applied the pedagogy of service-learning before I knew that it had a name or that it *was* pedagogy. It seemed common sense to me. To understand what a nonprofit is and how it might influence the community, you must see a nonprofit from the inside. I designed a project where my students would serve as consultants for a small nonprofit. The students developed plans for fund development and, in later service-learning classes, plans for public policy influence, financial analyses, training and development models, and donor recognition programs. I did not have a grand plan to make my students better citizens. I wanted the students to learn how to do something in a very realistic setting. I thought they could serve local nonprofits in the process. Having been on the community partner side in my past, I understood that the community partners would be providing a service to the students as well. It was important to me that the projects be relevant and helpful to the organizations we served. I did not think of this as civic engagement; I just thought of it as a great way to teach.

Ultimately, most of the students loved it. They felt all of the same frustrations that employees at small nonprofits feel when there is not enough time, money, or information to accomplish the task at hand. They felt as though they did not know what to do at every step during the project. I reassured them, and we ventured forward together. At the end, they could not believe how much they had learned about nonprofits and about the subject matter of the course. My students have served and learned from more than 25 different Salt Lake area nonprofits. However, not all of the projects were successful for both the students and the organizations. Not all community partners used the student projects, but many found them helpful. Some wrote me notes of thanks at the conclusion of the project.

As I grow as a civically engaged scholar, I realize that I need to adapt even more, to push myself beyond what is most comfortable to me and what I want my students to "give," and to explore what the community partners know they need. I also am learning that the students, when supported properly, can co-create knowledge that is far beyond what I can offer them on my own. In serving the needs of the community partners and the needs of the students, I am no longer the center of "my" class. This is difficult, and it can be uncomfortable and even frightening. Adopting a service-learning pedagogy means handing over control to others. I am still struggling with how to do this effectively while simultaneously having students realize the value of my role in the classroom and in the process of teaching and learning through service-learning.

After I had experienced service-learning from the student side, from the community partner side, and from the faculty side, I wanted to explore service-learning from all three perspectives. With a colleague, I examined the motivations, expectations, and satisfaction of nonprofit community partners in service-learning relationships (Basinger & Bartholomew, 2006). This work led to my first publication.

As I further explored these questions, I found colleagues at the University who helped me realize that nonprofits' needs may be met in additional ways through a broader definition of civic engagement by those in the academy. Beyond service-learning, faculty research and outreach serve our community. I have explored ways to serve through my research. I have completed a report on the state of the nonprofit sector in Utah and a wages and benefits survey of nonprofit employees in Utah—both applied research projects that benefit those in the nonprofit sector by providing information they can use in their organizations and to inform policymakers in our state. In addition, I have supervised master's research for several students interested in doing community-based research. In this way, my students and I not only serve through class-based projects but are also able to explore civically engaged scholarship. Through their community-based research, my students have explored such diverse topics as volunteer management, donor motivations, and board governance.

Civic engagement for me now means more than just joining a group. It means supervising service-learning students, engaging in participative and applied research for the nonprofit sector, and seeking outreach opportunities to help nonprofits build their own capacity through training and facilitation. As for being a civically engaged scholar, I do not see it as a choice, but rather a necessity. Without the benefits of my own direct service on boards and through applied research for the nonprofit community, and without the knowledge I gain through supervising service-learning projects, I cannot imagine how I would know what research is needed, interesting, and publishable. As is true for my students, I learn best by doing. There are countless opportunities for me in this regard. There are more than 1,000 public charities within a 90-minute driving radius of the University. My task now is to channel my new understanding of civic engagement and my passion for the work of charities into true civically engaged scholarship.

REFERENCES

Basinger, N., & Bartholomew, K. (2006). Service learning in nonprofit organizations: Motivations, expectations and outcomes. *The Michigan Journal of Community Service Learning, 12*, 15–26.

Clark, P. B., & Wilson, J. Q. (1961). Incentive systems: A theory of organization. *Administrative Science Quarterly, 6*, 129–166.

Douglas, J. (2001). Political theories of nonprofit organizations. In J. S. Ott (Ed.), *The nature of the nonprofit sector* (pp. 205–216). Boulder, CO: Westview.

Mount, J. (1996). Why donors give. *Nonprofit Management & Leadership 7*, 3–14.

Putnam, R. D. (2000). *Bowling alone: The collapse and revival of American community.* New York: Simon & Schuster.

Weitzman, M. S., Jalandoni, N. T., Lampkin, L. M., & Pollak, T. H. (2002). *The new nonprofit almanac & desk reference: The essential facts and figures for managers, researchers, and volunteers.* San Francisco: Jossey-Bass.

Wolfe, A. (1998). What is altruism? In W. Powell & E. Clemens (Eds.), *Private action and the public good* (pp. 36–46). New Haven, CT: Yale University Press.

Young, D. (2001). Government failure theory and contract failure theory. In J. S. Ott (Ed.), *The nature of the nonprofit sector* (pp. 190–197). Boulder, CO: Westview.

CHAPTER 9

THE CIVICALLY ENGAGED SCHOLAR

Identity, Relationship, and the RPT Process

Hank Liese

Inscrutably involved, we live in the currents of universal reciprocity.
—Martin Buber (1970, p. 67)

I attended college in the late 1960s, an exciting, turbulent, often confusing time. Two books I read during that period had a profound effect on me, and still do. One was *The Quest for Identity* by Allen Wheelis (1958) and the other was Martin Buber's *I and Thou* (1970).

Wheelis called his book "an essay on man in mid-twentieth-century America," concerned with "his changing character, with the loss of his old identity, and with his search for a new one" (p. 9). It's no surprise this book appealed to a twenty-something college student out to find himself and forge an identity separate and apart from his parents and siblings. For Wheelis, identity was a "coherent sense of self" and was dependent upon "the awareness that one's endeavors and one's life make sense, that they are meaningful in the context in which life is lived" (p. 19). A psychiatrist,

Finding Meaning in Civically Engaged Scholarship, pages 77–85
Copyright © 2009 by Information Age Publishing

77

Wheelis artfully tied his discussion of identity to the tenets of psychoanalysis. For a psychology major enamored by the writings of Freud and Jung, Wheelis touched a chord deep within.

Buber did the same, speaking to my parallel search for a spiritual self at a time when some were claiming that God was dead. A religious ethics course introduced me to Buber and other religious philosophers and theologians—Paul Tillich, Dietrich Bonhoeffer, Reinhold Niebuhr, and the Berrigan brothers, Daniel and Phillip—whose writings fashioned my values and steadied my moral compass during the public controversy and personal dilemmas engendered by the Vietnam War.

I and Thou (*Ich und Du* in Buber's native German) was written in 1923, and the book's first English translation appeared in 1937. Focused on human relationships and their reciprocity, the book is a difficult but rewarding read. Writes Walter Kaufmann in the prologue to his 1970 translation: "He [Buber] evidently did not wish to be read quickly, only once, for information. He tried to slow the reader down, to force him to read many sentences and paragraphs again, even to read the whole book more than once" (p. 43). For a young college student seeking meaningful connections to others, believing as I did that these relationships would give shape to an emerging sense of self, Buber was a beacon in a stormy sea—not to mention a lesson in patience.

GOING UP FOR TENURE: IDENTITY REVISITED

Fast forward to the present—40 years since college, 50 years since Wheelis wrote, 60 years since *I and Thou* was translated into English. I am an associate professor in my University's College of Social Work, have been tenured for five years, and am wearing the mantle of a civically engaged scholar. But this is not a mantle bestowed on me from the outside. It certainly was not a mantle described in my College's guidelines for retention, promotion, and tenure, or RPT. When I went up for tenure, I felt, to borrow from Wheelis, that I had to make sense of my endeavors and my life in the academic context in which I was living. I wanted my peers, those who would judge me, to understand my love for, and involvement in, the burgeoning field of service-learning and civic engagement. I went out on a limb, introducing the personal statement of my final tenure review with the following: "I have chosen to present myself here as a 'civically engaged scholar,' an identity which I believe is not only reflected in my research, teaching, and service but which, importantly, allows me to *integrate* my scholarly activities in these three critical areas."

It was risky. At about the same time, a group of like-minded colleagues and I had been conducting a review of the 50-plus sets of RPT guidelines from all the University's colleges and departments. Only five of them made specific mention of "service-learning," four of them listing it under service and only one under teaching. At my institution, junior faculty are often cautioned *not* to teach service-learning courses until *after* they are tenured. Doing so, they are told, may jeopardize getting tenure, since it detracts from the pursuit of "real" scholarship.

In my personal statement for tenure (18 pages, including references), I took the role of educator: I had to explain what it *meant* to be a "civically engaged scholar" to review committees, both within my College and the larger University, that might not grasp the nature and importance of this work. For me, the trick was to not go off the deep end, to not break the branch on which I was crawling. I did this by casting service-learning and civic engagement as best I could in the language and expectations of tenure review committees, which historically have focused on excellence and/or mastery in three areas: research, teaching, and service. The priority ranking of these three areas depends on the college or university. I list research first because the University of Utah, my home institution, is a Research I university.

REFLECTING ON CIVICALLY ENGAGED SCHOLARSHIP

Before summarizing the case I made in my personal statement—which, it is hoped, may assist the reader in a similar situation—I would like to recount my own understanding of civically engaged scholarship (CES) and the journey and side trips that got me here. Taking a page from psychoanalysis and engaging in a little free association, four words come to mind: *connection, reciprocity, authenticity,* and *service.*

When I think of civically engaged scholarship, I think of a Buber-like *connection* between me and my students, between colleagues doing similar work, between me and my discipline (social work), and, most importantly, between all of these constituencies and communities—small and large—outside the geographic boundaries of the university.

In a similar vein, CES, for me, is about *reciprocity,* defined by our dear friend Webster as "mutual exchange." Everyone engaged in this work, it seems to me, gives something to someone or something else, willingly and without artifice (see *authenticity* below). My expectation in giving is, quite simply, that a little will go a long way and that just as much, if not more, of what I give will come back to me in return. Old-school pedagogical methodology is too unidirectional in nature, as Paulo Freire (1970) observed. Reciprocity can and should take academicians and students alike outside themselves and quell a tendency toward egocentricity, a malaise that can unbalance both our personal and professional lives.

For *authenticity*, I return to the sixties, when the somewhat pejorative phrase "get real" was popularized. Demonstrating against the Vietnam War, we could have easily delivered that phrase to what we believed to be clueless and stubborn university administrations. Several generations later, college and university campuses look and feel much different. Protest is muted, if it exists at all. However, there seems to be a greater self-awareness among students today, the so-called "millennials," who seem to have a growing sense of who they are and what they must do to make the world a better place. In my college days, I might have designed a lapel button that read, "Get real." Today, I, and I think many of my students, would wear buttons reading, "*Be* real." To make civically engaged scholarship work, we must be real, we must be genuine—true to ourselves, true to others.

Taking yet another historical perspective, I hope we have forever banished the "me" generation; I like to think we're in the "us" generation. *Service* is quite different if approached with an "us," rather than a "me," mentality. We have to get outside ourselves to truly—authentically—serve others. One of my first jobs out of college was working in public relations for the prep school I attended in the Midwest. I wrote a feature article for the school's alumni magazine about a group of theater students who traveled by bus to area nursing homes to perform short plays for the residents. It was a wonderful intermingling of the generations; in fact, the young students (this was 1972) were ahead of their time—they were, quite literally, acting in an "us" fashion before "us" was fashionable. The theater director who organized and supervised these traveling minstrels held this motto up for his troupe: "Service above self." It was about transcendence. It was an antidote to egocentricity.

EDUCATING ON CIVICALLY ENGAGED SCHOLARSHIP

A year before my final tenure review, I participated in a small discussion group on campus called the Civically Engaged Scholars group (to be distinguished from the current Civically Engaged Scholar Cohort from which this collection of essays sprang). Comprising about a dozen faculty members and several doctoral students, the group met every other week for two hours. We immersed ourselves in the growing literature on what the late Ernest Boyer (1990) termed the "scholarship of engagement"; what Fear, Rosaen, Foster-Fishman, and Bawden (2001) called "outreach as scholarly expression"; and what Checkoway (2001) called "public scholarship" related to "the pressing problems of society" (p. 143).

Utilizing concepts and terms from the literature, each member of the group wrote a definition of "civically engaged scholarship." From these individual definitions, the group developed a collective definition: "Civically engaged scholarship is a dynamic and collaborative participatory process in which the rich resources of the university and community are combined to integrate research, learning, and service in identifying and addressing community-based issues and needs while promoting socially responsible knowledge. Faculty, staff, students, and members of the community forge relationships as meaningful partners in exploring those practices that produce tangible outcomes to benefit the partners and their communities and that disseminate new knowledge in a variety of ways."

I included this definition on the first page of my personal statement for my final tenure review. I noted that, although more and more universities were beginning to address the scholarship of engagement in the RPT review process (Gelmon & Agre-Keppenhan, 2002), most institutions of higher learning still emphasized the more traditional, and narrow, conceptualizations of research, teaching, and service. In my role as educator for the RPT review committees, I explained that Boyer (1990) had recast these three streams of the academic mission into four forms of scholarship—discovery, integration, application, and teaching—and argued that the academy needs to recognize all four categories.

Lest my reviewers get lost in Boyer's terminology, I presented Glassick, Huber, and Maeroff's summary (1997) of Boyer's schema. Following Glassick et al. (p. 9), I noted that the scholarship of discovery "comes closest to what academics mean when they speak of research," and that the scholarship of integration involves faculty members making connections "within and between the disciplines." The third element, the scholarship of application, "moves toward engagement as the scholar asks, 'How can knowledge be responsibly applied to consequential problems?'" Finally, the scholarship of teaching "initiates students into the best values of the academy, enabling them to comprehend better and participate more fully in the larger culture." My personal statement continued: "For the civically engaged scholar, the scholarship of application moves front and center, not to the exclusion of discovery, integration, and teaching, but as the next logical step once knowledge has been generated. If this is what we know and what we teach, how do we apply that knowledge, both within and outside of the classroom, to community-based issues in real-life settings? The scholarship of application can also serve as a mechanism for the integration of one's research, teaching, and service."

In my personal statement, I organized my academic accomplishments under the three traditional categories of research, teaching, and service, following my College's RPT guidelines. At the beginning of each major section—research, teaching, and service—I restated the College's criteria for promotion (to associate professor) and tenure. These were the "familiar" for my reviewers, and they would want to know I was addressing the appropriate criteria. "This format," I wrote, "is meant to capture the evolution of my work and thinking over the past nine years[1] and to illustrate how I intend to approach my research, teaching, and service as an engaged scholar."

My personal statement acknowledged the reluctance of many faculty to involve themselves in public scholarship and quoted Finkelstein (2001), who attributed this situation to "a prevailing view among academics that engaged work is less scholarly than traditional research" (p. 36). Finkelstein, I said, asserted that assessing community-based scholarship is difficult because it does not resemble research as taught by most disciplines: it "involves non-academic partners, is often multidisciplinary, and is usually problem- rather than theory-driven" (p. 36).

At the time I was going up for tenure, Finkelstein was calling on universities to articulate a single set of standards that would help faculty members document the scholarly value of their work, no matter what form it took. Earlier, Glassick et al. (1997) had articulated six standards that were eventually adopted as portfolio evaluation criteria by the National Review Board for the Scholarship of Engagement, which was created to review and evaluate the scholarship of engagement of faculty who were preparing for annual review, retention, and promotion. My personal statement used these standards to advantage. "While I understand that I am being reviewed under the [College's] existing RPT guidelines," I wrote, "I nonetheless would like to set forth Glassick et al.'s standards here, for they provide me with a guiding framework as I develop my future agenda as a civically engaged scholar:

- *Clear Goals.* Does the scholar: (1) state the basic purposes of his or her work clearly, (2) define objectives that are realistic and achievable, and (3) identify important questions in the field?
- *Adequate preparation.* Does the scholar (1) show an understanding of existing scholarship in the field, (2) bring the necessary skills to his or her work, and (3) bring together the resources necessary to move the project forward?
- *Appropriate methods.* Does the scholar (1) use methods appropriate to the goals, (2) apply effectively the methods selected, and (3) modify procedures in response to changing circumstances?
- *Significant results.* Does the scholar achieve the goals and does the scholar's work (1) add consequentially to the field and (2) open additional areas for further exploration?
- *Effective presentation.* Does the scholar (1) use a suitable style and effective organization to present his or her work, (2) use appropriate forums for communicating work to its intended audiences, and (3) present his or her message with clarity and integrity?

- *Reflective critique.* Does the scholar (1) critically evaluate his or her own work, (2) bring an appropriate breadth of evidence to his or her critique, and (3) use evaluation to improve the quality of future work?"

This recitation of Glassick et al.'s framework, I believe, helped my reviewers see how closely the College's own RPT criteria actually mapped against the emerging criteria for the scholarship of engagement. My gamble, apparently, paid off.

WHY CIVICALLY ENGAGED SCHOLARSHIP?

This "preflection" question was posed to the current Civically Engaged Scholar Cohort (CESC) at the outset of this writing project. I believe that when we choose to do one thing, we are choosing *not* to do something else. So I approach this question by considering what I am *not* choosing to do at this point in my academic career—with tenure, I might add, and comfortable now in the skin of a civically engaged scholar. I am not choosing to teach all my classes in a traditional classroom bounded by four walls, bounded in turn by the "invisible fence" that separates town from gown. I am not choosing to spoon feed information to my students in the hope that something will be digested, make a difference to them, and eventually find its way outward to make a difference in the community at large. I am not choosing to undertake traditional, positivistic research, which can be patronizing, holding *me* up as the expert, and which ignores the hopes and dreams of the community at large. I am not choosing to serve on boards and committees, within and outside the University, that don't serve a larger purpose in bettering that community. For me, it is *all* about community— the community that develops between me and my service-learning students, the community of engaged scholars that I hold so dear, and the community that all of us who do this type of work seek to serve, and through that service to embrace, embolden, and, ultimately, empower.

A second preflection question the CESC addressed was, "What would it mean if 'we' didn't do this type of work?" For me, it would mean doing all of the things above I am choosing *not* to do, and what fun would that be? For us, collectively, it would mean that we, as well as our students, would not be joining with the community to make a difference in addressing the pressing issues of our time: poverty, homelessness, the lack of affordable health care, environmental degradation, racism, sexism, homophobia, bullying in our schools, child abuse and neglect—and on and on. It would mean abandoning the stewardship of our society, indeed, our planet. If "we" didn't do this work, then who would?

BACK TO THE FUTURE

I could not have known 40 years ago that Allen Wheelis and Martin Buber would presage my future in the way they did. Through their words and now my own experiences, I have come to understand that identity is something we are always defining and refining, especially in new situations that call for new roles, whether personal, professional, or both. I know as well that our worlds—and our identities—to a large degree are shaped by the relationships we choose to develop and nurture. The deeper and more authentic those relationships are, the stronger and more authentic the identity will be. Entering academe 15 years ago, in my mid forties, I was thrust into new roles that demanded new relationships and a new identity. It took time to develop both, but the fit, for now, is remarkable and gratifying. May the quest continue; there is so much work to be done.

NOTE

1. I had taken an administrative leave of absence for four years to serve as the College's Director of Development and Alumni Relations, which extended my timeline for gaining tenure.

REFERENCES

Boyer, E. L. (1990). *Scholarship reconsidered: Priorities of the professoriate.* Princeton, NJ: The Carnegie Foundation for the Advancement of Teaching.

Buber, M. (1970). *I and thou.* New York: Simon and Shuster.

Checkoway, B. (2001). Renewing the civic mission of the American research university. *The Journal of Higher Education, 72*(2), 125–147.

Fear, F. A., Rosaen, C. L., Foster-Fishman, P., & Bawden, R. J. (2001). Outreach as scholarly expression: A faculty perspective. *Journal of Higher Education Outreach and Engagement, 6*(2), 21–33.

Finkelstein, M. A. (2001). Toward a unified view of scholarship: Eliminating tensions between traditional and engaged work. *Journal of Higher Education Outreach and Engagement, 6*(2), 36–44.

Freire, P. (1970). *Pedagogy of the oppressed.* New York: The Continuum Publishing Company.

Gelmon, S., & Agre-Keppenhan, S. (2002, January). Promotion, tenure, and the engaged scholar: Keeping the scholarship of engagement in the review process. *AAHE Bulletin.*

Glassick, C. E., Huber, M. T., & Maeroff, G. I. (1997). *Scholarship assessed: Evaluation of the professoriate.* San Francisco: Jossey-Bass.

Wheelis, A. (1958). *The quest for identity.* New York: W.W. Norton and Company.

PART II

CIVIC ENGAGEMENT IN ACTION: COMMUNITY-BASED RESEARCH AND SERVICE-LEARNING

CHAPTER 10

CHILDREN'S DEVELOPMENT IN CONTEXT

Understanding through Service Learning

Marissa L. Diener

ABSTRACT

This chapter describes how service-learning has been integrated into a general education, undergraduate course on Child Development. Students provide service individually working directly with children from underserved populations. The choice of community partners is determined by the professor. Students generally find greater meaning in the course material as a result of the service and also feel a greater connection to their community. They also develop a sense of responsible citizenship. Challenges to service-learning include time demands on students, ethical issues in working with children, communication among students, faculty, and community partners, and staff turnover.

Finding Meaning in Civically Engaged Scholarship, pages 89–102

I can easily say the greatest optimal experience I have had in college was in my service-learning last semester. I would dare say it was one of the largest in my life. It was as though the curriculum fit with the project so well and it changed me for life. I think it was learning in class the emotions that people experience and then going out and actually watching it. (Female Student; Spring '08)

THE COURSE: DEVELOPMENT IN INFANCY AND CHILDHOOD

Development in Infancy and Childhood is a 3000-level course with no prerequisites that meets a general education requirement and serves majors across campus. The course is also required for the Early Childhood Education program. Because of their diverse backgrounds, students vary tremendously in the extent of experience with, interest in, and knowledge of child development as well as their understanding of social science methodology. Most recently, students from anthropology, biology, chemical engineering, early childhood education, history, human development and family studies, international studies, modern dance, nursing, political science, psychology, sociology, and Spanish enrolled in the course, as well as those who had not yet declared their majors. Thus, an issue that I face is how to bring the course material to life for students who may have little experience with children and are planning careers in fields unrelated to children. Service-learning has been the answer to this challenge, although incorporating service-learning into the course has presented other challenges.

My goal for the course is for students to understand normal physical, cognitive, and social development and the interrelations among these aspects of development. Before I incorporated service-learning into my course, although I hate to admit this, I lectured on many facets of child development, and then asked the students to memorize these facts. Not only was I boring the students, I was boring myself! There had to be a better way. It seems obvious now. How better to experience the magic of a 3-year-olds' thinking than to work in a classroom of 3-year-olds? How better to learn the sequence of language milestones than to talk with children of different ages? How better to understand emotional development than to try to soothe a crying child? Service-learning provides the opportunity to apply research findings on children's development to real children, and to see how the course material applies to and can improve the lives of real children, as well as inform public policies involving children and their families. Another goal is for students to see themselves as part of a larger community from which they can learn and to which they can contribute.

In addition to the regular class time, students in the course are required to provide 30 hours of service over the course of the semester, write a weekly reflection paper, and participate in three in-class reflection sessions. The in-class reflection sessions vary in format; many of them are drawn from Reed and Koliba (1995). For example, one reflection session involves presenting students with a question, such as, "What has been your greatest challenge at your service site?" Students respond in written format, and place their responses in a fishbowl. Next, a student draws a response from the fish-bowl and reads it aloud, then responds to it. Other students also provide responses and suggestions. This enables students' opinions to be heard on topics about which they might be reluctant to share in class. I usually use this reflection technique at the beginning of the semester before students know each other well.

Another reflection session poses a series of statements to students, such as, "Learning about the course material is the most important part of service learning," "I will have a long term impact on the children with whom I am working," and "The children at the volunteer sites will end up just like their parents." The desks in the classroom are pushed out of the way, and on one wall of the classroom a sign states "strongly agree," and on the other side of the classroom, another sign indicates "strongly disagree." "Agree" and "Disagree" are in the middle of the room. After each statement is presented, students are asked to move around the room to indicate the extent to which they agree or disagree with the statement. By simply looking around the room at students' positions in the classroom, everyone can see how many students agree and disagree with each statement. Then students are asked to explain their position in the classroom, and a discussion ensues, considering multiple perspectives on the issue. Students are allowed to move if their own opinion changes. Another reflection involves small group discussions among staff from community partners and students.

Reflection papers are designed to connect students' service to the course material. Students are sometimes given "free reign" to write about connections between their service experiences and course material, and other times are asked to respond to a specific statement or set of questions such as "What have you learned about yourself?" "How has this experience challenged your assumptions and stereotypes?" or "If you were one of the people receiving services (e.g., a parent of a child you are caring for), what would you think of yourself? How do the parents perceive the volunteers?"

Students choose from a variety of community partners that best fit their interests and schedule. In all cases, students provide direct service working with infants or children from underserved populations, including recent immigrants, refugees, homeless families, children experiencing abuse and neglect, and teen mothers and their children. With approximately 35–45 students each semester, I have found it overwhelming to let them choose any community partner they want. Furthermore, when the students choose their own service sites, I don't have a relationship with the staff at the site, and the staff may or may not have an understanding of service-learning. When the staff doesn't understand the goals behind service-learning, they may perceive the students as simply volunteers, who can be assigned any task with which they need help, such as stuffing envelopes or filing.

However, students need to be able to apply the course concepts to their service, and thus, need direct interaction with children. Consequently, I have found it much more effective when I set up the partnerships in advance and provide several options to the students. Nonetheless, I believe providing students a choice of service sites is critical to meet their interests and schedules, capitalize on their strengths, and give them a sense of ownership over their service project. In a practical sense, this means providing a choice of community partners that can provide evening, weekend, and daytime hours to meet every student's busy schedule, as well as organizations that serve a range of ages and provide more or less structure in determining student roles. By providing choices to the students, they have a feeling of control over their service. I usually have approximately five community partners, which allows students choice and provides sufficient service placements for the number of students in the course.

These community partners have changed over the years depending upon needs in the community and student interest. The Lowell Bennion Community Service Center at the University of Utah has provided me with some of the contacts and connections, and others have come directly to me from the community. Still, other partnerships have been driven by student interest. I meet with an individual from each community partner before the semester starts and discuss and identify how we can form a partnership that will meet the needs of my students as well as the needs of the organization. This dialogue is critical to forging a successful partnership. Each semester I generally include the most successful partners from past semesters and usually forge at least one new partnership.

The partners and I work together to create a contract that all parties involved sign, so that expectations are clear from the beginning. The contract often specifies the number of hours that the student will be at the agency, the type of clothing that is appropriate at the service site, how far in advance students will notify their supervisor if they cannot make it, the appropriate (and inappropriate) use of electronic devices such as cell phones, and the maintenance of confidentiality of the children and their families. In turn, the contract usually specifies that the agency will provide an orientation to the student about procedures, as well as the agency's mission and goals, provide opportunities for the student to work directly with infants or young children, complete an evaluation at the end of the semester, and communicate with me and the student about any problems.

The community partners that I have worked with recently include The Road Home, the child care center at Horizonte Young Parents' Alternative High School, Parkview Elementary School, the Christmas Box House, and The Children's Center. Horizonte Young Parents' program provides child-care for adolescent parents while they complete their high school diplomas. Students in the course volunteer alongside the teen parents in the childcare center, giving infants and children one-on-one attention. The informal interaction in the childcare center between the students and the teen parents allows the students to learn from the young parents. One semester, after witnessing how difficult it was for the teen parents to buy presents for their children at the holidays, students conducted a book drive. New books were distributed to 90 young parents to give to their children for the holiday season. This met the needs for both the parents and for Horizonte, whose goal is to increase family literacy and improve reading skills. The students better understood the challenges young parents face, and also were able to see the complexity of factors affecting academic achievement.

Parkview Elementary is a Title I school in which 14 different languages are spoken by the children and their families. English language learners make up about half of the school population, and the other half primarily consists of Spanish-speaking students who, in many cases, come from homes where only Spanish is spoken. Students staff Parkview's before-school reading club, which allows parents to bring their children to school early for help with homework and literacy and provides one-on-one instruction. The service-learning students enable the teachers to be able to refer children to the club to receive additional support and instruction in a personalized, one-on-one atmosphere.

The Road Home is a homeless shelter which serves 31 families with an average of 65 children. Students design curriculum and activities for children from ages 3–10 years and implement them in the evening. This childcare that the students provide is staffed entirely on volunteers, and enables the parents to attend life skills programs and other programs designed to enable the family to move out of the shelter. Students are often shocked to realize for the first time that families in their own community are homeless.

The Christmas Box House provides temporary shelter to children of all ages who have been removed from their home because of abuse or neglect. Students provide one-on-one attention to children who have been placed in this traumatic situation, as the state does not provide enough funding to provide this type of staff:child ratio. The students' volunteer efforts enable children's emotional needs to be met, in addition to their physical needs. For example, volunteers might read to a child before bed, or rock an infant, activities for which the staff has little time.

Finally, the Children's Center provides a therapeutic preschool program to children with emotional and behavioral challenges. Students in the class assist the therapists in providing positive feedback for good behavior, modeling appropriate behavior, and giving individual children as much attention as they can. In addition to seeing the course concepts, students learn strategies for managing disruptive behavior and about therapeutic goal setting. Many of the therapists at the Center start as volunteers.

THE IMPORTANCE OF INSTITUTIONAL SUPPORT

The University's Bennion Center has been critical to the success of the course. When I first began service-learning, I had a general concept of what it was, but no idea how to go about implementing it. The first semester I taught the course with a service-learning component, the Bennion Center provided a service-learning coordinator who helped me develop partnerships, write a contract, and evaluate the program. She was invaluable. She had taken service-learning courses herself and had assisted other service-learning faculty as well. Without her, I would have made so many more mistakes. Since then, the Bennion Center has provided funds for a service-learning coordinator each semester. The service-learning coordinator helps track students and their service placements and communicates frequently with community partners to troubleshoot problems, greatly reducing the demands on my time.

IMPACT OF SERVICE-LEARNING ON STUDENTS

When I started teaching my class as a service-learning class 10 years ago, I allowed students to choose between being involved in the service-learning option or doing several applied papers instead of the service. It soon became clear that the service-learning students were getting much more out of the class. I became convinced that service-learning is a better way for students to learn about issues facing children and their families today. Over time, service-learning has become an integral part of the course, and has been mandatory for the past five or six years.

One semester I taught two sections of the same course, and required service-learning in only one of the sections. There is great pressure on our department (and others within the University) to increase student credit hours since our budget is based upon the number of students we serve. Thus, my department discourages any decisions that might deter students from taking our courses, especially general education courses that draw students from outside our major. The fear is that if we require service-learning, some students will be displeased by the extra work and choose to take another course, and we will lose the student credit hours. Increasingly, we see our courses as a consumer product that we sell to our students.

It was in this context of consumerism that I agreed to teach a section of my course that did not involve service-learning. However, soon after the start of the semester, I came to dread teaching the non-service-learning section because the students (and I) were less connected with the material. The course was just not as rich. Students didn't have the real-life examples in their minds. They were less engaged with the course material because they couldn't see the relevance of it to their lives. They were just learning the material to perform well on the exams, not because it had any larger meaning or application beyond a grade.

Service-learning takes the course material from the theoretical to the practical realm, enabling students to see that it has relevance to children in their own community. One student in the service-learning section of the course indicated that "... where we go and volunteer three hours a week, is the most significant part of this course, because it's given the opportunity to take the information I've learned in the course and to see it in real-life situations, and I think for me that makes it easier to remember and easier to understand..." In fact, quantitative data support this conclusion. A comparison of the two sections of the course, one which incorporated service-learning, and one which did not, indicated that, by the end of the semester, students in the service-learning section performed better on the final exam, although there were no differences between the two sections on the first exam or in terms of GPA at the start of the semester.

Service-learning students always dread the time commitment at the beginning of the semester, but by the end of the semester, report that it has been worthwhile. Said one student, "At the beginning I was not too fond of having to volunteer three hours a week since I have a full-time job and school, and believed that it would be too much to handle. However, since I have started I have realized that it has benefitted me probably more than the kids that I have been working with because they may not remember me or what we did together but I believe I will." Another student commented at the end of the semester: "The service-learning with this class was absolutely remarkable in showing me the need for a knowledge of the course material." Seeing that they can use the course material to improve children's everyday lives can be empowering.

While increasing student learning is one goal of service-learning, the human connection is critical in developing a student's sense of social justice and responsibility to the community. I want students to understand that not all children have an equal chance of successful development and that this occurs through no fault of their own, but rather because of the circumstances into which they are born, because of public policies that benefit certain children over others, and because of prejudice and discrimination.

Students will be more likely to adopt this sense of social justice if they see children from different backgrounds as individuals, rather than as members of a given category. Students come to recognize the importance of the human connection over the course of the semester: "... I've really got to know the kids that I've worked with. And that's the reason it made such a difference. I got to spend so much time with them. In the beginning I'll admit I was like 'Three hours a week?! It's like a third job...' But I ended up loving it." Another student commented about a past service-learning class: "... I've had a service-learning class before, and I hated it because I never got to connect with the people I was working with. But now I'm working at the elementary school, and I love those kids. I mean I've connected so well with the community. It's been really great." Another student argued a similar point, "I think the biggest benefit in service-learning is seeing the different needs of the community.... The biggest part of it is your getting involved in the community." This sense of being involved in something larger than oneself is an important outcome of the class.

Through the service, students gain insight not only into themselves, but also into the broader issues facing their community. Service-learning can help break down some of the divisive barriers we face in Utah—e.g., immigration, religion, language. One student wrote in her service-learning reflection, "I have really grown attached to the children and I find that I talk about them everywhere I go. I also used to stereotype (the) underprivileged, and people from different ethnic backgrounds. I didn't like being around them, and I didn't want to talk to them. These kids have changed my feelings... I learned that it doesn't matter how much the parents make, or where their ancestors came from..." Another student commented, "One of the biggest life lessons that struck me while at the Children's Center is that my attitude of judgment was totally unfounded. When I first started there, I was surprised at my own judgments that I was passing on these children as well as on their families. These judgments fell by the wayside.... I came to understand how much of a need there is for programs such as this in our communities. SO many families are in positions where they have no support." This same student acknowledged that she was initially reluctant about the service: "At the beginning of my service-learning experience I was very skeptical about what was to come." By the end of the semester, she considered it "one of the most fulfilling experiences of my life." Given that the minority population in Utah, which until recently has been quite homogeneous in terms of ethnicity and religion, has more than doubled (Perlich, 1996) and that Salt Lake City is a refugee resettlement city; given globalization; and given the disparities in education between ethnic minority and majority children, it is critical that students become aware of the challenges facing children in their own community.

Service-learning also demonstrates to students the way in which a child's development is situated in a larger context. Students see firsthand how a child's development is affected by race, class, immigration status, and other social issues. They see the effects of homelessness, the dilemmas in foster care and child protective services, the effects of immigration and ESL on schools, and the implications of various funding scenarios on schools and teachers. Students also start to see themselves as part of a larger community to which they have some responsibility. For example, one student commented, "I think service-learning is not just integrating the course material but us building connections with the community and feeling as though we can do something rather than just be students." Another student wrote, "I can be a part of any community if I am willing to put myself out there and try to relate to people around me. What I learned about myself is that one person can really have a great effect on the community." A pre-medical student saw the benefit of service-learning this way: "I think the biggest benefit in service-learning is seeing the different needs of the community. I'm at Horizonte, and it's amazing how many young mothers there are, who are trying to go to school, to continue their education. It's a learning process because you're using the course material. But I think the biggest part of it is getting involved in the community, your giving service to people. And doing it in a selfless way."

In teaching this course, I hope that students will become more tolerant of people, whatever their background or situation. I believe students become less judgmental after seeing teenage parents at Horizonte working hard to finish school and be good parents. I also hope students gain a greater connection to their community. When I describe the nonprofit organizations they will be working with, most of the students have never heard of them and seem unaware of the many issues facing our community. By involving students in the community, I hope that they will become better citizens.

IMPACT OF SERVICE-LEARNING ON THE COMMUNITY

My students' service helps community partners give the children they serve one-on-one attention they might not otherwise receive, and community partners have generally been pleased with the service they have received. Many community partners have contacted me during semesters when I am not teaching the class to ask if I can send them some volunteers because they desperately need them. Some community partners have eventually hired students who have served at their agency. One agency commented, "Emily has been a great asset to our therapy group...She give valuable feedback to us. I would not hesitate recommending her as an employee here." In several cases, the students allowed a community partner to provide a service they wouldn't have otherwise. For example, the volunteer coordinator for the homeless shelter wrote, "Kathryn has been a wonderful volunteer. Each week she took the initiative to plan an activity for the kids and took an active role in running the playroom on Tuesdays. All of us, staff and children, have loved having Kathryn come in. She has done an excellent job." Without Kathryn there, the playroom would not have been open to children, and parents would have had to job search, apartment hunt, and complete other tasks with their children in tow.

In a similar fashion, children often become attached to the students, especially when the student works closely with one child over the course of an entire semester. This is good and bad. As a class, we have debated the ethical issues surrounding a child's forming a strong attachment to an individual, who will then leave at the end of the semester. In many cases, the children have already experienced the loss of an important relationship, and we struggle with how the children might interpret the students' departure, especially the young children who may not have the cognitive abilities to understand why the student is leaving. This dilemma is also an opportunity for students to better understand the course material on attachment relationships and apply what they know about attachment relationships to hopefully alleviate the potential harm. We talk in class about preparing the children for the student's departure and how to frame that departure in a way that helps children understand it is not a reflection on them. I also require a minimum of three hours per week with the children over the course of at least 10 weeks, so that students and children alike experience a certain degree of continuity. Other students are required by the community partner to make a six-month commitment, even though the course only lasts about 4 months.

IMPACT OF SERVICE-LEARNING ON FACULTY

I gain personally from teaching my course as a service-learning course in many ways. First, I feel that I am a more effective teacher, because the students see the course concepts in action. This provides real life examples that the students see and can share in class. It makes the class more dynamic and more connected to the real world. I don't have to convince the students about the course material because they see it for themselves. This makes my job easier in many ways. Second, I benefit by getting to know people in the community who work with kids on a daily basis. I can hear their perspective on the important issues facing kids and their families. This puts the rest of my research in perspective, and hopefully will help shape my research questions in the future. Despite the work involved in coordinating the logistics of the service-learning, I am more engaged and excited about the course material. Another benefit is getting to know faculty and staff from outside of my department as part of a larger university community. Hearing what other faculty are doing is really inspiring. There are faculty members in my own department whose approach I don't understand, so it is interesting to see how I can feel much more connected to faculty members from much more diverse disciplines. This is a very unanticipated, unexpected benefit to myself.

There are also more negative impacts. The dean of our college has publicly admonished non-tenured faculty for teaching service-learning courses and discouraged them from spending too much time on their courses when they should be focusing on research. This attitude makes my efforts feel undervalued. On the other hand, over time, I have seen greater support for service-learning. The chair of my department has been willing to cap the enrollment in my course to keep the number of students manageable. She has pushed to make my service-learning course required for the Early Childhood Education students because she recognizes the benefits of it. Thus, the climate in my department has become more favorable, despite pressures of maintaining high student credit hours.

Over time, I've let go of some of the traditional course material taught in a course on child development in order to make room in the course curriculum for larger social and economic issues and how they affect children's development. I have become more informed about public policy so that the course content better reflects the experiences of the students in their service. My course has become more interdisciplinary to address the complex issues that children face, and less focused on basic psychological processes devoid of contextual factors. As such, the readings and course discussions have evolved to mirror the emphasis on understanding development in context.

CHALLENGES OF INCORPORATING SERVICE-LEARNING

Despite the benefits of service-learning, there are challenges. Most of our students work full-time, and many of them are parents. School in general, and my course in particular, may be lower on students' priority list than I would like. The demands on students' time are enormous, and when they feel like they are wasting their time, they resent the service. I have learned that the service needs to be meaningful, and students need to see a connection with the course material. On the first day of class, I hear many complaints and really have to "sell" the experience so that a large proportion of the students don't drop the class. For example, a student in my non-service-learning section said about a previous service-learning class, "I had a class where you had to do 3 hours, and I did it at the food bank. And all I did was sort food and boxes in a warehouse. And so, I mean, I got my hours in but I didn't learn anything. So if I would have actually delivered the food or did hands on with the people that needed it, it would be a different experience. . . . And in my defense, I'm not saying that boxing food is a bad thing in this world, I'm just saying it was not applicable to the class I was taking." The service-learning fails when students do not see the meaning behind it or how it relates to the course material. I try to make explicit connections with students' experiences and the course material each class period, as well as soliciting examples from students in the course. Furthermore, all the community partners with whom I work have limited resources. They have to devote some of these resources to training and supervising the students, and thus, students who don't follow through, who aren't dependable, or who have a bad attitude about being there, tax the staff and the resources of the organization. The organization has invested in the student and is relying on them, and if the student doesn't show up, it is incredibly frustrating and puts the whole partnership at risk. It is at these times that I wonder whether I am doing more harm than good?

Reflection has been critical to help students understand and make sense of their experiences, but some students continue to resent the time commitment of the service-learning, and this attitude shows in their poor quality of work. When students are forced to do the service, and don't want to be there, they perform poorly, and do more harm than good for both the community partner and those they are serving. Their poor attitude can further alienate families who already feel disenfranchised from the community. In one case, a community partner asked a student to leave the organization. Our partnership survived that crisis, but it required an extra commitment and time on everyone's part. Often, students in the course are my most effective allies in that they challenge the other students in the class during class discussions and reflection sessions to consider how their own contribution affects their experience. Students often recognize that "you get out of it what you put into it," and they challenge other students in the course to consider their own role in the success or failure of the project.

Although students generally report positive outcomes despite initial reluctance, not all students find a comfortable placement. A female student wrote in a reflection paper, "Many times in volunteering at this institution, I have felt a little useless . . . And I really have a hard time getting comfortable with the kids, regardless. I have come to realize through this volunteering that I unconsciously try to stay aloof from the children . . . Thinking about the parents' perspective also makes me wonder how they would view me if we ever interacted. I imagine it is the same as how I think the staff view me. I already mentioned that I feel pretty useless at times. Well, I also act that way. I think that if I ever saw myself volunteering, I would think I was pretty ineffective." It is critical to get frequent feedback from students and community partners so that I have the opportunity to intervene in situations before they ruin the experience for either the community partner or the student.

As the pervious comment suggests, one set of challenges of service-learning involve ensuring good communication among students, professor, staff, and children. Many students, when asked about how to improve the experience, mention a more thorough orientation that explains the rules of behavior for staff and children, how to handle certain events, and what level of interaction (e.g., physical contact) is appropriate for the children and students. The organizations often provide orientations, but early in the semester the students do not even know the questions to ask or the situations to anticipate. Even when an orientation is provided, students sometimes are unaware of important information at their service site. For example, the last time I taught the course, several students contracted contagious diseases from the children with whom they were working, including head lice and impetigo, which, although not serious, were frustrating. Although the staff were aware of the children's health issues, the students were not, and were unable to take appropriate precautions. Also, sometimes the volunteer coordinator or director at an agency knows what the students are doing, but doesn't communicate that to other staff members. One student wrote: "I think the staff just kind of expects me and the other volunteers to know what to do in some cases and when we do not and the situation is out of control, then they will take over, but they do not explain what we could have done differently. I think if they would do that I would feel more comfortable in what I am allowed to do and not to do." To address this issue, I try to attend a staff meeting before the semester starts to explain the goals of the service and the needs of the students to the staff. Although this takes a little bit of time, I have found that it pays off down the road in terms of preventing problems on all ends. Students also learn communication and problem solving skills in these situations, as other students in the class brainstorm ways to address the problems that students identify in class. The problem becomes one for the class to solve, rather than the problem of any individual student.

Another challenge is that many nonprofit agencies have high staff turnover and are often understaffed. This makes the partnership a constant learning process, and involves reeducation each semester. On the other hand, students are often desperately needed, and really get satisfaction from the fact that they are helping the organization and the children they serve. A different challenge is that most community partners don't follow the University calendar, and thus, the ebb and flow of students don't necessarily match their needs. For example, students might leave on Spring Break when the community partner has come to rely on their attendance.

Feedback from all perspectives has been critical to improving the experience each semester. Students complete an evaluation form of their experience which is shared with me and the agency, and the agency completes an evaluation form. One of the newer additions to my class is to invite my community partners into class discussions throughout the semester. I never wanted to bother them previously, knowing how valuable their time is. However, the class has evolved to encourage more communication among all the partners in the endeavor. One of the best parts of the semester is having a reflection session in class in which the professor, students, and community partners discuss the benefits and challenges of the service. It helps for students to hear the perspective of the community partner and vice versa. It also helps me to know how to facilitate the relationships, prepare the students, and what to focus on in our reflection sessions.

In conclusion, there have been a number of rewards to incorporating service learning into the course. Students appear to find greater meaning in the course material, feel more connected to their community, and may develop a sense of responsible citizenship. The professor finds the course more rewarding. Nonetheless, there are challenges, such as the time demands on students and the professor, ethical issues in working with children, and the challenge of maintaining communication among students, faculty, and community partners.

REFERENCES

Perlich, P. S. (2006). Immigration: Contributions to Utah population growth and diversity. In C. D. Zick & K. R. Smith (Eds.), *Utah at the beginning of the new millenium: A demographic perspective.* Salt Lake City: The University of Utah Press.

Reed, J., & Koliba, C. (1995). *Facilitating reflection: A manual for leaders and educators.* Georgetown University. Retrieved 7-8-08 from http://www.uvm.edu/~dewey/reflection_manual/

CHAPTER 11

THE STORY OF THE WESTSIDE STUDIO

Maged Senbel

ABSTRACT

The Westside Studio was both a service learning course for architecture, urban planning, and business students and a center for community-based research. It was designed to provide professional planning services to area residents on the west side of Salt Lake City. The evolution of the Westside Studio is explained in terms of partners, projects, planning issues, students, program, and the faculty member's own personal context. This chapter also describes lessons and conclusions from the three-year project.

It's too bad that we have to dumb things down for people who don't care and don't show. It's too bad that we have to begin with the practical before we begin to dream. It's too bad that we have to play the chess game by its rules and its boundaries instead of defining our own game.

A graduate architecture student expressed these words of frustration in his reflection notebook. The course had failed him on many fronts. First and foremost, I had not articulated for him, or his classmates, the importance

Finding Meaning in Civically Engaged Scholarship, pages 103–115
103

of community engagement. To them, it was an impediment to unfettered creativity. It was an unnecessary dose of reality.

A year later, another graduate student wrote,

> I have a heightened awareness of west side issues since the beginning of class: an understanding of neighborhood that extends beyond geographic boundaries and imposed stereotypes. This will stick with me wherever I go.

What happened in that intervening year? What was the difference that created such divergent views on public participation? Of course, there are unpredictable and complex qualities to teaching that preclude a complete understanding of cause and effect in the classroom (Palmer, 1998). The views presented above are also an oversimplification of the spectrum of reactions and responses by the students. Some students in the first year drew greater satisfaction than the first quote implies, whereas some students in the second year were more frustrated than the second quote suggests. However, by and large, in the first year students were not given the opportunity to appreciate the significance of public participation in neighborhood design. In the second year, public participation, even when it was inadequate, was understood to be an essential and powerful tool for community planning and development. The class was called the Westside Studio. This chapter seeks to draw some lessons and conclusions from the three-year project.

In addition to being a service-learning course for architecture, urban planning and business students, the Westside Studio was a center for community-based research. It was a place and a space for partnership between student groups and community organizations to address real world problems of urban and social planning and community development. It was also a storefront space used by students, researchers, and a number of nonprofit organizations in Salt Lake City's west side, in one of the city's lowest income neighborhoods. In addition to University teaching and research, the space was used for numerous services such as ESL classes and tax assistance for low-income families.

The Westside Studio was a natural evolution of several independent trajectories. Neighborhoods on Salt Lake City's West side were clearly less served than their more privileged eastern counterparts (Buendia, Ares, Juarez, & Peercy, 2004). Institutional capacity at the University of Utah had recently matured enough to support a variety of initiatives, and the Graduate School of Architecture had just absorbed urban planning to become the College of Architecture + Planning (CA+P). A nonprofit organization with a long list of accomplishments at revitalizing neighborhoods had enjoyed significant success working with service-learning students. I had been just hired as an assistant professor in the College of Architecture & Planning and was eager to bridge the two newly combined areas in my teaching and research. The first class in the Master's of Urban Planning program was admitted, and they were as determined as the rest of us, and more courageous, to start the difficult work of translating theory into practice.

THE INSTITUTIONAL CONTEXT

University Neighborhood Partners (UNP), the University of Utah's first formalized campus-community partnership, was just two years old when the idea of the Westside Studio was conceived. Reporting to the Office of the President, UNP was created to better connect the University to underserved westside communities. UNP's mission is "to bring together University and westside resources for reciprocal learning, action, and benefit... a community coming together." Through my various projects and initiatives I have come to understand this mission as comprising three parts: (1) bringing University resources to communities where such resources were needed; (2) increasing awareness among westside residents of the University and the opportunities of higher education, thereby increasing enrollment of minority students: and (3) raising the profile of the University in the community and at the state legislature and developing a reputation as a critical service provider for the state's underserved. The Westside Studio, as a long-term sustained effort, was crafted in such a way as to contribute to these goals.

The formal partnerships that came together to support the Westside Studio were well balanced compared to the long tradition of community design centers that began in the 1970s. University Neighborhood Partners and the CA+P secured commitments from the School of Business and from Neighborhood Housing Services (NHS) to help fund the initiative. NHS, in partnership with the Bridge Group, a real estate development firm, donated space in a jointly-funded, newly-constructed building to house a storefront classroom. The School of Business provided teaching support as well as a modest sum, $5,000, to help set up the space. The College of Architecture + Planning provided the teaching staff and logistical support and integrated the course into the Masters of Urban Planning curriculum. UNP was the main contact and liaison between the course instructor and community groups and area residents. They also played the role of facilitator of the entire collaboration. UNP subsequently took the lead on writing a proposal for an HUD Community Outreach Partnerships Centers, Community Academic Partnerships grant. They were successful in obtaining almost $500,000 in funding over three years. Only a small portion of that grant, less than 10%, was allocated toward the Westside Studio project, but this money was not insignificant. The Dean of CA+P was to use the funds to hire an adjunct professor to teach the course. The foundations of institutional support were in place.

THE COMMUNITY CONTEXT

Salt Lake County's west side is home to Utah's greatest economic and ethnic diversity (Perlich, 2004; Westside Studio Students, 2005) Poverty is certainly not the exclusive domain of westside neighborhoods. Rural poverty may well be a more insidious and less discussed problem (Perlich, 2004), but urban poverty in Salt Lake has many of the characteristics of inner city poverty without the acute sense of destitution that plagues other major cities in the U.S. The west side is home to a large Latino population that reaches 45% in some census block areas. It is home to concentrations of refugee populations from Bosnia, Somalia, and Sudan. It is home to young families and immigrants who are slowly working their way up the ladder of financial stability or mortgage eligibility. It is also home to a group of old-time residents who have had the world change around them. They used to live in a peri-urban, semi-rural pastoral setting where all their neighbors went to the same church and had a similar outlook on life and the afterlife. Household incomes in west side neighborhoods range from the low teens to the hundreds of thousands (U.S. Census Bureau, 2000). This degree of diversity is not unique in metropolitan regions in countries of the North, but it is certainly unique in Utah.

Planners and policymakers in Salt Lake City were involved early in the process of crafting a vision for the Westside Studio. For a variety of reasons, the planning department at the city was going through a period of transition and was understaffed. The Mayor's office had simultaneously made it a priority to address issues of diversity and representation in the city. Through the process of hosting the Winter Olympic Games in 2002 and in building all the requisite infrastructure, the needs of the city's least affluent residents had been deliberately overlooked, but not with indifference. The time had come to allocate nonexisting resources toward addressing issues that were specific to westside neighborhoods. Graduate students from the University of Utah would help fill this shortfall.

Although everyone seemed delighted at the prospect of giving our graduate students this wonderful and rare opportunity of applying their skills to real world problems and providing a needed service, it seemed a perpetuation of injustice to have students doing the work that professionals should be doing to serve those most in need. The very success of our efforts might cause the status quo of imbalanced service to continue, rather than prompting a rebalancing of budgets and priorities across different areas of the city. Neighborhoods with wealthy and powerful residents would be served by the very best the city had to offer and poorer neighborhoods would be served by students with little or no experience. In the short term, there were communities in need with no one serving their interests. Although cognizant of these long-term concerns, we set them aside and went about our work serving those with the greatest need.

OUR MISSION

The mission of the Westside Studio from the outset was twofold: to collaborate with local area residents to provide professional planning services and to heighten the awareness and incidence of civic engagement. We were committed to applying student and faculty resources to westside neighborhood planning while simultaneously fostering civic engagement. We sought to empower residents to become engaged in the planning and decision-making processes that affect the neighborhoods within which they live, work, and play. I knew this would not be easy and would require years of trust and capacity building, but all the players in the process indicated that this was a long-term project in which they were willingly investing. I shared this sentiment and made a conscious decision that I would commit to this goal for five or six years. The emphasis of the Westside Studio and my own confidence in delivering a community-based curriculum evolved considerably over the three years that I taught the course. The following sections outline the evolution of the Westside studio along the six factors of partners, projects, planning issues, students, program, and my own personal context.

PARTNERS

Ours was a rather unusual case of community-based collaboration in that we owed our very existence, in part, to a community organization. NHS—Neighborhood Housing Services, now NeighborWorks Salt Lake, is that special caliber of community partner who is partly responsible for the existence of this class. They were supportive from the beginning, first with the provision of free space and then with facilitating our connection with the development community in the westside neighborhoods of Guadalupe, Jackson, and Fairpark. NHS worked with us every year, whether or not they were an officially designated partner. Their knowledge of the area and of the leaders in the area was invaluable. They also provided free workshop space for us to host public design workshops and public exhibitions of our work. Put simply, they were always involved.

It eventually became clear that NHS had expectations that we couldn't meet. They are development oriented. They revitalize neighborhoods, renovating run-down houses or tearing them down and building new ones. They provide instruction and advice for first-time homebuyers and finance loans to low-income individuals. They run after-school construction programs for youth and hold events to beautify homes and neighborhoods. Their success at this low-scale, incremental growth has been remarkable. According to Wakan (2007), their revitalization efforts raised home values at a considerably faster rate than surrounding communities. The building in which they donated space for us to use as a classroom, Citifront Apartments, was their first venture in a large-scale housing development project. It marked a transition into driving development and partnering with for-profit developers for even larger projects that would quickly transform neighborhoods. NHS was therefore eager to have us be catalysts of their vision for growth.

We had a slow, and at times rough, start. A few community partners seemed to treat our efforts as intrusions on their already full agendas. They did not see the benefits of our collaboration. In fairness to them, we also grew skeptical of our ability to marry our objective of facilitating community participation in neighborhood development with their organizational missions. While the various partners over the years supported the general goal of fostering civic engagement among the various constituencies they served, this goal was secondary to the specific projects and programs they were administering. The partnerships, particularly our nebulous goal of increased public involvement in neighborhood development, eventually became a distraction for two of the partners.

In the second year, the Westside Studio's focus was giving voice to the concerns of high school youth in the planning of their underserved neighborhood. I had 12 graduate students taking the course and four community partners: one that trained youth in filmmaking, one that employed at-risk youth to build houses after school, one that sought to increase youth participation in local governance, and a community garden that delivered programs for the youth. The organizations had varying hierarchies and different styles of governance (Senbel, 2007).

PLANNING ISSUES

Today, looming industrial complexes reside next door to homeless shelters, soup kitchens, and railroad depots. Hip warehouse conversions bring a new urban chic population to this downtown neighborhood, with coffee shops, art galleries, and an eclectic collection of small shops. Ethnic neighborhoods stretch farther to the west in the shadow of sound walls built to both sides of the freeway, which forms a swath through the landscape some long-time residents call their homes. (Bradley, 2004)

The conversion of light industrial space and the renovation of old redbrick buildings was an important revitalizing event in the recent history of the Western edge of downtown. This area has a long history of being on the wrong side of the tracks and, therefore, more risky for capital investment. Recent investments have changed the character of the neighborhood and encouraged a variety of uses and a diversity of residents. Planners and community organizers saw this and imagined a parallel kind of investment further west. Instead of warehouse conversions, area leaders envisioned renovations of historic homes and the building of large housing developments that included a certain percentage of subsidized housing and ground floor commercial activity. The vision was one of investment and empowerment that would help alleviate both racial tensions and geographical isolation.

Community planners and organizers implicitly knew that racial tensions existed in the neighborhood. Tensions appeared in a variety of forums, from community council meetings to development proposals to sensationalist newspaper articles. Racial issues also became evident through a door-to-door survey that a multidisciplinary research group conducted on Salt Lake City's west side. Until we started working with youth from the neighborhood, however, we had no way of talking through the issues in a non-confrontational way. Adults had always been either too courteous or too angry to constructively discuss the fears and insecurities that gave rise to prejudice. The youth, however, talked more freely about their experiences (Senbel, 2007). The most significant fact was that we heard about racial tensions from an ethnically diverse group; our previous exposure to these tensions had been through public meetings which were notoriously and exclusively white in a neighborhood that was only 40% Caucasian (Westside Studio Students, 2005).

Another set of planning challenges were structural land use problems. The West Side of Salt Lake City is crisscrossed with three major freeways. Some neighborhoods have freeways on three sides and others are sandwiched between heavy industrial plants on one side and a freeway on the other. Westside studio students built on research linking childhood asthma rates to residential proximity to freeways and mapped the area to find that every neighborhood on the West Side was at higher risk of childhood health complications. Elementary schools are also located within this at-risk distance. With every passing year the students and I became ever more aware that revitalization efforts have to include a deep understanding of land-use dependent environmental injustice. Development has to attempt to include mitigation strategies as a priority and has to creatively include the entire region in financing risk reduction.

STUDENTS

I taught the Westside Studio with three different combinations of students. The first year, in 2005, I had a business student, two architecture students, and 12 urban planning students. The second year, I had three architecture students and nine urban planning students, and the third year I had 12 urban planning students and none from architecture or business. This evolution was forced upon us by the growth of the Master's of Urban Planning (MUP) program. The course was one of the required capstones, and we did not have enough seats to achieve the model of integrated and interdisciplinary teaching while simultaneously admitting the entire graduating MUP class.

The interdisciplinary nature of the first year was a success in achieving the learning objective of exposing students to real world ideological clashes between collaborating professionals. We reached out to business students and promoted the class amongst business faculty. On the first day of class 3 business students came to class but only one could stomach the social justice agenda of the class. The others were more interested in real estate development. The business student who did stay was an asset to the class and ended up purchasing a property in one of the new neighborhoods. He understood the opportunities for synergistic relationships between revitalization, affordable housing, and real estate development. He produced a number of redevelopment plans and became a West Side real estate specialist.

The quote from the architecture student at the beginning of this chapter reflects another type of unresolved tension that I should have better addressed. This is the tension between uninhibited expression of a building's program on the part of architects and measured constraints for the sake of neighborhood harmony and cohesion on the part of planners. My own training in architecture was so well steeped in planning's concern for the "public good" that I failed to recognize that the solitary search for an inspiring functional design continues to be the sole driver for many architecture students. They could not, then, see the benefit of community involvement. When they did concede that public participation was important, they were apathetic about soliciting involvement from those who seemed reluctant to participate. As my student clearly stated, "it's too bad that we have to dumb things down for people who don't care and don't show."

In the second year of the course, I was more deliberate in discussing the extensive benefits of public involvement. I attempted to inspire the students using the examples of Doug Aberley (Campbell, 1997), Wendy Sarkissian (Sandercock, 2000) and Ann Forsyth (Forsyth, 2007). Public participation as demonstrated through the work of these practitioners is a way to achieve community empowerment and ownership over the decisions that affect their home neighborhoods.

One of the challenges of teaching this course was deliberate ambiguity of the objectives so that we could adapt to the needs of partners and area residents as we learned them. This was compounded by the uncertain usefulness of our proposed designs. The resulting environment of uncertainty made it difficult for my students and for some of our partners. As with any task performed by a group, uncertain goals led to uncertain outcomes. One of my students wrote in her journal, "This class is seriously stressing me out right now. I feel like all my other courses are being neglected, that our group hates each other, and that nothing we are doing is going to make a difference anyway." I noticed a certain tendency, on my part and on the part of my students and the organizations with which we worked, to sometimes tread water by simply going through the motions of participatory and inclusive decision making.

PROGRAM

Earlier in this chapter I presented the institutional context that provided the groundwork for the Westside Studio. This support contributed to an accelerated integration of the Westside Studio into the curriculum. The newly approved Master's of Urban Planning Program included a required graduate workshop, and the Westside Studio fulfilled that role. We had commitment from the School of Business for financial and teaching support. The money materialized quickly, but the teacher promised to us was already overcommitted. Nevertheless, at that early stage we maintained our own commitment to cater to students from architecture, urban planning and business. We had a modest start-up budget, that, in retrospect, could have been better used to equip the studio. However, I was new to the business of managing a program and was overly cautious about waiting to determine the long term needs of the program before spending the money.

In the second year it had become obvious that, given the limited capacity and budget of the Westside Studio, a full partnership with the business school to deliver planning, design, development and business services would not occur. We also would have needed a champion from the School of Business who could deliver the business curriculum. Despite the very positive experience I had with the business student who took the class in its first year, I stopped promoting the class with business faculty and students. I focused instead on increasing the numbers of architecture students using my access to them in other courses to introduce issues of planning and participatory design. In that year, architecture students also had fewer options for their elective studio, and the College allowed the Westside studio to count as an alternative. We, therefore, achieved the goal of having an architecture student in each of the four teams of students working on different projects.

By the third year our ability to be interdisciplinary was further diminished. In a sense, we were the victims of our own success in promoting and growing the MUP program. We had a graduating class of 12 planning students and did not have sufficient space to include a cohort of architecture students. The college was also undergoing an evolution in its internal structure. Architecture faculty were organizing to form a department within the college and the planning faculty were looking ahead to becoming a department and to gaining accreditation by the national professional association. Although the general tenor of the college in my first year was one of building strong connections between architecture and planning, by the third year, the culture had shifted to one of strong disciplinary boundaries. These boundaries further cemented the Westside Studio course as a planning endeavor exclusively.

PERSONAL CONTEXT

I went from nervous trepidation to exuberant over-extension to stoic reserve, all in the space of 3 years. In my first year, I was anxious about working with a community in a city that was new to me. I had only just met our project partners and the storefront classroom was not ready on the first day of class. I drove around the city with one of my students looking for desk parts. In the second week of the semester, we were still assembling the desks in class. It was a fun project, but it cost us precious time. I had to defy my tendency to be precise and organized with my curriculum and simply adjusted to circumstances as they arose. I was outside of my comfort zone and was not confident in my ability to achieve the rather lofty goal of contributing anything meaningful to the community. I also learned a tremendous amount about working with community partners and neighborhood residents. Most of all, I learned to be patient and to focus on building relationships rather than specific project outcomes. A rather significant impediment to my ability to flourish in the first year was the burden of having to finish and defend my doctoral dissertation.

By the second year, I was free of the self-doubt that had plagued me in the first year, and I had successfully defended my dissertation. I was hungry for partners and contacted many organizations in search of the right combination of partner and project. I had learned enough about my students' capacity to contribute that I was more confident in approaching organizations with offers of potential partnership. University Neighborhood Partners of the University of Utah had also used their rather extensive network to spread word about the Westside Studio. This opened up all sorts of doors and opportunities for us that otherwise wouldn't have existed. I had also started to develop strong ties and lasting friendships with faculty and staff from across campus. They advised me, inspired me, energized me and ultimately enabled me to do more. My ties to Salt Lake City and to the University of Utah had become surprisingly strong by my second year, and that was reflected in my enthusiasm for my work and for my channeling considerable energy toward the Westside studio.

Things changed considerably in my third year. In the process of preparing my third year review documents, and with my tenure review looming ever closer, it became obvious that my time and energy spent on the Westside Studio were not translating into proportionate output of tenure worthy publications. I was spending too much time managing and administering the studio, teaching the graduate workshop and not enough time writing. I mentally and emotionally had to shift my emphasis toward research. Halfway through teaching in my third year, I accepted an offer of a tenure track position from my alma mater in my home city of Vancouver. The offer was very much a surprise. Throughout the application and interview process I was convinced that it was too soon after my doctorate to be hired back. The only reason I applied was that it was an academic job in my home city. As hard as tried to reduce the impact of my impending departure on my teaching, it did have an impact. I was distracted by having to wrap up my work and package it for my successor. Adding to this feeling of closure was the unrelated expiry of our lease, which necessitated having to physically vacate the storefront premises that had been the identity of the Westside Studio from the outset.

OUTCOME

Planning students had a slightly better appreciation for the importance of community participation in the design process as a result of the West Side Studio experience. The following quote, which appeared in the University of Utah's official news bulletin, exemplifies the experience, "I feel that going out into a community and finding out about their wants and needs is essential in understanding the diverse people that may use something like a community garden. When people are connected and heard by people that are making decisions for their community, they may feel more invested in their place and happier with changes that may come" (University News Center, 2006).

The second year of the Westside Studio was by far the most successful in creating a meaningful connection between students and area residents. This connection occurred for a number of reasons. Even though we held public meetings, design workshops, and catered exhibitions, public participation was all but completely absent. But this isn't a story of measuring success against effort exerted.

The youth knew from the very beginning that they and the graduate students would be making presentations to two community councils about their work. In a statement to the Salt Lake City Council, a youth leader spoke about how her attitude toward the project transformed: "At first I didn't really think that anything we did would have any real effect whatsoever on the community. But after meeting with the University of Utah graduate students, I realized we really could make a difference" (Senbel, 2006). The youth knew their efforts would lead to something official, and it helped them take our collaborative work more seriously. We were also clear from the outset that our designs for the neighborhood were intended to represent the diversity of the community, and that the youth themselves constituted that diversity. Without youth input, our plans would fall short of meeting our intended goals.

Our participatory processes were most successful with residents who were eager to be included and who had a clearly defined role. For example, one group of residents was involved in a municipal revision of a neighborhood master plan. Their input into the ultimate design was known to be limited, but the parameters were clear. They were to help us scope the issues, understand community priorities, make their own suggestions and program proposals, and then give feedback on the work of the graduate students. Other groups had more ambitious roles planned for youth in the design process but time limitations prevented them from realizing those ambitions. It became clear that having clear goals, and being able to follow through on those goals, were more important than promising larger roles for both community residents and students.

REFERENCES

Bradley, M. S. (2004). Colliding interests: Mapping Salt Lake City's west side. *Journal of Urban History, 31,* 47–74.

Buendia, E., Ares, N. Juarez, B. G., & Peercy, M. (2004). The geographies of difference: The production of the east side, west side and central city school. *American Educational Research Journal, 41,* 833–863.

Campbell, P. (1997). Maps with teeth. *Ways we live: Exploring community.* USA, Bullfrog Films.

Forsyth, A. (2007). The rise of the nerds? Interdisciplinary research in architecture. *International Journal of Architectural Research, 1,* 177–182.

Palmer, P. (1998). *The courage to teach: Exploring the inner landscape of a teacher's life.* San Francisco, Jossey-Bass.

Perlich, P. (2004). Immigrants transform Utah: Entering a new era of diversity. *Utah Economic and Business Review, 64,* 5–6.

Sandercock, L. (2000). When strangers become neighbours: Managing cities of difference. *Planning Theory and Practice, 1,* 13–30.

Senbel, M. (2006). Unpublished field notes from Salt Lake City Council meeting held on April 20th, 2006. Salt Lake City, UT.

Senbel, M. (2007). Engaging youth to engage community in sustainable grassroots planning. *Children, Youth and Environments, 17,* 454–460.

U.S. Census Bureau. (2000). *Median household income, 1999.* Washington, DC.

University of Utah. (2006). *U of U students join community in designing Fairpark Garden. Salt Lake City.* U News Center, The University of Utah.

Wakan, D. (2007). *Real estate impacts of Salt Lake City's neighborhood housing services redevelopment projects.* Unpublished Master's of Urban Planning Professional Project, University of Utah.

Westside Studio Students. (2005). *North Temple Atlas 2005.* University of Utah College of Architecture & Planning.

CHAPTER 12

THE PROFESSIONAL JOURNEY

Neighborhood Democracy

Luke Garrott

ABSTRACT

The present chapter describes a Political Science service-learning course, Neighborhood Democracy, which engages 20 students a year who study different facets of democracy—democratic theory, leadership, neighborhood councils, community development and organizing. In the field, they, with community partners, plan and carry out a community-building activity. Notable among the first two years of the class were the Rose Park Community Festival, an inclusive celebration of the northwest SLC neighborhood of Rose Park, and a door-to-door neighborhood survey that gave substantive feedback to multiple SLC community councils about their constituencies. A number of institutional and community factors enabled the success of the course. Impacts on students and the community are discussed.

Finding Meaning in Civically Engaged Scholarship, pages 117–129
Copyright © 2009 by Information Age Publishing
117

INTRODUCTION: FROM THE PERSONAL
TO THE PROFESSIONAL

Civic engagement is common among the political science faculty I know, and it varies widely, from foster care for children in state's custody to umpiring adult baseball games. Unlike the political engagement usually practiced by academics—public service unrelated to their scholarship—I have always felt a pull to educate in a way that changed the world. Like reading my favorite philosophers for the first time, service learning, or engaged pedagogy, rang brilliantly true the first time I heard it. This chapter describes my journey in teaching Neighborhood Democracy, but first I'll discuss the influence of philosophy on that journey.

My development of engaged pedagogy took time. Early on, I was limited by my lack of imagination and loyalty to what I respected as the canon of my sub-discipline. I taught as my teachers had taught me. I tried to relate political theory to current reality as much as possible, which was well-received by my students. I recall, however, a revealing exchange with a faculty colleague. In routine small talk, he asked me if I was teaching that day, and I responded, "yeah, democracy, tonight." My shorthand for the course Democratic Theory amused him. Chortling at what he thought was my misspeaking, he parodied in an authoritative voice: "I AM GOING TO TEACH YOU DEMOCRACY." His point, a good one, was that democracy, a vastly complicated social, economic, cultural, political phenomenon, could hardly be represented in a class syllabus. I had not misspoken, however. My shorthand was meant to convey this very intention, to teach the experience of democracy, although I didn't know it at the time.

The teaching of the experience of democracy became intentional following an "ah-ha moment" while rereading philosopher Hannah Arendt about five years ago. Arendt's (1963) extended ruminations on freedom in the ancient, early-modern, and contemporary eras eventually led her to write *On Revolution*. When I finally came around to reading it, I couldn't put it down, especially the sixth chapter, "The Revolutionary Tradition and Its Lost Treasure." It made me realize that the democratic theory that most attracted me, participatory democracy, had real roots in American history. Her reading of early American freedom catalyzed brilliantly with the philosophy of her mentor, Martin Heidegger, who had played a major role in my dissertation on authenticity. His advocacy of engagement with the world is one of discovery, disclosure, and redemption, rather than the typical modernist emphasis on newness and creation. Here was a theoretical interface with the historical past that would enable my progressive engagement with the future. It was nothing short of revelatory.

Arendt describes the tension between revolutionism and constitutionalism faced by the American Framers. They must have savored the historically unique opportunity to create a completely new polity, "the proud privilege of being beginners of something altogether new," as Arendt (1963, p. 232) puts it. Some of them were also aware that, by codifying their political achievements, they denied the same autonomy to future generations. Arendt brilliantly extrapolates on Jefferson's awareness of this dilemma. In short, there was a profound and permanent cost inflicted on political freedom in America. The federalists won, and Jefferson knew that to concretize political sovereignty in the central and state governments would forever insure that the hand of the dead would rule over the living. To maintain the autonomous spirit of 1776, democracy would have to be practiced on the smallest levels: "divide the counties into wards" Jefferson insisted. There, in "little republics," everyday citizens would keep alive the revolutionary spirit of self-rule by serving in offices "near and dear" to them, providing such public goods as justice, education, welfare, and roads (Arendt, 1963, p. 251).

Arendt calls this "freedom in its most exalted sense…the freedom to act" (p. 232). Thus Jefferson tried to overcome the paradox that "if foundation was the aim and end of revolution, then the revolutionary spirit was not merely the spirit of beginning something new but of starting something permanent and enduring; a *lasting* institution, embodying this spirit and encouraging it to new achievements, would be self-defeating" (p. 232). It is the very paradox of institutionalizing a revolution. Only the founders have the freedom to create something new; every generation that follows is subject to the original foundations. This dilemma is the source of Jefferson's playful exhortation to have a revolution every twenty years, to avoid the injustice of the dead ruling the living.

Without the possibility of revolutions, the best approximation of the "space for freedom" enjoyed by the constitutional convention were the elementary republics of the ward system (p. 235). These republics were not a utopian dream; they were already here. Self-government was the essence of the Revolutionary "Liberty" slogan" (Foner, 1999). Historian David Hackett Fischer relates a story of a conversation between an interviewer and a veteran of the Battle at Concord. The veteran was asked if it was the writings of Locke or Paine that had urged him into action. He responded that he had never heard of Locke and had to admit not reading Paine. He then explained that "New Englanders had always managed their own affairs, and Britain tried to stop them, and so the war began" (Shain, 1998).

Political freedom is no utopian dream. Ralph Waldo Emerson saw it in the New England town meeting, "the unit of the republic." Jefferson credited the Revolution to the townships, which had "thrown the entire nation into energetic action" (Shain, 1998, p. 251). I have seen it in Salt Lake City, in neighborhood councils and associations, in parades and protests, in ward houses and parishes, in avalanches of emails and packed city council chambers. As I read Dewey and Arendt, I wondered how my classroom might contribute to this traditional wellspring of American political freedom.

INSTITUTIONAL CONTEXT

As I described in Chapter 3, at a certain point in my professional development it became obvious that I had to employ service-learning as a medium to teach democratic theory and practice, i.e., "democracy." My life experience *and* my favorite philosophers had taught me this. To make their study of American democracy real, I had to take my students outside the classroom and teach "democracy" as well as democratic theory.

Although I suffered some isolation from a faculty obsessed with meeting tenure, retention, and promotion requirements, mine wasn't a solitary journey or independent academic entrepreneurship. Neighborhood Democracy was the result of confluence beyond my own design. I owe its success, if not its conception, to key agents and incentives in both the University and the community. First, my title and job description were not impediments. As a lecturer, I was expected to teach an increased course load, but was not reviewed for my research productivity. In addition, the disciplinary context of political science at Utah is quite amenable to civically-engaged work. Contrary to what many of this book's contributors have experienced, I haven't had to justify to my peers my concern with community. "Practical politics," as they call it here at Utah, has an unassailable cache among faculty members in the Department of Political Science and its partner across the hall, the Hinckley Institute of Politics. I have, at times, enjoyed the support, and the valuable freedom of being left alone, from my colleagues, department chair, and dean over the last several years.

Indeed, this is a story of partnerships. To a trace a "beginning" is difficult and probably artificial. In 2002, University Neighborhood Partners (UNP), an outreach program of the University of Utah, was created out of the President's office, by Irene Fisher, former Director of the Lowell Bennion Community Service Center at Utah. Seeking to promote campus-community relationships that many considered long neglected in Salt Lake City, UNP works "To bring together University and west side resources for reciprocal learning, action, and benefit" (University Neighborhood Partners, 2008). Bolstered by a major grant from HUD's Community Outreach Program Center (COPC) fund in 2004, UNP continues to flourish today.

In 2003, I was asked to participate in a UNP-sponsored community-based research project in the Glendale neighborhood of Salt Lake. UNP had received a request from the newly-elected leadership of the Glendale community council to help discover the barriers to increased participation in the organization's activities. The young leadership cohort wanted the council to become more demographically representative of the neighborhood. The goal of the research group was to investigate and address these issues in Glendale, and by extension, other neighborhoods on the west side.

One of the key findings arising from the six focus groups convened was that "community" meant different things to different people. For some, community was based on geography or religion, but for others, it was defined by culture, language, or kin networks. The recommendation that followed was for neighborhood councils to focus on community-building instead of problem-solving. Activities suggested were street fairs and neighborhood festivals, neighborhood cleanups sponsored by a partnership of different organizations, and cultural performances at council meetings (Glendale Community Partnership, 2005). The first of these recommendations, the neighborhood festival, caught the wind and took flight under the aegis of Neighborhood Democracy.

COMMUNITY CONTEXT

The west side of Salt Lake City, home to neighborhoods such as Glendale and Rose Park, is in transition. Originally populated in the 1950s by the white, Mormon working class, "Glendale has been transformed from what might be thought of as a relatively *centralized* and homogeneous neighborhood—one in which most residents were part of the same overlapping ethnic, language, and religious networks that also shaped decision-making of the Community Council—to a *multi-centric* and much more diverse neighborhood in which there are multiple languages, backgrounds, religious and family networks, and arenas of local decision-making" (Glendale Community Partnership, 2005, p. 2).

The percentage of Hispanic residents on the west side, for example, increased from 16% in 1990 to 40% in 2000. The west side is also home to large numbers of Pacific Islanders, Asian-Americans, Native Americans, and international war refugees, including large numbers of Bosnians and Somalis. These demographic changes challenge west side communities to include these new residents in schools, social services, community groups, and political forums. In terms of political forums, it is no longer effective to rely on established networks or the World War II cohort who participate(d) in civic life in such impressive numbers.

These neighborhoods are also attracting increasing numbers of young Anglo couples who have been priced out of property on the east side and appreciate the west side's cultural and religious diversity. As political participation continues to correlate highly with education and socioeconomic status, short-term revival of neighborhood councils is probably dependent on this generation of young professionals becoming civically engaged. As such, the goals of Neighborhood Democracy were several-fold: to educate and help activate a generation of college students who were yet to find their place in civic life, and help reinvigorate neighborhood-level civic action in Salt Lake City through community partnerships with students.

DEPARTMENTAL ORIGINS AND INSTITUTIONAL INCENTIVES

I pitched POLS 3020 Neighborhood Democracy as a new class, fitting it between POLS 3010, Democratic Theory, a class which I taught frequently, and POLS 3030, State and Local Government. I was surprised at the facility of the approval process, and remember feeling pride in making my mark on the course catalogue. I had taught self-generated, unique courses before, but they were listed under general, pre-existing course numbers and titles like "Senior Seminar" or "Special Topics." Whether it was due to indifference or support on behalf of my colleagues, the seeds of my service-learning efforts found fertile ground in my department.

It is important to stress that this would not have happened if I were a tenure-track faculty. Although the course would still have been approved, my tenure reviews would have included admonitions to try this work *after* tenure. And my focus would have been different, i.e., racking up points toward tenure. Much of the book you hold is filled with stories of struggles to change the culture of retention and promotion within our departments and colleges at Utah. That burden, responsibility, and risk are not mine. In fact, service-learning fits very well with my role as a lecturer, where increased contact with students, especially in lower-division classes, serves to draw majors into the department and stimulate those with graduate school potential. For the faculty in my department, civically-engaged work is a tightrope walk above manifest *dis*incentives, unless, of course, one can meet publishing schedules with civically-engaged work.

In addition, it should go without saying that none of this would have happened without the Bennion Center at Utah. Their educational materials and the accessibility of staff, including then-Director Marshall Welch and Service-learning Coordinator Joani Shaver, guided me through key elements of course design and administrative approvals. In addition, their annual request for proposals provided incentive to verbally articulate my project earlier than I would have with a normal syllabus. Their financial support didn't hurt either. I applied for a Service-Learning Initiative Grant, from a funding pool aimed at sparking individual and departmental forays into service-learning. This was a significant small grant—up to $4000—and required the home department of the applicant to at least partially match funds. This requisite for departmental participation and college support brought my departmental chair and college dean into the process, forcing me to engage them in a topic I would not have otherwise.

IDENTIFYING COMMUNITY PARTNERS

In its four years of existence, Neighborhood Democracy has done 10 projects and had 5 different community partners. My original intention was to create unique, *sui generis* projects each year. I felt that students would receive richer experiences if they were involved as close as possible to the ground floor. As a result, I had an aversion to partnering with existing nonprofits at which students simply would be plugged in to existing initiatives. I wanted students to *own* their fieldwork. Since the preparation this required was immense, I have become less ambitious as the years have passed, sacrificing quality in some cases, but not in others.

The one community partner that has endured since the inaugural year has been the Rose Park Community Council. This partnership blossomed out of previous contact made by the aforementioned University Neighborhood Partners. Some of the leadership of the Rose Park Community Council participated in the Glendale participation study, and expressed interest in outreach to parts of their community who had not been active in the community council. A key cornerstone of UNP's philosophy is to respond to requests from the community, rather than offering to "fix problems" that the community may not recognize as such. With the Chair of the Council in particular, there was an enthusiasm for outreach, especially for the idea of a community festival. We met over lunch several times to get acquainted and synchronize our visions. I came to know and love the cohort of neighborhood participants whom he led.

Our visions, personalities, or process are not always identical, as I expressed in my first chapter. But what maintains the partnership, for me, is a sense of civic friendship. We share a *telos*, a common public end, which Aristotle marks as one of the qualities of the friendship found between citizens. I imagine that many engaged pedagogues develop these same civic relationships with their long-standing community partners. Other partners, whose projects ran only a year, have come from this same local tree, the entangled branches of Salt Lake civic life. These partners have varied from a City-sponsored after-school program for teens to a national nonprofit promoting financial responsibility for individuals and families. As I recall the partners involved, I am struck by how many of them are former students.

COURSE DESCRIPTION

Neighborhood Democracy (Political Science 3020) is a service-learning course that enrolls approximately 20 students each Spring semester. Currently, I have the help of one service-learning coordinator, a student of my choice whose $500 stipend I double from my research funds. For the course's second iteration in 2006, I had four assistants supervising four projects, and have since preferred a more manageable scope. The course is designed to combine the teaching of democratic theory and practice, with a focus on the local level. To try to convey the "experience" of democracy, I design the syllabus around readings, reflection essays, and fieldwork.

Readings focus on democratic theory, empirical accounts of democratic communities, and, when possible, project-specific material, e.g., on neighborhood planning or research methods. Jane Mansbridge's *Beyond Adversary Democracy* provides an excellent background of democratic theory as well as empirical accounts of democracy in township and workplace settings. Students gain language and concepts with which to understand and assess the neighborhood council meetings that they are required to attend and reflect on. In addition, a staple of the syllabus is *The Rebirth of Urban Democracy* (Berry, Portney, & Thomson, 1993), a text which weaves the political science concepts surrounding participation with empirical data from five American cities with strong neighborhood participation systems. Students gain, again, conceptual vocabulary as well as real-world examples with which to compare their Salt Lake experiences.

Reflection essays are the heart of assessment in service-learning. My assignments tend to revolve around two themes: (1) applying concepts gleaned from the readings to neighborhood council meetings and (2) reflecting on their group project. For example, Mansbridge's distinction between adversarial and unitary forms of democracy is a powerful tool to describe the personalities of diverse political communities. Commenting on decision-making procedures, the spatial organization of meeting rooms, and leadership styles, students are able to reflect on the comparative unitary or adversarial qualities of neighborhood councils in Salt Lake. Some reflection assignments are more open-ended and personal, encouraging students to articulate the most outstanding features of the experience to them. Sometimes the reflections are as open as, "What did you learn about democracy in this class?" Students are required to attend three different neighborhood council meetings over the course of the semester. Each time they are assigned specific elements on which to reflect. Far from rote regurgitation of readings through which the reader must suffer, they provide insight into this fascinating world.

Projects have varied greatly over the years. For some, like the Rose Park Community Festival and the documentary film project, I have done much legwork ahead of time, laying paving stones months before the semester started so that when students arrived in January, they could begin work immediately. In other cases, existing projects were complemented by college students' involvement, as in the youth planning initiative, where Neighborhood Democracy students became assistants to the project leader, a City employee, in supervising the high school students for whom the project was designed. This past semester, students were divided between the Rose Park Festival, a pre-existing but original project to the class, and initiatives of the local chapter of a national nonprofit. One of these involved the lobbying of the state legislature on the nonprofit's priorities, and barely engaged students outside of letter-writing to lawmakers. The other allowed students to have significant ownership, and they were able to sign up more than 50 students into a program to encourage personal savings and financial literacy.

Over the years I have learned the difference between full community partners and pseudo-partners. For a project to have staying power and meaning for students and community members, it must be conceived in a true partnership of mutual interest. The Rose Park Community Festival is the best example of a true partnership. The planning and execution of the festival occur through committees staffed by one student and one community member, who have sole responsibility for an element of the festival, such as food, entertainment, or children's activities. Given the public nature of the project, failure is not an option, and it is incredibly satisfying to see the differences that are bridged in order to realize the event. Not all projects have included genuine community partners. In the case of the various surveys, different neighborhood councils were only nominal partners, looking over suggested survey questions ahead of time and asked to suggest their own. Politeness, I think, resulted in more reticence than conversation. The idea of the surveys initiated with myself, and the interest on the part of the neighborhood councils was always limited. While the survey results were well received when they confirmed the communities' positive self-image, follow-up was limited because the research was not truly community-based.

STUDENT IMPACT

The term "service learning" carries an inherent sense of reciprocity within it. The financial supporters of this project, The Bennion Center and University Neighborhood Partners, are firmly grounded in this philosophy of reciprocal benefit for the university—students, faculty, and institution—and the community. Judging by students' comments on course evaluations and in reflection essays, there is no question that the students of Neighborhood Democracy were beneficiaries of their service in the community.

To read about the history and theory of participatory politics is one thing. Seeing a reflection of it in a neighborhood council meeting, one student struggled to articulate the aura of local democracy: "All in all I can say that my preconceptions of community council meetings were a tad off. This wasn't what I would call action packed, but it was entertaining at times watching the interaction between the citizens and the guest speakers. I enjoyed a certain feeling in the meeting. I felt like I was part of the 'grass roots' of politics in that room." His boredom had been pierced!

Self-reported pedagogical results have been impressive. In written evaluations, typically more than 90% of students strongly agree with the statement "I learned a great deal" in the course, and rate the effectiveness of the course equally strongly. Their responses reveal that they developed technical skill—through the *doing* of community work—as well as qualities of character like ingenuity and persistence in the face of intimidating challenges. In addition, communication and the other elements of cooperation were required skills to the pass the class's service component—and indeed, the grand majority of students said they developed their collaborative skills in the course. All agreed that they gained "a better understanding of diverse groups and issues related to diversity."

In some cases, misconceptions about Salt Lake's west side were challenged. "I have been able to first and foremost be educated on a part of the city I was originally unfamiliar with and because of that have changed my views on the Rose Park area itself. Before I started this class I had the same opinion of Rose Park that most people who are unfamiliar with the city do, that is, a negative outlook... at our first meeting I was impressed by the gorgeous library building... the brand new elementary school... and the well-lit streets and tidy homes. I have since learned however that Rose Park is a community full of citizens who are proud of their city and want to let others know it."

Students may be enthusiastic about stepping out of the traditional classroom, but they suffer much the similar apprehension I have. During the students' 2-month participation, misgivings frequently arise. The first year's Rose Park Community Festival team were self-conscious trailblazers. One enthusiastic festival team student who was in charge of the daunting task of festival publicity reported, "Going into this project I was under the notion that we would be operating under a preestablished framework. I quickly became aware however that we were pioneering the conception and implementation of this event." As if building the road as you walk isn't enough, this same student had to survive prolonged absences and negativity of his community partner: "I also found my community member partner to be quite adversarial. I noticed this because I was starting to take her skepticism personally since I at this point personally cared about the outcome of the project." But by the conclusion of the festival, there was no doubt in his mind. "This project blew my socks off and I'm proud to have been a part of it."

What about students' relationship to class material—readings on democratic theory, sub-municipal politics, leadership, and community development and organizing? How well did students' experience in the field enhance their learning? Anecdotally, again, the evidence is strong that some theoretical concepts were well illustrated in the field. Students generally reflect insightfully on concepts like efficacy, leadership style, and group procedure.

Starting from the political science concept of efficacy in his reflection on his group financial literacy project, a student from this year's class commented, "The experience of this project has taught me more than anything else in this class, because it brought everything I had read and learned into fruition and showed me that you create your own level of efficacy with community involvement." Referring back to his group project experience, he continued, "There were obstacles that each of us faced with our different assignments but we were able to brainstorm together to overcome the obstacles and establish a program at the University that will hopefully really take off and help students become better financially educated." The project mattered to him, and he had felt effective. Recognizing that action can have value beyond any expected outcome, he observed, "But even if that goal is not accomplished, I think that each of us learned what it takes to have efficacy in a group project, and I think that will make more of a difference in the future for each of us." He had understood the concentric and interdependent circles of community and his role in them. Only engaged pedagogy can teach such lessons.

COMMUNITY IMPACT

The explicit community-based normative goal of the Neighborhood Democracy class is to try to help build the democratic capacity of the community councils we partner with. Supporting projects of group problem-solving and community outreach, we try to accomplish this through bridge-building activities like the Rose Park Community Festival. I am very proud of the connections we've cultivated yet recognize that there's so much more to do.

I am acutely aware that expanding capacity through bridge-building is slow and difficult to measure. And in the absence of a controlled study, we are left to gauge our success in stories, rather than, say, tracing movement on a social capital index. How could we begin to record the consequences of a multitude of interactions? In one sense, all I have is the intuition that we are making a positive difference. Some projects, like the Rose Park Community Festival, have endured, and will be in its fifth year next Spring. Other projects, because of lack of real partnership or shared goals, have not been repeated. In sharing our survey results with our partners on the community councils, we have tried to increase self-knowledge, and that information-sharing (e.g., a list of new Festival contacts, an annotated directory of local organizations) has helped grow connections in the community.

I also hope we have helped grow social capital between the University and community organizations. Trust is only built over time; my experience with the Rose Park project has demonstrated the value of years of investment in building quality relationships. Two former students from the class are now on the executive committee of the Rose Park Community Council. One moved back to the area after graduation, and another was a recently-arrived resident at the time he took the class and has chosen to expand his involvement in the neighborhood. He will probably be next year's Festival Chair.

CONCLUSION: LESSONS LEARNED

Continuity, then, is essential for building democracy, just as it helps me teach students what a democratic experience feels like. As a result I think my students *are* learning about "democracy," in the classroom about its ideals and different forms, and in the field by participating in a hands-on group project. Without continuity with, of, and between community partners, the quality of students' field experience will suffer. And effectiveness increases as ties grow stronger; our Rose Park Festival team has lowered "transaction costs" significantly in our 5 years as we build on shared experiences and knowledge built cooperatively.

Communication is needed for continuity. Staying in touch with community partners keeps communication lines open for ordinary and extraordinary communication. The familiarity that frequent communication enables is exactly the tie you want to build with your community partner. Remember that communication styles differ; you may have to adjust to a style you're not used to. I have found that this challenge is especially acute for students, especially if they are 2 or more generations removed from their community partners. Personalities, technologies, mores, habits—all may be out of synch. Indeed, the Rose Park Festival is rich in the opportunities for partners, joined at the hip as co-chairs of an organizing committee, to bridge differences. I give my students the advice to carry out the little disciplines, like checking in frequently with your partner (and checking a couple of things off your list), that allow the garden to grow.

Finally, have *confidence in your vision* in the face of resistance and limited evidence of success. Change is slow and often imperceptible. The strength given me by Arendt's story of early American democracy enables me to act as an agent of democratic culture, encouraging democratic elements wherever I can within the course experience. For example, I have tried to assert my democratic dialogical style on group project dynamics. I encourage horizontally-oriented deliberation and governance in the student project groups, and remind them of the leadership reading we have done. This also comes out in my relationships with community partners. For one, I can't help but challenge the way Rose Park residents who are my parents' generation run a meeting. This meeting style, which I consider too formal and task-oriented, I have tried to push in the direction of a meeting as an *event* rather than merely a tool. Believing that this allows space for more sharing across differences that is so valuable to successful group dynamics, i.e., community-building, I feel a need to put as much theory into practice as possible.

Thanks to my ethical commitments to participatory democracy and engaged pedagogy, I have been willing to take risks with community partners on projects not terribly well defined because of my faith that *something* will be better than nothing. Great—and failed projects—have come about that way. Service-learning is certainly not for perfectionists and control-freaks. While I have worked hard to prepare the highest quality experience for students, it doesn't always come out that way. Yet I know it *will* help move them, at least some distance, down the road toward authentic citizenship.

REFERENCES

Arendt, H. (1963). *On revolution.* New York: Viking Press.

Berry, J. M., Portney, K. E., & Thomson, K. (1993). *The rebirth of urban democracy.* Washington, DC: Brookings Institute.

Foner, E. (1999). *The story of American freedom.* New York: W. W. Norton & Company.

Glendale Community Partnership. (2005). *Understanding community participation in the Glendale neighborhood.* Salt Lake City, UT: University Neighborhood Partners.

Shain, B. A. (1998). American community. In G. W. Carey & B. Frohen (Eds.), *Community and tradition: Conservative perspectives on the American experience* (pp. 39–62). New York: Rowman and Littlefield.

University Neighborhood Partners (2008). Retrieved 8–15–08 from www.partners.utah.edu/index.htm

CHAPTER 13

REFLECTIONS ON THE
EYE OF THE STORM

Marshall Welch

Over the years, I have created and taught three service-learning courses. My first course was a graduate-level, interdisciplinary course in which education students worked together in schools to identify a specific student need related and then collaboratively create, implement, and evaluate a program (Welch et al., 1996). The second class was on children at risk due to economic, cultural, health/ability factors. The third course, on civic engagement, involved students providing indirect service working for local nonprofits (Welch, 2007; Welch & Taylor, 2006; Welch, Chatwin, & Sudbury, 2005; Welch & Davies, 2004). I conducted research to assess the impact the course had on both students and their community partners. These courses were rewarding to me, my students, and the community partners. I was prepared to teach the course on civic engagement for a fourth time until my intentions were diverted by Hurricane Katrina.

Soon after the storm, a group of students gathered at the Lowell Bennion Community Service Center for a lunch meeting to explore how we could help. There were many ideas for providing immediate, direct assistance; however, the community and nation as a whole had already begun

Finding Meaning in Civically Engaged Scholarship, pages 131–143
Copyright © 2009 by Information Age Publishing
All rights of reproduction in any form reserved.

the helping process. Instead, I proposed we explore what we could do within a year's time, when the help had diminished.

A year went by. I decided to create a different kind of class in which the students and I would learn together. The course, *Katrina: The Eye of the Storm*, used the hurricane as a mirror of our society. I conceptualized the class as an opportunity for the students to teach one another; the only structure I implemented was to examine the complex issues of Katrina from economic, cultural, political, and environmental perspectives. I wanted the experience to teach us more about racism, classism, and privilege. I also wanted to make it personal and real, to put a face on it, so it was more than an academic exercise.

I arranged a week midway through the semester in which the class would gut houses in New Orleans. Obviously, the task of stripping the interior of houses was not tied to any instructional objective. In fact, the actual service may have been the most insignificant aspect of the whole experience. Instead, the physical work was simply a catalyst or a means of seeing abstract issues first hand. I wanted us to do more that acquire discrete facts, but rather, gain insight and understanding. The best way to do this was to go to New Orleans, feel the city, and talk to the people there. We met my initial instructional objectives of learning about Katrina from various contexts. However, we all came to learn much more.

THE OPERA OF KATRINA

I have created and used the simple first-letter mnemonic device of O.P.E.R.A. (Objectives, Partnerships, Engagement, Reflections, Assessment) as a rubric when I am organizing my own service-learning course or assisting colleagues as they conceptualize a course. To illustrate its utility, it will serve as the headings to describe this class.

OBJECTIVES

I wanted students to take an active role in creating their learning experience. The structure of the course was to form four teams of three students each which examined Katrina from a different perspective: health, policy, environment, and culture. Each team conducted research related to their topical area and taught the class and their instructor prior to the week of service in New Orleans midway through the semester. Upon our return, the plan was that each team would revisit their research with new insight and experience. A key aspect of the follow-up research was to identify what we had learned in New Orleans and apply it to our own community. Collectively, the class would create some kind of product or presentation that would be shared with the entire campus community.

The Director of the Honors program found my course compelling and provided $5,000 from her discretionary funds to cover the cost of the trip for 12 students, which was the enrollment cap. The cost for each student was approximately $380 which covered airfare, room and board at $15 a day at a local church, the cost of high-end ventilator masks, and van rentals. The 3 ½ hour class sessions met weekly for 15 weeks with the trip to New Orleans at mid-semester during Fall Break.

The first class session provided a perfunctory overview of the service we would do in New Orleans and the objectives of the course. I made it clear that the students would be responsible for their own learning, and my role would be to facilitate the process. Once we had gone over the basic structure of the course outline and syllabus, we spent considerable time creating a class covenant. The discussion was frank and candid. I "put on the table" the array of volatile issues we would confront—race, class, poverty, and privilege. We collectively recognized and agreed upon the need for creating a safe environment for learning and dialogue, so we generated a list of principles to guide our actions for the next 15 weeks. Everyone in the room ratified the covenant by signing it. Intellectually, we knew this covenant was important, but we could not imagine how important this academic exercise would become later.

The students sincerely wanted to go and help the city; there was no doubt about their willingness to provide service. It also became abundantly clear, however, that this experience was viewed as an exciting "paid road trip for credit." After all, this was a trip to the "Big Easy." It soon became real work as the teams were expected to conduct and share research with the entire class. Student teams were taking on the responsibility of working together to teach one another. Two types of tasks had to be undertaken to accomplish this goal.

First began the more explicit academic focus of what constitutes "best practice" in teaching. We allocated considerable time in which I asked the students to generate "best practices" in teaching based upon their experiences. The plan was to use the ideas listed on the board to create a rubric to "evaluate" the quality of their teaching. Their list was full of activities such as using websites, video clips, simulations, preflection and reflection questions, and Power point slides. After nearly an hour of discussion, I brought up the fact they had not included any readings from articles or books. The inevitable question was finally posed, "Are you going to MAKE us include reading assignments?" I never imagined or anticipated that readings would NOT be part of their instruction. I gulped and said, "No, this is up to you but...you're all going to be held to whatever you decide and your evaluation is based on the criteria you come up with." I had to be consistent with what I had said or the trust established through our covenant would have been violated. The discussion continued, and they finally collectively created an evaluation rubric of their presentations. After each team made their multimedia presentations to the class, they were evaluated as both individual presenters and as a team.

Second, we focused on the hidden curriculum of learning how to work together in the research and teaching process. Each week we engaged in discussions and activities designed to help them identify their own working and communication styles. We talked candidly that conflict was inevitable and considered strategies for coping with disagreements. We learned how to make action plans. We allocated time at the end of each class session to assess the team's and individuals' function in sharing, communicating, and following through on tasks. The outcomes of this review process became goals for subsequent tasks and sessions.

PARTNERSHIPS

The St. Charles Avenue Presbyterian Church in New Orleans was coordinating a project known as Rebuilding Hope in New Orleans or RHINO. Working with college and church groups, they provided housing and food along with supervision of the work. I was able to secure a week with the project that coincided with our school's fall break. In hindsight, this was the most straightforward aspect of preparing for the course. Identifying a partner organization with experience and infrastructure was critical.

REFLECTION

Students had to reflect in writing on what they learned from their team presentation, how they felt about what they had learned, on how they might use this new information in the future. I used the ABCs rubric with points for addressing affect, behavior, and cognition (Welch, 1999). This written reflection, however, was only one small component of the entire reflection process for the course.

Because I wanted students to take major responsibility in co-creating new knowledge, I included them in designing the reflection activities for our time in New Orleans, although I had never done this previously. The week before we departed, the class generated reflection topics that would be used while we were in New Orleans. We eventually decided on six topics, one for each day. Dyads of students volunteered to be responsible for determining the format and conducting their reflection session at 5:00 P. M., following each day's work before the students were free for the evening. We agreed not to evaluate or grade the reflection discussions, another first for me. I also assigned students a personal daily journal. Although it was not graded, I wanted them to keep track of their array of experiences and emotions. In what seemed no time at all, we were on our way to New Orleans.

ENGAGEMENT

Classroom Engagement. The classroom was the initial setting for engaged learning. The student teams worked on thematic topics and presentations. Although I assigned the 4 broad topical areas, the students chose the specific focus of their project. They reported on what could be learned from Katrina and applied in our own community. The environmental team taught the class the role of the natural swamplands as a "sponge" to absorb the effect of hurricanes. These students then illustrated how the wetlands had been "reclaimed" for agricultural and industrial use, essentially removing the terrestrial buffer zone. Their presentation also reported on the environmental blight and pollution that resulted from the disaster.

The group of students examining health chose the novel topic of medical records, discussing how medical records are usually archived as hard copy paper files. Since many of these documents were lost or damaged, not only was providing medical care a challenge, but merely knowing the type of treatment provided previously to elderly or poor patients was difficult. The group also reported on the emotional stress and mental health issues that surfaced for survivors after the flood waters had receded.

Another group focused on culture, ethnicity, and race. They began by reporting on the history of various groups settling in what became New Orleans. Important traditions and heritage were presented to gain insight into New Orleans. This discussion led to examination of diversity, assimilation, tolerance and blending of traditions—not only in New Orleans, but in our own community as well.

Another team led the class to reflect on how policy is shaped by culture and race and vice versa. This included examination of policy breakdown between city, state, and federal officials, providing insight into the infrastructural causes of the post-Katrina rescue and recovery efforts.

Being There. Once we arrived in the ravaged 8th and 9th wards in New Orleans, it all became very real, very quickly. Katrina was no longer an abstract concept for intellectual dialogue. We got an overview of the type of work we'd being doing the first morning. Beyond the rudimentary instructions of how to gut a house down to its stud walls, we were reminded by our community partner that our mission was to rebuild hope. We were engaging in the invasive act of salvaging the personal belongings of strangers. We also would be literally dismantling the house. We were asked that we work with respect and to remember these were the remnants of shattered lives. We were forewarned that we might ask—either to ourselves or openly—why not simply bulldoze these houses? Some were nothing more than shacks, so why not just knock them down and start over? Instead of using our frame of reference of affluence and privilege to judge, we were encouraged to recall that these were the homes of people who wanted to return and rebuild. Our task and mission was to give these people hope to return. We went in with open hearts and strong hands. Despite the orientation, none of us could truly imagine the impact of what we were about to do.

Our initial foray into our first house was surreal and full of contradictions. It became very personal but in a detached sort of way. In 90-degree heat, we began to tear down the home of strangers so they could rebuild. It was all quite voyeuristic, especially because on that first day the owners were not actually present as we worked. In their absence, we saw the intimate and personal pieces of people's lives—some salvageable, some lost forever. We also saw poverty. We saw the ravaged residue of the storm and floods. We saw mold, mud, filth, and shattered lives.

None of us were ready for this. Looking back, we thought we were prepared. We had discussed all of this for weeks prior to coming to New Orleans. We had read about it, talked about, and made presentations in class about it. We emerged from our first hour of labor for a break, physically and emotionally exhausted. I looked at my students and I knew that none of us would ever be the same again.

The Little Things.   I started noticing the little things as soon as our work began. When I say little things, I mean the type of things we take for granted and don't even notice in our daily routine. Things like breathing. I rarely give the simple act of breathing much thought. But this work required respirators. These masks served as constant reminders that I couldn't even take breathing for granted. We encountered mold and filth like I had never seen. The odor of rotting food and standing water after 13 months is overwhelming. Learning to get used to masks strapped across the face took time as well. Coupled with wearing safety goggles, one couldn't but help feel inoculated to an extent. I began to realize this shielding was more than physical protection because it also served as a kind of psychological and emotional buffer but in a futile sort of way.

There was no water or electricity or plumbing at the work sites. If we had to urinate, we had to walk either to port-a-potties located out and about or to a nearby convenience store. This was an inconvenience. But it paled in comparison to what the people of this amazing city endured for weeks and many continue to do so to this day.

Likewise, I realized this "inconvenience" of no water and electricity—as temporary as it was for me—is a daily reality for many people around the world. One spray painted graffiti I saw in the 9th ward reminded me of this. It said in its crude lettering, "this is America's Baghdad."

And then there were the actual tiny objects and the seemingly trivial remnants of personal lives we found or recovered. Many were fragile, like the lives we came to know. We did our best to salvage some of those things and to return them to the people we were helping. Despite losing almost everything, these individuals celebrated when the little things were saved. We found a photo album that belonged to a woman named Elaine. She cried and rejoiced as she thumbed through the photo albums with us, telling us her stories. She said we had given a part of her life back. How can something like that not change you?

I was so proud of the students who carefully brought out everything, even the trashed materials, and carefully placed them outside. All of us began to see the objects with new eyes, wondering about their apparent value that was lost on us. We had, in small way, become a part of these people's lives. The students' sensitivity, care, and awareness of those we were helping was one of the more profound learning moments. They were relating to the otherness and plight of total strangers. How does one teach this in a class or from a textbook?

Here's the thing; after awhile, I got used to it all. I soon forgot about the mask, the lack of water, the conditions, the huge spiders we simply whacked with our hammers as we worked, the mold and smell, the rat feces, and the spray paint codes on the side of every house. Each day we became more familiar and skilled with the work itself. Soon, we worked our way past the initial shock we encountered on the first day. It's not so much that we got used to it. I don't think that ever happened. Instead, we . . . I . . . came to accept and grasp the reality of it all, to an extent.

So this is what I've been trying to sort out and I'm still working through it. Did I just become numb to it all to the point I just didn't want to think about it? And if so, to what extent do I do the same thing in other aspects of my life? Is this what we as a people in this great nation have come to do? Simply anesthetize ourselves from these things to keep us sane or to absolve ourselves from any kind of responsibility? Or is this a way of persevering and moving on in the face of adverse conditions? Does it actually make us stronger? It's probably a little of both. I don't know. I'm still working on this.

The Big Things. Katrina reminded America that its dirty secrets of poverty, classism, and racism are very much alive. It took this human tragedy to make America realize we have a long way to go. As my students said so eloquently and succinctly, it took a hurricane to make us rediscover the oppressive systems and cultural norms that still exist to perpetuate poverty and injustice.

Seeing New Orleans and the enormity of interrelated issues and challenges is overwhelming. We saw the botched bureaucracy and the short attention span of a nation to see and realize that economic, environmental, political, and cultural issues are inextricably linked and intertwined. The fundamental way we do things and teach about these issues have to change.

In asking their deep questions, many of the students pondered if our efforts were merely perpetuating that oppressive system . . . if our work was simply rebuilding the same unjust infrastructure and cultural norms that spawned this poverty. There is some credence to their speculation. At the same time, in their own small way, they are making a difference in the lives of people they are helping as they rebuild.

It is this professor's dream come true to have students ask these probing questions. They wanted answers. And they wanted to change things—not merely reinstate the status quo. They wanted a revolution—their exact wording. But they also realized there was little or nothing they could do to impact the deeper issues that created this situation. They could provide direct assistance, but they could not impact the cultural norms or political policy of that place. So, they resolved to identify something they felt they *could* do. They recognized they were the beneficiaries of an amazing learning experience. And so, at four in the morning, they decided the undergraduate experience *had* to change.

Squirm and Learn.   As mentioned previously, the students developed and conducted their own reflection activities conducted each day following the day's experience. Some sessions involved dialogue, others asked students to find objects during the day that symbolically represented what they had learned, experienced, or felt. Another session was a guided meditation led by a student who embraced Zen Buddhism. Sometimes we listened to audio recordings of the people we were helping. These reflection sessions generated an array of emotions, and some were steeped in profound silence. During one of our reflection sessions a student questioned whether we were merely perpetuating the status quo by "rebuilding" the same unjust, classist, racist system that existed before Katrina. This question resulted in a deep and emotional discussion, fraught with cognitive dissonance. During the final reflection session at the airport as we prepared to depart New Orleans, we considered how our own experience was a microcosm of what New Orleans experienced: chaos, exhaustion, frustration, inspiration, anger. We also examined three fundamental questions of "what did we learn?" "so what?" and "now what?"

These deep discussions clearly manifest what I call "squirm and learn." Students were out of their comfort zone; they experienced significant discomfort and expressed shock and dismay that they felt this way when they expected to have a "good time" while "helping others." This was, for many, the first time they had ever experienced true cognitive dissonance in figuring out who they were and what their role was in the world. The learning process was very disorienting. It was not, for perhaps the first time, a simple matter of completing an assignment and getting a grade. That kind of learning was familiar and straight forward to them. This was new, messy, scary, and very natural in the true developmental evolution they were experiencing.

Suddenly, their somewhat naïve and optimistic perception of service had been turned on its head. They confronted the notion of charity versus justice. They confronted their own biases, a disconcerting process as they recognized traces of their own prejudices. My role at this point was to merely be there for them—to create a safe space and to help them make their own journey. Many students crossed an important developmental bridge as they evolved from their myopic, self-centered perspective to a broader recognition of others. This journey is described and characterized in many development models (Kegan, 1994). I saw it unfold before my eyes. This development was unnerving and not included in the syllabus. I had tried to warn them about this particular learning objective. They couldn't really understand or appreciate the "squirm and learn" until later, much later.

When the semester was over, I had a realization about the entire reflection component of the class. In all my teaching, I had never completely entrusted students with a major portion of the reflection process. In the past they may have had input on the topic, but they had never chosen or facilitated the format. An even more dramatic realization was that I was actually a participant in the reflection process rather than the leader. During the reflection on the fourth day, my students witnessed their instructor weep as I tried to process and articulate what I had experienced that day. The room got very quiet for a long, long time. This was a first for all of us. It revealed many things to all of us. Perhaps the most important revelation for the students was the discovery that their instructor was human with emotions, too. The power differential between instructor and student was obliterated. The squirming and learning was for everyone.

So What? Now What? What does all this mean? What do I personally take away from this experience as an instructor, a citizen, and human being? What did my students take from it? For the longest time after we returned, neither my students nor I could talk about what we saw, did, or felt to each other, family, or friends. We were truly getting our heads around the entire experience. Some students came away angry and confused. Some were inspired and motivated to make a difference. In any case, the students came away transformed. They began to make meaning of the world and their place in it. Along with them, I learned and questioned as much as they did. I learned as much *from* them as I did *with* them. How many instructors can say that?

The students from this class decided they wanted *all* students exposed to these bigger issues in a meaningful way. They wanted to create a pedagogy of engagement that transcended traditional civics courses that introduce principles of economics or government. They wanted students to have authentic experiences that gave them skills to empower them to be good citizens in a just and democratic society. Thus, upon our return, the class collectively decided to shift from the original project of merely providing a multimedia and interdisciplinary report of the experience to campus to bringing about policy change within the undergraduate experience. The remainder of class time was spent organizing a movement through issue mapping and asset mapping to create an action plan designed to revise the American Institutions requirement. Using strategies from community organizing, the students began exploring how they could work within the system to change it.

With that, they began drafting a call to action to revisit the undergraduate curriculum and a proposal to infuse deeper, civic engagement within the American Institutions requirement. They researched and compiled a tentative curriculum and sought instructors who might consider piloting new courses. They accumulated syllabi from existing courses and reviewed them. They organized and convened a forum to discuss their experience and present a rationale for their proposal. Planning the forum included logistical coordination of reserving a room, finding a caterer, creating an agenda and discussion format, writing press releases, and inviting faculty and students. Students identified who would facilitate certain segments of the discussion, whereas others drafted the call to action, and others had it printed on a large banner.

After the forum, the students approached the Undergraduate Council, the body responsible for oversight of the undergraduate curriculum, asking to be on the agenda. They were allotted 15 minutes to make their presentation. Again, class time was devoted to organizing how they would articulate their experience and proposal. Students created Power Point slides, used critical thinking skills to anticipate questions and resistance, and argued over the merits of proposing an overhaul of the American Institutions requirement or merely recommending development of a pilot course. Additionally, one student took it upon herself to propose a campus forum of faculty to explore civic engagement and community-based research. Understanding the political and institutional mission of the university, she proposed the creation of a research center on and for civic engagement. As she prepared to graduate and enter the Peace Corps, this student recruited junior students to carry the plan forward after she had left the campus. They discovered how difficult policy change was, even within the relatively confined environment of a single university. They had greater insight into the complexities associated with broader social change. In the process, they learned about themselves, how to work with one another, and how to work within a system to bring about change. They learned social change is messy and difficult. They came away from the entire experience realizing how easy it is to reduce major events such as Katrina to finger pointing and rhetoric because they were involved in moving beyond rhetoric to real policy change on campus. They learned how difficult it is to bring about change at their own institution, let alone in a city torn apart.

ASSESSMENT

There is no way to truly measure what we learned or felt. There are no authentic, meaningful ways to quantify how it changed us. There is no way to assess how and whether we made a difference in New Orleans, other than to say we helped rebuild the lives and homes of 5 families. Those statements sound odd coming from a professor who generates instructional objectives and attempts to assess to what extent they were achieved. Although I realize the comment is not very scholarly or empirical, I know that we are not the same people we were when we arrived.

I think and hope my students changed, and I take some degree of satisfaction knowing I played a small role in that. As an instructor, I noted that the students came away with more questions than answers. That means something happened as they struggled with the apparent contradictions and cognitive dissonance they experienced. When does that depth of reflection and learning take place in the traditional classroom? To me, these struggles are what true learning and deeper education is about—not to passively accept discrete facts and theories but to search for meaning and apply it to themselves as human beings. Did the students actually accomplish their goal of restructuring the undergraduate experience? At the time of this writing, they had not. Does that mean they failed? No. Did they learn about the change process? Indeed.

I certainly changed. That was not part of the plan or the course objectives. Isn't it the students, not the instructor, who are supposed to be transformed? Was that supposed to happen? Should it have happened? I went to New Orleans with preconceived notions of what we would learn, and what we would experience. I could not have imagined the extent to which the experience changed me or how it would impact my students. The learning was unscripted and uncontrolled, a scary notion to an instructor. I squirmed and learned right along with the students.

As I reflect on this amazing experience, I realize these students in my class were engaged in the same kind of deeper education as the junior high students trying to save the rain forest mentioned in Chapter 4. Simply put, I was doing what I had hoped to accomplish after seeing what this deeper education could be. It had all come full circle for me since the knock on my office door.

EPILOGUE

The experience forced me to reexamine my professional and personal priorities in terms of integrating social justice within my own civically engaged scholarship. I realized that social justice was inextricably linked to engaged scholarship, as it held the academy accountable for using its rich resources in addressing the underlying systemic causes for many of society's problems. Although the University of Utah promoted service-learning as a credible form of pedagogy, it demonstrated a reluctant support of civic engagement due to a lack of understanding of it. As a public research university, the institution was deliberate in its avoidance of social justice as it was viewed as too political. The University made a conscious effort to refrain from using that specific parlance. As a result, I left the University of Utah after 20 years to become the director of a service-learning center at a small, faith-based liberal arts college where I can also teach. The mission of both the institution and the center is to integrate social justice across the undergraduate experience through service-learning and community-based research. I am now the Director of the Catholic Institute of Lasallian Social Action at Saint Mary's College of California.

REFERENCES

Kegan, R. (1994). *In over our heads: The mental demands of modern life.* Cambridge, MA: Harvard Press.

Welch, M. (1999). The ABCs of reflection: A template for students and instructors to implement written reflection in service-learning. *National Society of Experiential Education Quarterly, 25,* 23–25.

Welch, M. (2007). Identifying and teaching civic engagement skills through service-learning. In L. McIlrath (Ed.), *Higher education and civic engagement: International perspectives* (pp. 103–120). Aldershot: Ashgate Publishing.

Welch, M., Chatwin, W., & Sudbury, N. (2005, April). *Service-politics and civic engagement: The development and evaluation of an innovative service-learning course.* Sponsored presentation at the American Association of Colleges and Universities Annual Conference of Engaged Pedagogy, College Park, MD.

Welch, M., & Davies, K. (2004, October). *Service politics and civic engagement: The development and evaluation of an innovative service-learning course.* Presentation at the 4th Annual International K-H Conference on Service-learning Research, Greenville, SC.

Welch, M., Sheridan, S.M., Wilson, B., Colton, D., & Mayhew, J.C. (1996). Site-based transdisciplinary educational partnerships: Development, implementation, and outcomes of a collaborative professional preparation program. *Journal of Educational and Psychological Consultation, 7,* 223–249.

Welch, M., & Taylor, N. (2006, October). *A three-year study of a service-learning course on civic engagement: Quantitative/qualitative results and student perspective.* Presentation at the 6th Annual International K-H Conference on Service-learning Research, Portland, OR

CHAPTER 14

INTEGRATING SERVICE-LEARNING FOR PHYSICAL THERAPY PROGRAMS

Frameworks & Opportunities

Gina Maria Musolino

The physical therapy program at the University of Utah has a long-standing tradition of excellence dating back to the admission of its first class in 1969, making the University of Utah program in physical therapy one of the oldest in the region. The Doctorate in Physical Therapy (DPT) program at the University of Utah reflects the breadth, depth, and rigor of the professional physical therapist education curriculum in response to the current and expected future health care environment. This health care environment includes an enhanced role and higher expectations for the physical therapist, including a commitment to evidence-based physical therapy services and patient care. These skills must be achieved by the completion of an entry-level professional program, which is the outcome expected of our students upon completion of the DPT.

Finding Meaning in Civically Engaged Scholarship, pages 145–159
Copyright © 2009 by Information Age Publishing
All rights of reproduction in any form reserved.

The faculty of the Department of Physical Therapy at the University of Utah considers their fundamental mission to be consistent with that of the University. The Department seeks to: (1) address the health care needs for physical therapy of the community, state, and region by educating physical therapy practitioners; (2) investigate, discover and transmit knowledge related to physical therapy; and (3) provide services to the academic, professional, and general communities in which the Department is involved. We regard physical therapy as a health care profession whose primary purpose is the promotion of human health and function through the application of scientific principles to identify, assess, correct, prevent, or alleviate acute or prolonged human impairment, functional limitation, and disability. The faculty believes that physical therapy education represents the initial commitment to professional service and life-long learning. Professional preparation should be based upon a liberal education in sciences and humanities which develop the values necessary to function effectively and humanely in an ever-changing society. The professional curriculum should prepare students to be confident in the multifaceted roles of clinical practitioner, teacher, researcher, consultant, administrator, and life-long learner. These goals align with the University of Utah's primary mission, which includes creating an environment where the highest standards of scholarship and professional practice are observed, and where the responsibilities to students are conscientiously met. The University of Utah, Department of Physical Therapy, Doctorate in Physical Therapy Program is accredited by the Commission on Accreditation of Physical Therapist Education (CAPTE), and is currently ranked 19th by *US News & World Report*, 2008 Rankings.

The entry-level Doctorate in Physical Therapy (DPT) Program at The University of Utah admits cohort classes of students beginning each summer for a 9-semester entry-level DPT degree. The program transitioned from an entry-level Master's Degree in Physical Therapy (MPT) with 36 students in each cohort to a Doctorate of Physical Therapy in 2005, with 42–44 DPT students in each cohort. DPT students enter each summer semester and complete the DPT curriculum, 116–120 total credit hours, in 3 years, graduating in May. Students complete several clinical education internships which together consist of 1440 clinical hours or 36 weeks of full-time internships. Successful completion of the DPT provides the opportunity for the DPT graduate to take the National Physical Therapist Examination and apply for licensure in the United States.

ENTRY-LEVEL DPT EVALUATIVE CRITERIA

The Evaluative Criteria for Accreditation of Education Programs for the Preparation of Physical Therapists (adopted October 2004) calls for education programs to evaluate specific criteria to both accredit programs and ensure that programs prepare graduates who will be effective contemporary practitioners of physical therapy. The Commission on Accreditation of Physical Therapist Education (CAPTE) calls for faculty to demonstrate scholarly agendas, that in part, contribute to the development of critically reflective knowledge about teaching and learning (Scholarship of Teaching); specifically demonstrating educational effectiveness studies. The SL Courses serve to address the accreditation need for the evaluation of the DPT program. Physical Therapists programs are evaluated in terms of four broad areas, (a) Program, (b) Faculty, (c) Curriculum, and (d) Curricular Outcomes related to the students and the communities they serve. Several program accreditation criteria are addressed (in partial fulfillment) through the service-learning courses (for more detail, see the Accreditation Criteria at http://www.apta.org/).

PIONEERING SERVICE-LEARNING FOR THE UNIVERSITY OF UTAH, DEPARTMENT OF PHYSICAL THERAPY

At the time of my arrival in Fall 2001, formal Service-Learning (SL) was a novel concept for the then Division of Physical Therapy. Certainly, there was a strong sense of volunteerism, with voluntary service being completed by students and faculty as opportunities arose. Yet connected SL, integrated with the curriculum and mutually engaged with the community and learning outcomes, was not yet in place. Hence, it was necessary to share the key concepts of SL with students and faculty. These concepts included that (a) service must meet an identified community need, (b) be congruent with the community served, and (c) the SL must correspond with specific course and community objectives for civic engagement. To uphold these basic tenets of SL, students would be required to complete a formal community needs assessment and link their findings back to course and community objectives, in order to defend the relevance of the civic engagement. The model for SL currently includes evidence of a balance of service and learning, a shared plan for educational and community service, identifying and agreeing upon needs, as well as opportunities for reflection, assessment and evaluation.

As Director of Clinical Education and then Assistant Professor (Clinical) a component of my teaching responsibilities included taking over the course *Physical Therapists as Educators,* a two-credit hour semester course, in the second year of the MPT program. With the transition to a Doctorate program on the horizon, it was the perfect time to implement a change. Although the current MPT content met the former MPT CAPTE standards, it did not meet the Doctorate standards, and the course came too late in the curriculum for many of the basic concepts that were needed by students on their first internships, which involved teaching and educating patients/clients and other health care providers. Hence, the first year interns were disadvantaged, and students' chief concern regarding the MPT course was that it lacked meaning or application. Having developed SL experiences as a at my former institution, I began to see the need for SL in the redevelopment of the DPT curriculum. Aligning my past experience with the changes in the profession and degree program, I proposed the infusion of SL within the new curriculum.

Therefore, the course was redesigned to incorporate SL. The MPT course went from a one semester, two credit hour course, to a two-semester course sequence of 3 total credit hours. The course sequence begins Fall semester of Year I as *Teaching and Learning I* for one credit hour and culminates Spring semester of Year II as *Teaching and Learning II* for two credit hours. Students propose, develop and receive approval for their SL project in Year I and implement and evaluate it from Year I to Spring of Year II. These changes address student needs for providing early didactic content, curricular exposure purposeful to clinical education internships, and a meaningful SL project for learning linked to community-based activities. It was at this time that I elected, as discussed in my journey in Chapter I, to propose this course series formally for SL designation through the Service-Learning Class Committee of the Lowell Bennion Community Service Center.

APPLYING THE CONCEPTS: TEACHING & LEARNING SERVICE-LEARNING DPT COURSE SERIES

An entry-level DPT curriculum is a heavily credit-hour based program. Therefore, it is important to enhance the professionalism and social science components of the curriculum with real-world applications to enforce meaning and relevance for clinically minded DPT students. The Teaching and Learning course series addresses theory and practical applications of educational principles in clinical and community environments and provides preparation for clinical internships and experiences. Students begin to: (a) examine curricular design, development, and evaluation; (b) apply principles of educational leadership; (c) begin the orientation process and preparation for clinical internships and experiences; (d) explore teaching and learning philosophies; (e) propose and plan a service-learning team teaching and learning project with plan for implementation and evaluation; (f) implement the SL plan and present and discuss the project and evaluation; and (g) discuss and evaluate clinical learning experiences. Learning is assessed through active participation, reflective discussion, peer, self, team, and faculty evaluations. (See Appendix A and B for evaluation forms and criteria). In addition, community-based learners and stakeholders also evaluate the SL projects.

The University of Utah, Department of Physical Therapy, Teaching & Learning (T&L) SL I and II course series builds upon Boyer's (1990) Model of Engagement for SL. This theoretical foundation is introduced in the first T & L course and linked to SL proposals and evaluation in the second course (see Figure 14.1). Engagement with communities enables the intersection of teaching, service and scholarship, and is consistent with these missions.

During the first course sequence, Teaching & Learning I, offered the second semester of the entry-level clinical Doctorate in Physical Therapy (DPT), students are introduced to the concepts, theories and definitions related to SL. Students also complete article critiques of published SL, peer-reviewed articles in the *Journal of Physical Therapy Education,* to begin to further understand the relevance, processes, and potential learning outcomes

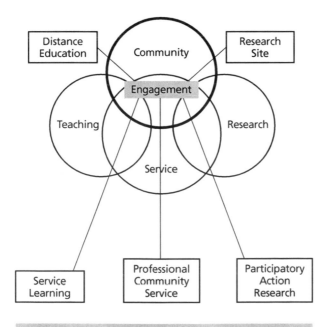

Figure 14.1   SL theoretical foundations based upon Boyer's model of engagement.

associated with SL within the profession. According to Siefer (1998), service learning involves a structured learning experience that meets identified needs in the community with explicit learning objectives, preparation and reflection. DPT students are expected to provide direct community service but also learn about the context in which the service is provided, the connection between the service and the academic course work, and their role as citizens. This community-based SL should not be confused with the traditional internships and/or clinical education. The latter focus more on students' skills for the profession and education, whereas SL provides a balance between service and learning and works to first meet community needs.

A contemporary DPT is recognized by the public as a doctoring profession, utilizing evidence-based practice and a practitioner of choice for movement related dysfunction. Evidence-based practice, as defined by Sackett et al. (1998), includes clients' preferences, values and beliefs, scientific evidence, professional experience and judgment, in addition to clinical and community circumstances. The obligation of professionalism in autonomous doctoring practice means to maintain active responsibility for the growth of the profession and the health of the people it serves (American Physical Therapy Association, 2008). During the first semester of the entry-level DPT program, students begin to learn of the professional commitments and APTA Code of Ethics for the profession, ideas which are also incorporated into the SL.

Based on our profession and our professional documents, it is clear that the DPT has a "*social responsibility*" and "*social obligation*" to serve not only our patients and clients but also society-at-large. Therefore, DPT's must '*value*' service; SL applications provide a venue for this enculturation to occur within the DPT program. The American Physical Therapy Association (APTA) Standards of Practice, Code of Ethics provides in PRINCIPLE 10: "A physical therapist shall endeavor to address the health needs of society. PRINCIPLE 10.1 Pro Bono Service: A physical therapist shall render pro bono publico (reduced or no fee) services to patients lacking the ability to pay for services, as each physical therapist's practice permits. PRINCIPLE 10.2 Individual and Community Health: (a) A physical therapist shall be aware of the patient's health-related needs and act in a manner that facilitates meeting those needs; (b) A physical therapist shall endeavor to support activities that benefit the health status of the community." These ethical principles and core values of the American Physical Therapy Association (APTA) are in parallel with the core values of community-based participatory research as described by Holland (1997). Note the similarities described in Table 14.1.

Through the examination of these foundational principles and profession directives, it is clear that the SL coursework is important for the

TABLE 14.1   Core Values of Community-Based Participatory Research

Holland (1997) Director, National SL Clearinghouse	APTA Core Values
Trust	Accountability
Respect	Altruism
Exchange of Expertise	Excellence
Shared Responsibility	Compassion/Caring
Clear Roles	Integrity
Involvement in all Phases of Work	Professional Duty
Value on Listening and Communicating	Social Responsibilities
Knowledge benefits for All	

post-professional clinical Doctorate in Physical Therapy (ppDPT), which also was implemented during the 2005 transition. The ppDPT is for PT practitioners who wish to return for education to bridge the curricular gap for contemporary practice. At the time of approval of the entry-level DPT, the Utah Board of Regents also approved the post-professional DPT for practicing physical therapists. As ppDPT students are already engaged in communities of practice, it was determined that they could more readily and rapidly complete SL projects within one semester. Table 14.2 provides the curricular sequence and course offering information for both the DPT and the ppDPT.

Silberman (2006) suggests that we retain little from lectures and readings, but substantially more from practice by doing and teaching others. As SL projects involve discussion, practice, and teaching, Silberman's argument further builds the case for civic-engagement as an integral instructional method for the T&L course sequence for both the entry-level DPT and ppDPT.

TABLE 14.2   Service Learning Coursework for the DPT and ppDPT Programs

Course Number & Credit Hrs ( )	Course Name	SL Designation	Education Level	Semester Offered
PH TH 7100-01 (1)	SL Teaching & Learning I	Yes	Entry-level DPT	Year 1
PH TH 7100-05 (1)	SL Teaching & Learning	Yes	Post-Professional DPT	Fall or Spring
PH TH 7270 (2)	SL Teaching & Learning II	Yes	Entry-level DPT	Year 2

TEACHING & LEARNING COURSE SERIES DESCRIBED

Our program has two entry-level DPT courses for those new to the profession of physical therapy, and one post-professional DPT course for practicing physical therapists. The first course for entry-level DPT students provides an introduction to theory and practical applications of educational principles in clinical and community environments and preparation for clinical internships and experiences. This course facilitates the active learner in understanding the theory and concepts related to teaching and learning with patients, clients, and the numerous health care stakeholders. Through this introductory course experience, students begin to: (a) examine curricular design, development, and evaluation; (b) apply principles of educational leadership with service learning proposals and needs assessments; (c) begin the orientation process and preparation for clinical internships and experiences; (d) explore teaching and learning philosophies; (e) propose a planned service-learning team teaching and learning project with reflection and plan for implementation and evaluation, and (f) discuss and evaluate clinical learning experiences. During the 2nd entry-level Teaching and Learning course, the entry-level DPT students implement the SL plan, reflect on it, and discuss and evaluate their service-learning experiences.

The post-professional Teaching & Learning course shares many of the same objectives as the introductory course for entry-level DPT students. It also requires students to propose a service-learning teaching and learning project, implement the SL plan and present and discuss the project and evaluation with reflection opportunities, as well as to complete the APTA Clinical Instructor Education and Credentialing Program (CIECP). The CIECP requires participants to have a minimum of one year of practice experience and is open to all health care professionals.

TEACHING & LEARNING COURSE SERIES:
COURSE OBJECTIVES

The following are samples of the course objectives that focus on service learning for the Teaching and Learning course series: discover and articulate in writing a personal teaching and learning philosophy with literature support, relating to the SL project, patient education, and professional career; understand and apply the various domains of learning for self, patient, and community service-learning; participate in a community-based needs assessment of a community health care need; develop, plan, implement, and evaluate the proposed teaching and learning SL project, incorporating a team-approach for a community-based service; select a leadership text and evaluate personal leadership inquires; present the outcomes of the SL project.

To meet the Lowell Bennion Community Service Center designation for SL, nine criteria must be met. A committee of faculty members, Bennion Center staff and students meets regularly to review the courses and provide feedback on implementing high quality service learning courses. This committee provides approval for the SL designation, which appears on students' transcripts. The following provides the summary of the criteria and how these are met within the T&L SL Course series:

1. *Students in the class provide a needed service to individuals, organizations, schools, or other entities in the community.* Students are required to complete a formal needs assessment with the community-based organization/s before developing the SL project.
2. *The service experience relates to the subject matter of the course.* Students are provided access via WebCT to previous SL project presentations, proposals, evaluations and needs assessments; the students are also provided the list of prior community partners and suggestions for additional community partners are discussed in class and discussion boards. The students must link the project to the APTA Guide to PT practice for health promotion and wellness and the Healthy People 2010 Objectives, assuring relationship to the subject matter, teaching and learning for physical therapists.
3. *Activities in the class provide a method or methods for students to think about what they learned through the service experience and how these experiences related to the subject of the class.* Students are asked to share and discuss projects, related hurdles and reflect through one-minute papers, pro/con response grids, and self-, peer- and team evaluations throughout the semesters.
4. *The course offers a method to assess the learning derived from the service. Credit is given for the learning and its relation to the course, not for the service alone.* Students are expected to complete approximately 4–12 hours of service for the community-based needs assessments and implementation of the service project. Students are assessed in terms of meeting course objectives and completion of related, graded assignments.
5. *Service interactions in the community recognize the needs of service recipients, and offer an opportunity for recipients to be involved in the evaluation of the service.* Proposals are not approved until they include an evaluation component. The evaluation component must include an age-appropriate evaluation of the learning achieved by the service recipient. Furthermore, the community partners must evaluate the students' skills as community leaders and change agents. Students develop the evaluation instruments in direct relation to the SL project.
6. *The service opportunities are aimed at the development of the civic education of students even though they may also be focused on career preparation.*

Students are expected to serve as change-agents and leaders as they meet a community need, rather than merely imposing their own agenda or perspectives; students are expected to be civically engaged in the community being served.

7. *Knowledge from the discipline informs the service experiences with which the students are involved.* Entry-level students complete the SL project in a two-phase process through PH TH 7100-01 and later in the second year of the DPT PH TH 7270, when students have more depth and breadth of understanding of the profession and 2 years of didactic curriculum completed. Post-professional DPT students complete the SL project in a one-phase process during PH TH 7100-05, because as practicing clinicians, these students already possess the requisite knowledge to implement the project. The novel components for these students are often the needs assessment and evaluation.

8. *The class offers a way to learn from other class members as well as from the instructor.* Students learn from one another and the instructor through classroom-based discussions, web-CT discussions and postings, and classroom-based presentations with peer-, self-, and team-assessments.

9. *Course options ensure that no student is required to participate in a service placement that creates a religious, political and/or moral conflict for the student.* Students are provided the opportunity to self-select and propose their SL projects and, if the need arises, may join another team or select another project. All University of Utah, students' rights, responsibilities, equal access and nondiscrimination are abided by in these courses.

FINAL REMARKS: THE VALUE OF INTEGRATING SL FOR YOUR PROFESSIONAL PRACTICE

Both current and former DPT and ppDPT examples of T&L SL Proposals and Presentations are available for review via: http://services.tacc.utah.edu/musolino/groupprojects.html. Students are also provided access to these successfully completed proposals and projects to enhance their project efforts and so they can consider continuing a former project. In all cases, students are encouraged to invite their peer successors to continue their project efforts. Several students have presented their SL projects including the proposal, development, implementation and evaluation phases at state and national levels, whereas others have been recognized with awards designating their project as 'best' for the particular community efforts. The SL projects continue to meet related course objectives and professional requirements, and students appreciate the benefits to the community partners and their own learning outcomes. Although additional learning occurs through this course sequence (on topics such as learning styles, personality types, leadership, behavior change, micro-teaching, and research critique), the culminating SL projects reinforce all course learning. Pre/post test assessments also reveal significant progressions in overall learning outcomes for the Teaching & Learning courses.

To date, from 2002–2008, our DPT & ppDPT students have served 50 different communities with SL projects. Examples of SL Projects include: *Injury Prevention & Exercise Initiatives, Exercise for Stress Management & Fitness, Body Mechanics for the Dental Hygienists and the Uninsured Clinics, Back Care & Body Mechanics: A Train-the-Trainer Initiative for a Good Samaritan Program, Gringo Lingo: Spanish for PT Practice to Serve Spanish-Speaking Patients/Clients, Therapeutic Recreation for Persons with Spinal Cord Injury: A Needs Assessment with follow-up Implementation, Educating Elementary School Students in Disadvantaged Regions on the Benefits of Cardiovascular Health and Methods to Achieve through Mentorship, and Educating Somali Refugee Children about the Human Body through Interactive Learning.*

The course series continues to receive positive evaluative feedback, specifically in terms of the SL projects. The entry-level DPT graduates include the SL projects on their resumes, making them more competitive for careers, especially when the organization embraces community-based engagement. The ppDPT students, while initially reluctant to further examine these community-based efforts, find that they have improved teaching and learning skills as well as the ability to evaluate community programs. These evaluation skills, which can be used to justify time and effort, have enabled several students to obtain foundation grants for continuing these efforts with community partners.

REFERENCES

American Physical Therapy Association. (2008). *APTA guide for professional conduct.* Retrieved 8-1-08 from http://www.apta.org/AM/Template.cfm?Section=Core_Documents1&Template=/CM/HTMLDisplay.cfm&ContentID=24781.

Boyer, E. L. (1990). *Scholarship reconsidered: Priorities of the professorate.* Princeton, NJ: The Carnegie Foundation for the Advancement of Teaching.

Holland, B. A. (1997). Analyzing institutional commitment to engagement. *Michigan Journal of Community Engagement Learning, 4,* 30–41.

Sackett, D. L., Haynes, R. B., Rosenberg, W., Richardson, W. S. (1998). *Evidence based Medicine: How to practice and teach EBM.* New York: Harcourt Press.

Seifer, S. D. (1998). Service-learning: Community campus partnerships for health professions education. *Academic Medicine, 73,* 273–277.

Silberman, M. (2006). *Active training: A handbook of techniques, designs, case examples, and tips.* New York: John Wiley & Sons, Inc.

APPENDIX A
Peer Review Form for the Service Learning Proposals

Instructions: Provide a quantitative numerical score where indicated; check box areas addressed and provided narrative comment to support rating in each category; total numerical score and deduct for any form and style issues

A. Statement of Needs Assessment

☐ States the purpose of the needs assessment effort related to overall purpose of proposed project
☐ Good highlighting of key points
☐ Identifies specific audience(s) targeted for learning needs
☐ Succinct summary of needs of all stakeholders both internal and external that should be involved in the process and/or are affected by the project
☐ Discusses plan to assess learning needs of participants in proposal
☐ Discusses necessary resources, financial and personnel, available for needs assessment
☐ Considers all relevant questions for stakeholders for needs
☐ Clear statement of problem addressed
☐ Clear time frame for needs assessment and appropriate in relation to overall proposal
☐ Shares what form the report of the results of the needs assessment will take and who will have access to this information
☐ Provides a clear and succinct relationship /tie to the APTA Guide to PT Practice and Healthy People 2010 Initiatives and Objectives
_____ | 15pts

B. T&L Project Proposal

☐ Includes intro & summary
☐ Logical flow of project plan
☐ Objectives clearly identified with appropriate learning domains and incorporation of Bloom's Taxonomy – Appropriate number of objectives for plan

☐ Includes citations as appropriate

☐ Discusses Proposed Design of Project and Instructional Strategies

☐ Includes timeline of project, budget PRN, notation of necessary permissions/support i.e. principal, PT, managers, directors, etc…

☐ Evidence of project proposal is shared with evidence of equal participation of ALL Team Members both in oral/class presentation & throughout project proposal phase

_____ | 10pts

C. T&L Evaluation of Project Proposal

☐ Clearly illustrates evaluation of project goals & related to needs assessment for the project

☐ Proposed Evaluation is age and client appropriate

☐ Proposed Evaluation is appropriate for outlined project/needs/goals

☐ Proposed Evaluation is both qualitative and quantitative in perspective

_____ | 10pts

D. Deductions

– _____ (subtract from sum score)

Deductions Less 10 pts maximum

☐ Compliance with AMA form & Style (up to 10 pts deducted)

☐ Writing Style—grammar, punctuation, spelling, etc. . . .
per *AMA Manual of Style* 9th ed.

☐ Literature support citations as needed and referenced in presentation

Total Peer Rating:

(less deductions PRN)

_____ | 35pts

APPENDIX B
Peer Review Form for Evaluation of Final Project Presentations and Evaluations

Instructions: Provide a quantitative numerical score where indicated; check box areas addressed and provided narrative comment to support rating in each category; total numerical score and deduct for any form and style issues.

PRN Team Project: _____

Team Members: _____

_____| 5pts

A. Restatement of Needs Assessment—Summarized

☐ Good highlighting of key points
☐ Restatement only not complete revisit of needs assessment/proposal
☐ Succinct summary of needs of all stakeholders
☐ Clear statement of problem addressed
Comments:

_____| 15pts

B. T&L Project Implementation

☐ Includes intro & summary
☐ Logical flow of project implementation
☐ Objectives clearly identified with appropriate learning domains and incorporation of Bloom's Taxonomy
☐ Includes citations as appropriate
☐ Discusses procedures, design, & hurdles encountered
☐ Includes timeline of project, budget PRN, notation of necessary permissions/support
☐ Evidence of project implementation is shared (pictures/recordings, other)
☐ Evidence of equal participation of ALL Team Members both in oral/class presentation & throughout project
☐ Evidence of ongoing mentoring not just one time event
Comments:

_____ | 15pts

C. T&L Evaluation of Project Implementation

☐ Clearly illustrates evaluation of project goals & related to needs assessment for the project
☐ Evaluation is age and client appropriate
☐ Evaluation is appropriate for outlined project/needs/goals
☐ Evaluation is both qualitative and quantitative in perspective

Comments:

D. Deductions:

– _____ (subtract from sum score)

Deductions Less 10 pts maximum
☐ Compliance with AMA form & Style (up to 10 pts deducted)
☐ Writing Style—grammar, punctuation, spelling, etc. . . .
    per *AMA Manual of Style* 9th ed.
☐ Literature support citations as needed and referenced in presentation

Comments:

Total Peer Rating: (less deductions PRN)

_____ | 35pts

Peer Name: _____

CHAPTER 15

PLANNING FOR CHANGE

Community-Based Urban Research with Young People

Caitlin Cahill

ABSTRACT

Community-based participatory action research and practice offers a promising new framework for scholars who are committed to social justice. In this chapter, I reflect upon my experiences doing a place-based participatory action research process with young people entitled the *Growing Up in Salt Lake City* research project. Specifically, I address my concerns as to how to position research strategically to contribute to social change movements and how this position shifts the planning process, the role of the researcher, and the development of research presentations.

FALL 2006

The last Thursday in October we took a field trip to explore Salt Lake City's West Side neighborhoods of Glendale, Poplar Grove, and Rose Park, the communities where our youth researchers live. Our objective was to inves-

Finding Meaning in Civically Engaged Scholarship, pages 161–172

Figure 15.1   My favorite place: My friend's house. (Photo credit: Growing Up in Salt Lake City, 2008).

tigate, document, and analyze local conditions, and identify priority issues for young people. First we spent time discussing and practicing how to take field notes, and the significance of noting both objective and subjective perspectives on what we observe. We talked about how our own bodies are research instruments that can tell us about a place: Do we feel stimulated? engaged? afraid? bored? What do these feelings tell us about a place and, in turn, about "our place" in this place? In other words, who is this place for? Is it "youth-friendly? How? In what ways?

Each youth researcher was also given a camera, and we shared strategies for taking photos. For example, we discussed the different feelings and information conveyed when taking pictures close up versus far away. The youth researchers were also given an actual photo frame to use, in order to raise consciousness about "framing" their perspective and thinking about what to include and exclude in the image (see Figure 15.1) (see Driskell, 2002).

We split into teams with three youth researchers in each car (we had to drive because the West Side neighborhood is quite large). We brought with us maps of "significant places" the youth researchers had created the day before as a starting point for our tour of the neighborhood. Significant places included fast food restaurants, their schools, the supermarket, the library and boundaries to their neighborhood (the highways). At each of the significant places, the research teams spent at least ten minutes exploring the neighborhood on foot documenting what was most striking to them. The adult mentors/research assistants would ask the youth researchers to close their eyes and just listen. The youth researchers took notes on what they felt/heard/smelled/saw and even what the place would taste like if they could taste it (e.g., like metal because it was industrial, or like fresh salad because it was so green). This exercise engaged all the senses to experience the neighborhood. The youth researchers also took notes on what was most interesting, what they noticed, the places that made them feel uncomfortable and why.

WHAT WE LEARNED

The youth researchers' favorite places included Wal-mart, the library, their friends' houses, and the local recreation center. Places that made them feel uncomfortable included a local park, dilapidated houses, and the major highways. None of the youth researchers discussed spending much time outdoors in their neighborhood. Most don't have cars (as they are at the age where some are just starting to get their driver's licenses), and for the most part the youth researchers do not walk in or around their neighborhood. Instead, the youth researchers depend on others for rides to friends' houses, school, the recreation center, and other places. Walking in Salt Lake City is stigmatized because it means you don't have money to own a car, and so walking around, in and of itself, made the youth feel uncomfortable. Because nobody walks in the neighborhood, it felt strange for them to do so. But what was most noticeable was how disinterested the youth researchers were in their neighborhood. No one was excited about their neighborhood, or about any particular place, for that matter. In fact, our "field trip" was revelatory for the youth researchers because many had never really walked around their neighborhood or studied it. None of the youth researchers expressed feeling connected to their neighborhood.

This is how we began our research project, investigating what the youth researchers shared, their community. The youth researchers participating in the *Growing up in Salt Lake City* project expressed a profound disinterest in their neighborhood environment. We wondered whether this was because of their age (14–18 years), and if so, what we could learn from this information. What are the interests of young people growing up on the west side of Salt Lake City? What are they engaged with? What can we learn from young people about our cities? Although the *Growing Up in Salt Lake City* project is a place-based research program, the youth researchers decided not to focus upon the physical environment in their research, but instead upon their most pressing social concerns: the intersection of racism, immigration, and education. These are, of course, some of the most important issues in the United States at this political moment, but they play out in very specific ways in the particular geopolitical context of Salt Lake City, as we will discuss further.

BACKGROUND

Salt Lake City, Utah is an interesting place to research young people's experiences because Utah has the youngest population in the country (U.S. Census, 2000). Utah is also on the cusp of major urban (and suburban) development and dramatic demographic changes. Although the population is still almost 90% Caucasian, Utah's demographics have changed significantly in the last ten years (U.S. Census, 2000). We were interested in what these changes mean for young people, and for young people of color in particular. The *Growing Up in Salt Lake City* project focused on Salt Lake's West Side, in the most diverse zip code in Utah, where almost 40% of the residents are ethnic minorities, the majority of whom are Latino. There has been little research focused on young people's experiences in Utah and even less on young people's own concerns. The aim of the *Growing Up in Salt Lake City* project was to address this lack of information by involving young people as agents of change in researching their own communities. We hoped not only to learn more about young people's concerns about their social and environmental contexts, but also to improve urban conditions for young people and influence municipal policy.

Civic engagement is one of primary goals of the *Growing Up in Salt Lake City* project. The project is part of the international UNESCO-affiliated Growing Up in Cities project, which has actively engaged young people in community evaluation, action and change in low income communities in more than fifty sites around the world (Chawla, 2002; Driskell, 2002; Lynch, 1977). The objective is to involve young people in researching the places they live in, and identifying and responding to issues they face in their communities. This scholarship contributes to urban planning and public policy a much needed understanding of young people's experiences and needs in urban environments. This research is especially significant now as the majority of the world's population lives in cities (Bartlett et al., 1999). In addition to developing a growing global database on young people's perspectives on cities and their ability to create change, the Growing Up in Cities projects have led to many substantive changes in local communities. Because young people determine the focus of the projects, outcomes have varied widely, from physical changes (such as improving green spaces or proposing skate parks) to larger scale policy and program initiatives (such as municipal youth policies) (Chawla et al., 2005).

The *Growing Up in Salt Lake City* project adopts a participatory action research epistemological and pedagogical framework. Participatory action research (PAR) approaches pry open a space for youth agency, making them 'subjects [and] architects, of research . . . researchers [not just] the "researched"' (Torre & Fine, 2006, p. 458). Repositioned as co-researchers, young people are involved in all aspects of the research process: they frame the questions to be investigated, document and collect data, collectively analyze their findings, and develop proposals for change. Participatory practices are already widely used by child rights advocates, critical educators, youth workers, and community organizers working on problems of educational inequities, media portrayals of youth, violence in the community, police brutality, and discrimination based on sex/race/class. This work contributes to, and builds upon, the growing, multidisciplinary support for youth participation and more inclusive collaborative research practices in the social sciences, planning and public policy (Cahill & Hart, 2007; Cammarota & Fine, 2008; Ginwright et al., 2006; Hart, 1997; Torre & Fine, 2006). Engaging young people in research works to democratize the research process and build the capacity of young people to analyze and transform their own lives and communities (Cahill, 2007).

PLANNING THE PROJECT

As a community-based researcher focused on urban and youth studies, the decision to initiate the *Growing Up in Salt Lake City* project was a natural extension of my participatory work with young women in New York City researching gentrification and racial representations (Cahill et al., 2008; www.fed-up-honeys.org). New to Salt Lake City, I had no idea of what direction the project would take or what issues would be of concern to young people here. However, my personal/professional goal was to think through and work toward explicitly addressing the challenges of how research, and youth research in particular, might influence public policy and affect change. Whereas changes within the immediate scope of the neighborhood context may be easier to achieve, the long-term impact of action-oriented research is less clear (Chawla et al., 2005).

How can we position research strategically to be "of use" and make a difference (Cahill & Torre, 2007; Fine & Barreras, 2001; Torre & Fine 2007; Pain, 2006; Staehli & Mitchell, 2005)? Personally, as an aspiring activist/ scholar, new to academia and somewhat cynical of the intentions and impact of academic knowledge production, I wanted to understand how research might contribute to social change movements. Scholar's recommendations (Chawla et al., 2005) included having adequate funding in place to "follow where youth lead," in other words, budgeting in potential project money for realizing the action oriented ideas of young people. In our case, having sufficient funding was significant because we ended up producing two documentaries which involved purchasing equipment and extended the timeline for our project. Scholars suggest building upon the significant lobbying power of families and communities, which also has proved to be central to our efforts to reach larger audiences. Another recommendation involves the need to work with local government decision-makers, and not rely upon particular individuals (Chawla et al., 2005). Most important, the role of the researcher, my role, was not only to facilitate a collaborative youth-led research process, but also to create a plan for sustainability and a network of advocates for the project, to root the project within local organizations and strengthen local capacity to act upon research findings (Chawla et al., 2005). As Fine and Barreras (2001) argue, social change "is a long haul that demands the engagement of multiple players, relying upon multiple discourses, working on multiple levels and constantly (re)forming allies" (p. 5).

With this in mind at the outset, I developed partnerships for the project. Establishing partnerships made sense, not only in terms of thinking through the long term goals for the project, but also from a practical standpoint. As I was new to Salt Lake City, I had few contacts and didn't know my way around (literally and figuratively). I had (and still have) a lot to learn. In addition, as a community-based participatory researcher, I am invested in the power of collaborative work at all levels of the project. I started my planning process six months before the project officially started, meeting with community leaders, nonprofit organizations, scholars, and youth workers to discuss my proposal and explore potential ideas. These meetings were critical for shaping the project. I developed relationships with people who continue to act as informal advisors for the *Growing Up in Salt Lake City* project and me personally, and who generously offered to share advice and resources. As a result of informal conversations, partnerships organically developed out of shared interests. Two individuals, in particular, became key collaborators on the *Growing Up in Salt Lake City* project: Matt Bradley, an activist scholar with an expertise in youth media and documentary filmmaking, and Angela Romero, the Project Coordinator for YouthCity Government, Salt Lake City Mayor's Office. I feel fortunate to have had the privilege to work and learn from both of them.

The *Growing Up in Salt Lake City* project was made possible by an initial community-based research grant from the University's Lowell Bennion Community Service Center. This funding allowed us to move forward with the project, to pay the youth researchers stipends and purchase equipment and food for the project. In turn, University Neighborhood Partners, a campus community partnership of the University of Utah based on the west side of Salt Lake, generously offered us the use of space to meet twice a week and later became a key partner/supporter of the project. The importance of this support points to another critical task for the action researcher/activist scholar: grant writing and resource development. Funding and donations of time/space/resources make everything possible. Thus, I am learning another skill, the art of asking, or at least not being afraid to ask. On a practical level, doing community-based action research involves garnering resources and building upon community-assets and collaborations to create diverse and relevant presentations to reach broader audiences (beyond the journal article), such as websites, documentaries, theater productions, or public art projects (Cahill & Torre, 2007). These activities may involve engaging 'experts' to help; for example, without Matt Bradley's expertise in youth media we never could, or would, have considered embarking on our documentary projects.

THE PROJECT

The *Growing Up in Salt Lake City* project began in Fall 2006. To begin, we recruited youth researchers from schools and community centers on the west side. To participate, youth had to be between the ages of 14 and 18 years, live on the West Side of Salt Lake City, be available to participate two afternoons a week, and complete an application. The research was originally structured as a year-long project, and youth researchers were paid a stipend for their participation and ongoing commitment. A diverse team of eight youth researchers (six ended up staying with the project for the duration) were selected representing different ethnic, racial, and religious backgrounds: African American, Latino, White, African, Catholic, Muslim, and Mormon. We met after school in the basement of University Neighborhood Partners, which was conveniently located in Glendale, a neighborhood on the West Side of Salt Lake where the youth researchers lived. Most days we would begin with a snack and a reflection on a question or issue that would provide a starting point for our discussion; for example, describe your neighborhood to another person who has never been here before. Or, what are the most fun things for a young person to do in Salt Lake City? Or, if you were principal of your school what would you change and why? The process of collective sharing and discussion provided an opportunity for the youth researchers to reflect upon their everyday experiences and identify issues of significance.

The first few months of the *Growing Up in Salt Lake City* project was dedicated to exploration and developing the research capacity of all involved. We structured our process to build upon the knowledge and experience of the youth researchers. For the youth researchers to know the process, it was imperative that they were involved in defining the focus and the purpose of the project from the beginning. Through the process of exploring their community and analyzing their everyday life experiences, the youth researchers learned through doing, developing research skills in an applied way. In addition to photography and the walking tour discussed earlier, our research methods included journal writing, group discussions, interviews, community mapping, identity mapping and archival/internet research (see Cahill, 2007; Driskell, 2002; Hart, 1997 for descriptions of research methods). This preliminary research informed the development of our research questions.

Our PAR process followed a Freirian model of critical pedagogy, starting with the concerns and questions of the youth researchers: What matters to you? What are your concerns? You are the experts in your everyday life experiences (Freire, [1970] 1997; Hooks, 1994). As part of our research process we engaged in an ongoing cycle of dialogue and critical reflection toward the goal of conscientization (critical consciousness). Our research engaged the youth researchers in the analysis and investigation of the conditions and contradictions of their everyday lives. As part of this preliminary research process, the research team members identified many issues of significance to young people including police-community relations, access to education for teen moms, the quality of schools, and interfaith and racial relations. But two issues were identified as most critical for young people growing up on the west side of Salt Lake: (1) Stereotyping and racism in the schools—titled "Red Flags," and (2) Access to higher education for undocumented students—titled "Easy Targets."

These research projects reflect the young people's concerns with access to education and the role of education to create access to opportunities. Their interviews with students of color and undocumented students give qualitative texture to the unconscionably high drop out, or push out, rate for students of color in Utah (Alemán & Rorrer, 2006). The 'achievement gap,' or better put 'the race/class and opportunity gap' (Fine et al., 2004), reflects the inequitable educational outcomes of white and Latino students and the structural failures of Utah's already overwhelmed public school system to adequately serve *all* students. As Alemán and Rorrer (2006) suggest: "If the state is to benefit from a well-educated workforce and fully active citizenry, political and educational leadership will have to overcome its deficit notions of those that are different and, instead, commit to changing current educational practices and policies" (p. 9).

Racism and immigration are two of the most contested contemporary social issues in the U.S., but in Salt Lake City, they can also be understood as urban issues reflecting a geographic confluence of structural poverty, institutional racism, and immigration. The West Side of Salt Lake City is home to Latino and immigrant communities and is the most diverse census tract in the state. In our project "place-based research" reveals a broader definition of the environment that is at once social, political, physical, and emotional. The youth researchers' investigation of their community reveals "how the intimate and global intertwine" (Pratt & Rosner, 2006, p. 15) on the ground and in the everyday lives of young people.

The *Growing Up in Salt Lake City* research team split into two and each project followed its own rich, messy path of discovery, twisting and turning with new insights. As part of this process, we turned on the questions of purpose and audience: Why are we doing this research? What do we want our research to "do?" And, to whom do we want to speak? Is the goal of our research to educate? Motivate? Provoke? How do we do this? Grappling with these questions informed our collective decision to create video documentaries as a way to reach a broad public audience, to share our findings with other young people in particular, and to create a platform for young people's voices to be heard.

The decision to create video research documentaries had important ramifications for our research process: it significantly extended our time-frame as it involved learning new technical skills (e.g., how to use the camera, lighting, and editing equipment), and it changed the nature of the research. For both projects, the youth researchers conducted interviews, focus groups, and attended community meetings. In addition, the youth researchers developed other creative ways to tell their stories. For example, the "Red Flags" researchers also re-enacted their own experiences as part of their documentary (as discussed in Chapter 6). Labors of love, the research teams shot more than twenty hours of film that they then worked collaboratively to edit. This was a long, involved process, especially because each decision was collectively negotiated. Our project, which was initially scheduled to be completed at the end of the academic year, May 2007, was extended through the Fall because of these challenges.

It was worth it. We have been invited to share our research with school community councils, at nonprofit organizations, and in places around the state. How exciting to screen our research documentaries to local audiences, at national conferences, and in our schools. Sharing our research with the public has been a very powerful experience. Most interesting to us has been the different ways people respond to our findings and the conversations that follow. Many of the opportunities to share our work developed out of relationships with people who were involved in our research, the families of the youth researchers, and local nonprofits that have a stake in the issues we address. For example, in Spring 2008, the law protecting undocumented students' rights to in state tuition was challenged in the state legislature. Working with a coalition of immigration rights advocates, Utahns for the American Dream, we staged a press conference at which we released a shorter version of the "Easy Targets" documentary to every state legislator. The "Easy Targets" video created a safe space for undocumented students, whose voices are silenced in the mainstream media, to speak to the decision-makers about a public policy that would dramatically impact their lives. This exciting experience was a tangible example of how research might contribute to a larger social change movement.

Nonetheless, there is much more work to do, which raises one of the challenges of doing participatory action research. When the funding is gone, when the research project is "over," the critical work of doing community outreach to affect change begins. Over a year later, we are still piecing together resources and time to most effectively reach out with our action projects so that they are "received." We struggle to find the time for the team to get together to prepare presentations for new audiences, conferences, and public meetings. The same challenge holds true for our collective scholarship. The issue of time and support is critical to being able to continue the work. These challenges speak to the ongoing, long-term commitments involved with community-based activist research and civic engagement. What a privilege, however, to be part of this! As Alice Walker (2004) put it beautifully:

> There is always a moment in any kind of struggle when one feels in full bloom. Vivid. Alive. One might be blown to bits in such a moment and still be at peace...To be such a person or to witness anyone at this moment of transcendent presence is to know that what is human is linked, by a daring compassion, to what is divine. During my years of being close to people engaged in changing the world I have seen fear turn into courage. Sorrow into joy. Funerals into celebrations. Because whatever the consequences, people, standing side by side, have expressed who they really are, and that ultimately they believe in the love of the world and each other....

ACKNOWLEDGMENTS

I love, and give thanks to, everyone involved with the Growing Up in Salt Lake City project: the incredible youth research team, my warm colleagues/ co-collaborators with whom I was privileged to work with: Matt Bradley, Denise Castañeda , Sonia Caraveo, Ariana Prazen, Angela Romero and Roberta Targino. It has been a privilege to collaborate with the University of Utah's University Neighborhood Partners. We are most grateful to everyone else who has been involved in the Red Flags and Easy Targets projects as this includes many generous, interested, and brave young and old people who shared their experiences with us.

This research was supported by a community-based research grant from the Bennion Center of the University of Utah, the American Association of Geographers, Dr. Octavio Villalpando, Assistant Vice President for Diversity, University of Utah; Dr. Theresa Martinez, Vice President, Office of Academic Outreach, University of Utah; Dr. Cheryl Wright, Chair, Family &

Consumer Studies, University of Utah; and University Neighborhood Partners, University of Utah. Heartfelt thanks to all of you!

Thanks also to the Civically Engaged Scholarship Cohort for their support and Marissa Diener for her editorial work and project coordination.

REFERENCES

Alemán, E., & Rorrer, A. K. (2006). *Closing educational gaps for Latino/a students in Utah: Initiating a policy discourse and framework*. Utah Education Policy Center, Salt Lake City.

Bartlett, S., Hart, R. A., Satterthwaite, D., & de la Barra, M. (1999). *Cities for children: Children's rights, poverty and urban management*. London: Earthscan.

Cahill, C. (2007). Doing research *with* young people: Participatory research and the rituals of collective work. *Children's Geographies, 5*, 297–312.

Cahill, C. (2006). 'At risk'? The fed up honeys re-present the gentrification of the Lower East Side. *Women Studies Quarterly* (special issue *The Global & the Intimate* edited by G. Pratt & V. Rosner), *34*, 334–363.

Cahill, C., Rios-Moore, I., & Threatts, T. (2008). Different eyes/open eyes: Community-based PAR. In J. Cammarota & M. Fine (Eds.), *Revolutionizing education: Youth participatory action research in motion* (pp. 89–124). London: Routledge.

Cahill, C., & Hart, R. A. (2007). Re-thinking the boundaries of civic participation by children and youth in North America. *Children, Youth and Environments, 17*, 213–225. Retrieved [July 1, 2008] from http://www.colorado.edu/journals/cye.

Cahill, C., & Torre, M. E. (2007). Beyond the journal article: Representations, audience, and the presentation of participatory research. In S. Kindon, R. Pain, & M. Kesby (Eds.), *Connecting people, participation and place: Participatory action research approaches and methods* (pp. 196–205). London: Routledge.

Cammarota, J., & Fine. M. (Eds.). (2008). *Revolutionizing education: Youth participatory action research in motion*. London: Routledge.

Chawla, L. (2002). *Growing up in an urbanising world*. London: Earthscan and Paris: UNESCO.

Chawla, L., Blanchet-Cohen, N., Cosco, N., Driskell, D., Kruger, J., Malone, K., Moore, R., & Percy-Smith, B. (2005). Don't just listen—do something! Lessons learned about governance from the "Growing Up in Cities project." *Children, Youth and Environments, 15*(2), 53–88. Retrieved 2/1/06 from http://www.colorado.edu/journals/cye/.

Driskell, D. (2002). *Creating better cities with children and youth: A manual for participation*. London: Earthscan and Paris: UNESCO.

Fine, M., & Barreras, R. (2001). To be of use. *Analyses of Social Issues and Public Policy, 1*, 1. Retrieved from: http://www.asap-spssi.org/issue2.htm)

Fine, M., Roberts, R. A., Torre, M. E., Bloom, J., Burns, A., Chajet, L., Guishard, M., & Payne, Y. (2004). *Echoes: Youth documenting and performing the legacy of Brown v. Board of Education*. New York: Teachers College Press.

Freire, P. ([1970] 1997). *Pedagogy of the oppressed.* Harmondsworth, Middlesex: Penguin Books.

Ginwright, S., Noguera, P., & Cammarota J. (Eds.). (2006). *Beyond resistance! Youth activism and community change: New democratic possibilities for practice and policy for America's youth.* New York: Routledge.

Hart, R. (1997). *Children's participation: The theory and practice of involving young citizens in community development and environmental care.* New York: UNICEF.

Hooks, B. (1994). *Teaching to transgress: Education as the practice of freedom.* New York: Routledge.

Lynch, K. (1977). *Growing up in cities.* Cambridge, MA: MIT Press.

Pain, R. (2006). Social geography: Seven deadly myths in policy research. *Progress in Human Geography, 30,* 250–260.

Pratt, G., & Rosner, V. (2006). The global and the intimate. *Women Studies Quarterly, 34*(1–2).

Staeheli, L. A., & Mitchell, D. (2005). The complex politics of relevance in geography. *Annals of the Association American Geographers, 95,* 357–372.

Torre, M. E., & Fine, M. (2006). Participatory action research (PAR) by youth. In L. Sherrod (Ed.), *Youth activism: An international encyclopedia* (pp. 456–462). Westport, CT: Greenwood Publishing Group.

Torre, M. E., & Fine, M. (2007). Theorizing audience, products and provocation. In P. Reason & H. Bradbury (Eds.), *Handbook of action research* (pp. 407–419). Thousand Oaks, CA: Sage.

U.S. Census. (2000). http://quickfacts.census.gov/qfd/states/49000.html

Walker, A. (2004). In full bloom. *The Nation.* September 20. Retrieved 7–21–08 from http://www.thenation.com/doc/20040920/walker

CHAPTER 16

LITERACY CENTER

Partnership and Learning for All

Janet Kaufman

ABSTRACT

Describing the history and evolution of the Family Literacy Center, a service-learning program for pre-service secondary English/Language Arts teachers, this essay addresses questions about the practical aspects of running and sustaining a long-term service-learning project within teacher education Methods courses, the nature of student learning through the Family Literacy Center, university–community partnerships, and the professional challenges for faculty engaging in this work.

The time spent driving from place to place is as valuable to me, if not more so.
These interludes are spent talking to Hector in Spanish about his life and my life.
I have to admit that I do a lot more listening than I do speaking....
The implications of this on my teaching are immense.

—Jamie, Methods student

Finding Meaning in Civically Engaged Scholarship, pages 173–183
173

> *On the days that I help out with the after school program, I spend time*
> *with each group of students to make sure things are running smoothly*
> *and I am the resident "problem solver."*
>
> —Alison, Methods student

BACKGROUND AND BEGINNINGS

Methods of Teaching English/Language Arts I and II strives to prepare undergraduate English majors to teach secondary English/Language Arts (grades 6–12). Students generally take these courses in the two semesters before they begin a year-long program for secondary licensure, in which they do their student teaching. Thus, it is my goal to help them in all ways possible to think practically as well as theoretically about teaching English/Language Arts. They read about diverse models of teaching; study the state Core Curriculum and develop corresponding curricular plans; learn about reading interpretation and writing in multiple genres; role-play lesson plans; learn about creating classroom community and working with diverse students; study assessment as a tool for curriculum development; and grapple with political aspects of English/Language Arts such as the "No Child Left Behind Act." To help students acquire their learning in real-world contexts, I began integrating a service-learning component into my courses in 1998.

My work in service-learning started off as and has remained a project with a central focus: the Family Literacy Center, a program housed at a large urban high school to meet a diverse range of needs expressed by students, teachers, and families. It changes each year as my students change and the needs in the community evolve and express themselves in new ways. In practice, university undergraduates in my Methods courses serve in secondary classrooms, in after school literacy projects, as tutors in a juvenile court tutoring program, and in ongoing projects in neighborhood elementary, middle, and high schools. In exchange for their service, the students learn about the complexities of English/Language Arts teaching; the bureaucracies and politics of public education; adolescents; social issues such as immigration and second-language learning; and their roles as citizen/teacher.

In his essay titled "Strong Democracy," Benjamin Barber (1994) says that "to be a citizen is to participate in a certain conscious fashion that presumes awareness of and engagement in activity with others" (p. 215). And then he makes three generalizations: First, strong democratic talk entails listening no less than speaking; second, it is affective as well as cognitive; and third, its intentionalism draws it out of the domain of pure reflection into the world of action.

Teaching English/Language Arts (E/LA) involves all these components: teaching listening as well as speaking; addressing the affective with the cognitive, as much of what we do in reading interpretation is to develop sympathy and empathy; identifying personally with literature and writing; and making the reflection in E/LA classes meaningful for our lives and the world we live in. To think, thus, about E/LA in the context of civic engagement is to go beyond thinking about the discipline as encompassing isolated skills of reading, writing, and thinking, but to consider that the language arts, among other vital goals, can help us create strong democracy. Developing conversation about this in the Methods class becomes part of our challenge.

The Methods course is a 3-credit course and, when students register for it, they also register for an additional credit specified for service-learning. During the course, students are required to serve the equivalent of two hours each week, which they negotiate according to their own scheduling needs with their respective placements. Students might serve a month in an intensive project, two hours per week, or any variation thereof. While the FLC began, in 1998, as a research project in which students gathered information and learned as much as they could about the school, neighborhood, and accompanying needs, it grew to be a Center in its own space within the largest and most diverse urban high school in Salt Lake City.

By latest count, students at the high school speak 52 languages. The school enrolls approximately 2,500 7–12th grade students, performing at all levels. The middle school group is in the ELP (Extended Learning Program, for accelerated students), and the high school students range from those in the International Baccalaureate program to those recently arrived from war-torn African countries, just learning to speak English and grapple with our culture. Forty-five percent are identified as low income and 46% identify as ethnic minorities. Ultimately, our program seeks to: (1) increase the number of students who perform well in school, graduate, and go on to higher education through curricular, extracurricular, and leadership opportunities; (2) provide support and advocacy to youth and families in need (immigrants, refugees, low-income, students in crisis); (3) create curricular enhancement, i.e., bringing in visiting writers, artists, photographers, etc.; and (4) partner with other neighborhood schools and community organizations to create learning opportunities for youth and families.

The Family Literacy Center started somewhat accidentally, or serendipitously, when I went with a colleague to meet with the high school's Community Education staff, to see if we might find a way to give our students experience in the high school while meeting school needs. Service-learning staff from the University of Utah's Lowell Bennion Community Service Center brought us to West High; they were clearly oriented toward service-learning as a partnership that serves each partner's needs. We were hoping eventually to develop a long-term project with the school, but imagined it would take some extended time of partnership before the idea and need for a larger project expressed itself. In the course of our first meeting, one of the Community Education staff said, hesitantly but with a dreaming voice, that she'd always wanted to have a Family Literacy Center. None of us knew what she meant—it was a vision for which she didn't have a specific picture. But at that moment we all decided we would take on the project of creating the Center. Without a model for this project, it developed, and still develops, organically. We began with a year of planning with our students and with the support of an undergraduate teaching assistant experienced in service-learning. Working in small groups, Methods students spent time at the high school interviewing teachers and students to determine their needs, speaking with community members, attending various school and Community Council meetings, and listening to parents and administrators. By the start of the following academic year, the school principal offered us a large classroom to use as the Center, and thus our doors have been opened since the fall of 1998.

For the first several years, the partners included the English Education program at the University (me, as my colleague soon left the university), West High, and the Bennion Center. Through the support of the Bennion Center, I was able to staff a part-time position at West High to run the Family Literacy Center, and usually had two to three other students who assisted this staff member to fulfill their Methods course service-learning requirement. This enabled us to keep the Center open during school hours and manage it on-site. Five years into the project, I obtained sufficient grant money to fund a full-time onsite director; this director has developed the work of the Family Literacy Center in ways we could not have imagined and, each year, I raise funds to sustain her position. The on-site director, coordinates the Methods students placements, keeps track of the university students' hours served through the Center, works with me to develop new ideas and to problem-solve when challenges arise. These can range from a student having difficulty in a particular placement to the collapse of a collaboration within the school or neighborhood, to concerns about sustainability of the Center. She maintains that faculty and staff at the high school have gained trust in the FLC project because we have stayed committed to our initial agenda: to make the project a collaborative partnership, serving students, staff, and community members in the school while offering pedagogical experiences to our pre-service teachers from the University.

Our partnership has thus come to be nearly ten years old as of this writing, and we have a formal Center: a room with books and soft lighting, comfortable seating and meeting corners, student art and photography, a wall adorned with lines of poetry and photo essays featuring individual students in the school. The core of the FLC partnership includes me, as representative of the English Education program at the University of Utah; the onsite director of the FLC at the high school; and the high school as an entity. The high school, specifically, includes the principal, who agrees to host us, give us space, allow us a degree of free reign in the school to place the university students in projects, and encourage the participation of the faculty and students; the faculty, who work with the director to place service-learning students in classes and with students, and who collaborate on individual projects; directors of extracurricular and Community Education programs within the school who design projects in partnership with us—these enable us to contribute more to the school and sometimes make possible curricular enhancements that would not otherwise exist; and the students, who use the Center in an extraordinarily broad range of ways. The Center has gone through many phases as we have collaborated with different individuals and organizations within the school, seen changes of leadership, seen priorities for the school shift at the district level, and seen changes in attention and focus due to the impact, nationally, of high-stakes testing. The larger partnership includes the University of Utah English Department, the University's College of Humanities, the Lowell Bennion Community Service Center, and the foundations that have sustained us and enabled our success.

The way the partnership works, practically, is that I teach the Methods classes on the University campus. The site director comes to my classes to meet my students at the beginning of each semester, and together we introduce the FLC project to them and the opportunities for placement through it. The site director follows through by placing the students in appropriate projects, taking into consideration students' professional interests, schedules, talents, and desires for contribution, and the current expressed needs and interests for collaboration in the high school. Recently we have developed new sites of outreach for the FLC at the Juvenile Court, a middle school, and a neighborhood literacy project for children. We generally take a week or two at the start of each semester to arrange placements, so starting in the second or third week students begin service-learning. We then both work with and follow the students over the course of the semester: I work on academic and personal reflection with my students, brainstorm with them about bringing their classroom knowledge to bear on their placements, and coach them when they get stymied by a particular situation; the on-site director follows their work, sometimes helps them find a new placement if the original one doesn't work, sometimes serves as a mediator if there is a problem in a student's placement, and tracks the university students' hours of participation. She and I go both together and separately to meet with partners new and old, such as the principal of the intermediate school or representatives from the juvenile court.

TWO STORIES: STUDENT LEARNING, AND LEARNING FROM STUDENTS

As my students learn about teaching, they also learn about the fuller lives of their students, and what the stakes are of teaching English/Language Arts—reading, interpretation, writing, communication, and thinking. Thus, a subtle shift occurs from thinking about the discipline as an isolated entity; to serving the community and reflecting on questions that emerge regarding education, race, class, and the discipline itself; to considering our and our students' roles as citizens in a democracy.

Student I: Driving.   For his service-learning project, Jamie, whose reflection is excerpted for the first epigraph of this paper, worked with Hector, the parent of a 10th grader at West High. Hector was participating in the evening ESL classes that my students helped to teach for families of West High students; he worked in a meat-packing plant and was trying to translate information about health care and other social services into Spanish for his coworkers at his and other industries in our city. Jamie offered to help by going with Hector to speak with workers and managers, and then helping Hector to delivering the information he had gathered and translated. So Jamie spent Monday afternoons in the car with Hector, speaking in his developing Spanish and Hector's developing English, getting to know about Hector's history, his education (he had an advanced degree from his own country and had been a teacher), meeting his family, networking at the high school to support his daughter's academic life, and learning about the complex forces in immigrants' lives and educations. In these realms, service-learning and civic-engagement merge.

In an ongoing inquiry, I ask myself how service-learning contributes to my students' education more or differently than student-teaching or the hours they observe secondary classrooms in their teacher licensure program. Jamie's reflection speaks directly to this question when he writes, "The time spent driving from place to place is as valuable to me, if not more so [than actual classroom teaching practice]. He then adds, "I have to admit that I do a lot more listening than I do speaking." The opportunity to learn about individuals' lives—to meet them in encounters outside of the classroom and experience them as whole human beings beyond the roles of student/teacher, which are rife with assumptions, expectations, power relations, and institutional boundaries—better prepares my students, I hope, to meet and face the complexities of their own future students, and to be able to better imagine that their students, indeed, will have complex stories of their own that bear on their learning.

Student II: From the university to the high school classroom.   It is the intention of service-learning that students take what they are learning in class and be able to test it out, experiment with it, add to it, and internalize it through reflection. David Kolb's (1984) well-known learning cirlce model, in which students move from experience to reflection to abstraction to active testing of new insight and ideas, speaks directly to this. One can, in fact, start at any point on the circle, but generally in the Methods class, we begin by reflecting on new experiences the students have had in the field, raising questions and developing insight from it in relation to English Education theory and textbook methods. This leads to the return to the placement experience, where students test out their new thinking and then again bring back new experiences to share with the class. In a semester-long exploration of how to create, develop, and sustain classroom community in English/Language Arts, we read D. Kay Johnston's (2006) *Education for a Caring Society*. Amy, a student in a recent course, became fascinated with Johnston's discussion of personal and communal responsibility in a classroom, and the moral weight of this responsibility when it involves our help or hindrance of each other's learning. In a written reflection on this subject, Amy wrote:

> Pondering this has first affected me personally as a student sharing the class-room with others. I also often stop to wonder if [a question I ask] lacks per-tinence or insightfulness, and having discussed [this] in our class has helped me to overcome my fears. By making it a responsibility as a student and a peer to ask my question, I can overcome the fear of looking less intelligent and instead feel like I am sharing the learning environment.

Gathering both curiosity and courage as well as personal insight from her classroom learning, Amy then found herself placed in a class at West High, carrying the Methods discussion to a few girls whom she was assigned to help with their writing. She recounts that the girls, from "Hispanic and Indian backgrounds," began telling her about their Advanced Placement classes in which "they found themselves severely racially outnumbered by Caucasian students" and that "the white students look at them as if they are speaking another language." As Amy recounted, "they feel different and less qualified, and therefore, choose to hold themselves back by not speaking up when they don't understand." Amy then wrote: I was encour-aged to see an opportunity to share what I was learning with these girls and share my fears and doubts with them as a student. I encouraged them to overcome this fear in the ways that I myself was trying to practice. We both agreed that it is easier said than done, but we would all work at it.

This story shows Kolb's (1984) experiential learning circle embodied, and it raises questions about participation, voice, race, difference, inclu-sion, and exclusion—questions we have in our democracy, too. While con-templating the abstract concept of classroom community in the Methods course, we were taken into one class member's experience through hearing Amy's story and reflection, considering the complexities of it, and then expanding ideas about classroom community to ideas about participatory democracy. There are no answers here, but instead what we have learned to think of as "essential questions" (Wiggins & McTighe, 2001).

Moving as a teacher between the discipline of English, the teaching of teachers, and civic engagement, I always return to poetry. Rilke (1987) wrote in his *Letters to a Young Poet,* "Live the questions." Indeed, it seems my job to help my students move from their intellectual and tangible experiences to questions that will perpetuate both their learning and their contribution to public life.

PROJECTS: CREATIVITY, GENERATIVITY, FLEXIBILITY, AND TRUST

Having an onsite director enables the Family Literacy Center to have eyes and ears at the school, and the nature and success of the FLC depends on our ability to support the efforts and needs of the school in practical ways. This director's presence at the high school allows her to learn daily about the community and, in turn, to address and attempt to meet those needs. In a recent example, she found out in casual conversation that one math class started the year with 47 students in it; besides the challenge of teaching too many students, 47 desks in the room left no walking space for the teacher to move around and help students individually. As I had initiated conversation with the university's math teaching program that semester to invite their partnership with the FLC, the site director was able to draw upon math pre-service teaching students to help this situation. The teacher identified a small group of students all in need of help with their times tables and set them up working with a university student in the FLC space.

In another recent example, the director noticed that her efforts to get English language learners involved in the school's literary magazine came to little fruition. The social and language differences among the students, as well as the culture and tradition of the magazine itself, seemed too complex for the students to negotiate comfortably. Yet helping in an English Language Learner (ELL) class one day, she noticed bits of student writing on the blackboard—honest, poignant expression that gave her the idea for creating a new literary magazine at the school. Why couldn't there be room for more than one magazine, addressing different needs and interests? Extending the FLC partnership, the site director connected with the Utah Arts Council, who gave the FLC a small grant to publish a magazine with writing by ELL students. Through this project, it became apparent that the students lived with anxiety about their budding English skills, but working on the new magazine helped them discover that they knew more about English than they thought. They expressed surprise and pleasure at being able to express themselves and be understood through their poetry. Their success in creating the magazine—the title of the first issue was "Things about Life"—became important to their academic progress. Through means less formal and threatening than conventional classroom work, their knowledge of English deepened and they performed better in school. Now heading toward the fourth annual edition, the magazine gives students a voice in the school that the traditional literary magazine has not. And while the latter sells, the new one is given away for free and enthusiastically circulated.

Attuning ourselves to the needs and opportunities in the school as well to our university students, and responding practically and creatively, remains the goal of the FLC. One of the earliest FLC projects demonstrates the strengths and challenges of our efforts over time. One Methods student in the second year of the FLC, an artist, learned through conversation that a group of high school students, also artists, had the idea of painting a mural on the walls of the FLC to make it feel more their own. The principal, having granted us a large classroom to use as the FLC, accepted the high school students' idea, pending approval of their design. Thus it happened that over several years, many high school students participated in covering most of the wall space in the room. The theme was hands—hands making, building, holding, touching, creating. A couple years into the mural project, the students stayed with the theme only loosely, but the art remained peaceful, joyful, vibrant.

The mural project, over several years, had become a site of engagement not only for successful students who were talented artists or simply had a desire to paint, but also for students who were in personal crisis or on the verge of dropping out. They would come to paint after school and, while there, ended up talking with the university service-learning students coordinating the project. On one occasion, one of the high school students was told by the juvenile court judge that if he painted the walls at the high school instead of the street, he could stay out of juvenile court. Others ended up staying in school, as they reasoned, with the help of a university student, that if they were coming to paint after school, they might as well go to 4th period, and if they were going to 4th period, why not come a little earlier for 3rd.... They listened to diverse music while they painted and talked with their peers and adults. Some brought guitars; they brought and completed homework during painting time; and they carried on a kind of informal, thoughtful, personal dialogue that they expressed was new for them in school.

Thus, early on, the FLC became a space for all kinds of students. Dana, the daughter of migrant workers, came to paint and challenged her younger peers to do their homework and respect their parents. An out lesbian, she graduated and went on to college in a neighboring state. The students who came to paint interacted with students of diverse ages, abilities, and backgrounds, and in ways explicit and implicit, they said the mural project helped them feel connected to the school and each other, and helped dissolve what they perceived as rigidity in the school. The school administration, wonderfully, had the flexibility and trust to honor the students' needs and the informal but powerful way the university students had of working with the adolescents who came to paint. While the results of such work are not measurable on a standardized test, they can be immeasurable to the quality of individuals' lives. Indeed, several students graduated who might otherwise not have, and occasionally suicidal teens found a home at the FLC and found enough strength and support there to stay alive.

DISAPPOINTMENT

The success of the FLC depends on multiple factors. The FLC is a fragile endeavor because, as a project founded in the desire to learn and meet human needs, it depends upon the good will and commitment of individuals and their ability to grapple with and negotiate diverse and complex desires. Thus the mural project, which had such an auspicious beginning and an extraordinary four years, came to a very disappointing end. At the start of one particular school year that came with a surge in enrollment, the room that had originally been granted to the FLC was deemed necessary to house a social studies class. We worried about what would happen to the mural, whether the new administration would be willing to keep it, and how the students would react to potentially having the mural painted over. The students who had created it were incredibly proud of the mural, bringing siblings and parents to look at their artwork, and returning as alumni to see it. They took pride in the way they had transformed the empty walls of a former classroom to the creative, inspiring, intimate space of the Family Literacy Center. For a year, though the FLC space was moved to a smaller space in the school, the mural stayed on the walls through ardent appeals to the principal by students and faculty alike.

But the next summer, just before the start of school, the walls were painted over. Through this experience and other successes and failures, equally strong, we continually assess what is happening, talk to each other as best we can, renegotiate agreements, and explore new possibilities.

CONCLUSION

Teachers have talked about public education being "under siege." Class sizes are far too large; high-stakes testing takes an inordinate amount of time and distracts from curriculum; funding is too low. As we knew from the beginning of the FLC project, we can meet only a very small portion of needs at the high school and it cannot be the job of a university service-learning project to compensate for the gaps in public education. Yet we see needs that we can address, and it is an honor and privilege to be able to do so. The partnership we have with the high school undoubtedly would be stronger if we all had more time to work personally with each other and had more funding. When we do come together, the enthusiasm for the project is tangible; yet it is sometimes difficult to carry out the possibilities we envision due to the logistical demands we all face.

Through the ongoing evolution of the Family Literacy Center, we know the partnership is strong when we have open communication, collaboration, trust that the university is not coming to the high school to impose a particular agenda, and confidence that the university service-learning students will be reliable. We know the partnership is weak when we experience a lack of trust, a lack of partnership, concerns about funding, and subsequent fear about the survival of the Center.

We do believe, though, that over time, the FLC has been successful because the high school and university constituents have seen reason to trust each other. Individuals have come together to learn, to support ongoing efforts, and to attune ourselves to what is needed and wanted practically and humanly. In this way, we continue to develop our own knowledge of English Education, as deeply and broadly as possible.

NOTE

Names in this article have been changed to protect anonymity.

REFERENCES

Barber, B. (1994). Strong democracy: Participatory politics for a new age. In M. Daly (Ed.), *Communitarianism: A new public ethics* (pp. 213–224). Belmont, CA: Wadsworth.

Johnston, D. K. (2006). *Education for a caring society: Classroom relationships and moral action.* New York: Teachers College Press.

Kolb, D. A. (1984). *Experiential learning: Experience as the source of learning and development.* Eaglewood Cliffs, NJ: Prentice Hall.

Rilke, R. T. (1987). *Letters to a young poet.* New York: Libri. [First published 1929]

Wiggins, G., & McTighe, J. (2001). *Understanding by design* (2nd ed.). Alexandria, VA: ASCD.

CHAPTER 17

FINDING STUDENT SATISFACTION IN SERVICE-LEARNING

Implementing Service-Learning in a Graduate Nonprofit Management Class

Nancy Winemiller Basinger

ABSTRACT

Student course evaluations, one from each of the three semesters I have taught a graduate nonprofit advocacy course, exhibit the widely varying opinions of my course, although each were written by students who took the same service-learning class from the same professor on a subject they profess an interest in. Why is there such a disparity in their attitudes toward the benefits of service-learning? A mismatch between teaching styles and learning styles, the composition of the class, life events—many factors that are largely unrelated to service-learning may cause a student to be dissatisfied with a course. The very strong reactions to this element of the class, however, deserve more attention; an in-depth examination of the implementation of the service-learning project may reveal lessons that will benefit future implementation

Finding Meaning in Civically Engaged Scholarship, pages 185–196
Copyright © 2009 by Information Age Publishing

efforts. In this essay, I discuss the details of the service-learning project I use in this class, and I also highlight some of the implementation choices, their rationales, and student satisfaction outcomes in order to better understand student satisfaction with service-learning.

1. I hated the class project. It monopolized our time and always felt unorganized. I will avoid service learning projects from this point on.
2. This was by far the most practical course that I have taken. It will be a fantastic addition to my resume because it can be applied in the "real" world.
3. The hands-on learning [was effective]—We HAD to understand the course because we were out in the community.

INTRODUCTION—THE BEST AND THE WORST OF TIMES

Reading over my student evaluations from Fall 2004 for my course entitled "Nonprofits and their Public Policy influence" was "the best of times." There are only two numbers from the student evaluations that my department focuses on: "overall, this was an effective course" and "overall, this was an effective instructor." My scores on a 6-point scale were 5.2 and 5.47 respectively for the graduate section of the class and 6.00s for the undergraduate section of the course. Furthermore, my scores were higher than the all important departmental average—5.15 and 5.21 for that semester. Cause for celebration! I had broken the teaching code. I had arrived. I called my husband, and we went out to dinner.

Sitting in my office two years later, reading over my evaluations from Fall 2006 for the same course was, in stark contrast, "the worst of times." That semester the graduate students rated the course and my effectiveness a 4.86 and 5.00, below the departmental averages of 5.18 and 5.34. The undergraduate assessments were down as well, to 5.00 and 5.00. I shut my office door, and I cried. I could not help it. I was distraught. The scores were from what I lovingly refer to as "my advocacy class." It is my favorite topic in the study of nonprofit organizations, the issue I know the most about. I wrote my dissertation on this topic. I am at my most passionate, energetic, and creative when I teach this topic. But when I took a step back, I realized that I should have anticipated these evaluations. That semester, the third I had taught the class, it had fewer students (10 graduate and 5 undergraduate), many of whom did not attend regularly. I struggled all semester to think how *else* to engage them. When I walked to my car after each class session, I felt frustrated. The students did not read; they did not talk; they did not care. (How could they not care? Weren't we studying one of the most engaging topics ever?) I asked them to lead discussions, and they simply read each other the book. I held out hope that the service-learning project would increase their interest and excitement. Instead, it only made the ball of flame hurl more quickly toward my particular spot on the earth. Thus, I learned not only did I think it was a miserable class, but my students did too. What was a poor, beleaguered assistant professor to do? I thought about it. I talked to colleagues. I worried. Finally, I decided to write about this service-learning class at its best and at its worst so that I, and others, might learn from it.

CLASS DESCRIPTION

The course, Nonprofits and their Public Policy Influence, is offered in the Master of Public Administration (MPA) program. It is primarily designed to prepare students who are running or preparing to lead charitable nonprofit organizations. These students are predominantly adults (mean age = 34 yrs) who are five to ten years into their career. They continue to work full time and manage family obligations while pursuing their MPA degree. It is also offered to upper-level undergraduates, up to 5, such that undergraduates and graduate students with vastly different experience levels are enrolled in the same course.

The course focuses on the legal framework of charity advocacy, theories of interest groups, mechanics of the policy process within the legislative, administrative and judicial branches of government, and the importance of issue framing. The students read books and articles, listen to guest speakers and lectures, and discuss charity advocacy. The biggest and most important assignment they have is developing a one- to five-year advocacy plan for a local nonprofit charity. Thus, the model of service-learning I use in this class is the consulting model. Students are expected to research the organization, the policy environment, and plan for how the organization, within existing constraints, can implement the plan. They work in groups of four to five and are expected to meet with their community partners two to three times over the course the semester to gather information and get feedback from them. The goal of the project is to maximize student learning while at the same time providing a needed service to the community. I have designed a project that I think will be useful to nonprofits in the community who are not aware of the best practices and legal framework around charity advocacy.

THE ADVOCACY PLAN

It is critical to emphasize good communication with both the students and the community partners. Box 17.1 is a copy of the handout I give to community partners and to students to clarify expectations for the service-learning project.

Box 17.1
Advocacy Class Service-Learning Description
RE: Advocacy Plan Development

What is the point?

- Students in this class will benefit by learning how to apply the theories and skills vital to advocacy for nonprofit organizations and will be able to learn about working in a (another) local nonprofit.
- Community nonprofits will benefit from working with students because they will spread knowledge of their organization to community members with an interest in their mission and will receive an advocacy plan that their organization can use to prepare for future advocacy activities.

Relevant Parameters:

- The products produced by this project are two: First, students will assess the nonprofit's organizational readiness for advocacy using the best practices suggested in academic research as the benchmark and second, students will prepare a comprehensive advocacy plan as detailed below.
- The purpose of this project is NOT for students to serve as staff, or to make advocacy appeals on behalf of the nonprofit, or to investigate only one type of advocacy (e.g., solicit funds from government funders) for the organization. Rather, the service to the organizations who participate in this process will be the receipt of a written advocacy plan based on an assessment of the markets, organizational readiness, and knowledge of the various advocacy strategies available.
- Finally, students groups will be expected to do their OWN work. The purpose of this project is to provide learning to students and assistance to nonprofits. Students must not expect the organization's representatives to do their work. Each nonprofit will provide information and the students will do their own analysis. Analysis is the responsibility of the entire group.

What students will be required to do:

- Using course materials, research into the organization and the community, and drawing on expertise from guest speakers, students will work in teams (about 4 students per group) with one local nonprofit over the course of the semester. The students will work with the organization in order to complete an assessment of needs and readiness as well as write an advocacy plan according to the following criteria:

1. Assess organizational readiness.
2. Based on the academic literature assess readiness and ability of the group to interact with various policy makers.
3. Analyze needs of the group.
4. What does the organization know about its potential advocacy outlets and strategies and what can we learn through research about the overall market in which the organization operates that might help assess potential?
5. Prepare advocacy goals.
6. Based on information drawn from the organization, identify two or three areas in which the organization may want to advocate and identify targets and strategies appropriate to those goals.
7. Define objectives.
8. What would the organization like to accomplish within its advocacy goals and what should be done to better prepare for these objectives?
9. Assess "role" assignments.
10. Who will be needed to accomplish the goals of the plan? What is the role of the board? Other volunteers? Will involved parties need training? What will be the role of various members of paid staff? Etc.
11. Select appropriate advocacy strategies and relevant timeline for implementation of various programs.
12. Prepare comprehensive advocacy plan.
13. This pulls together all of the above information into a clear, professional written and oral presentation to key leadership of the organization.

What the organization will be required to do:
- Provide access to relevant personnel and information
- Meet with students twice (or more if needed) during the course of the semester to discuss plan progress and its relevance to the organization.
- Commit to continue to work with students throughout the entire semester.
- Provide feedback on the process and end-product of the students.

In addition, the syllabus describes the project as follows:

> Service-learning project: The service learning project in this class is a group project that allows each student to directly apply, in a practical setting, the exact information you are learning in the class. The course teaches the theories and best practices in policy influence for charitable nonprofits, while the service-learning project will help you learn how to apply them. By working as a team, you will learn from each other about class materials and how to apply them. You may not fully understand the intricacies of devising an advocacy campaign for a nonprofit until you have done so. This project is designed to teach you from the "inside/out" of an organization about why "great intentions" and "being right" are not sufficient to achieve policy influence.
>
> The project will be the (1) composition and (2) presentation of an advocacy plan for a local nonprofit organization. The advocacy plan will first analyze the "needs and assets" of organizational capacity to become involved in the public policy process and will describe and analyze some or all of the following aspects of their work: the public policy objectives chosen, the analysis used, the tactics employed, the resources managed and leveraged from internal and outside sources, the internal decision making process, and the overall strategy (e.g., working alone, in coalition). The paper should provide a critique and recommendations for changes as appropriate. Each group will present their plan to the class. In addition each member of the group will be required to evaluate both the effort and quality levels of the contributions made by their fellow group members.

Armed with this advice, in-class discussion and group guidance, the students work with the nonprofits to gather information and to develop a plan to help the organization prepare to influence the policy process in the ways that are most appropriate and attainable for that organization.

TOWARD STUDENT SATISFACTION IN THE SERVICE-LEARNING PROJECT

As I analyze the student evaluations of the class and the service-learning component in particular, I find that there are three elements that receive the most attention: the project design, the group element, and the community partner. I believe that student satisfaction with the overall project is largely driven by the satisfaction with these three elements. I will address each in turn from their perspective and from my own.

PROJECT DESIGN

One issue in any service-learning experience that is project-based, is who should define the project? Will it be the community partner, the students, the professor, or a combination of these? In this advocacy class I have adopted two different models—one professor defined and one community partner and student defined. As I learned more about civic engagement, my project evolved to be more of a community-based project in the sense that we, the students and I, allowed the community partner to tell us what they needed. During the first two semesters I taught the class, I defined what the students would provide, and then communicated this to potential community partners through the listserv of the state nonprofits association. Organizations applied for consideration if they felt they could benefit from our project. In the third semester, I chose one nonprofit to work with and asked the students to work with the community partner to define the parameters of the plan.

Ultimately, the community-based approach was far less effective for the community-partner and less appealing to the students. Many students were quite dissatisfied with this experience, and their research missed some key elements related to advocacy for the organization. The students expressed a desire for greater organization of the project up front. One student put it this way in the course evaluations:

> ... the service-learning portion of the course was disorganized. Unfortunately, I know this is the case with many service-learning courses, we were unable to begin working for the [community partner name omitted] until over 2/3 into the quarter, because we were unable to develop an action plan for helping. In the future, the service-learning portion of this class (which should definitely be kept, because it provides a hands-on executable learning experience) should be decided prior to the beginning of the semester—that way work can begin to execute that plan as soon as possible.

Based on the outcomes of the two approaches, I now favor a professor-designed approach for classes limited to one semester for several reasons, including the need to educate the leaders in the sector, the importance of clarity and timing of expectations for students, and the ability to choose community partners that will promote broad learning. First, the nature of the topic can be controversial in the nonprofit sector. A majority of nonprofit leaders still believe that lobbying is illegal and that advocacy of any sort is risky. In part, this advocacy class is a way for the students to teach the community partner about the legalities of charity advocacy and the importance of engaging in advocacy. Many leaders fail to recognize the importance of building relationships over time that would enable the organization to exert influence if a crisis arose. Although I certainly want to avoid the "university knows best" approach with the community partners, the knowledge communicated by the students through their plan can be invaluable to the community in ways the community may not be aware of in the planning stages of the project.

Students often express frustration at the beginning of the semester because the project is, even when well defined, difficult for them to grasp. Presenting the expectations for the elements of the plan at the beginning of the semester is comforting. Even when parameters are known, some struggle. A common complaint is illustrated through this student evaluation, "I had *no idea* what was going on with the Advocacy Plan (let alone what it was) until the last month," (emphasis original). By having all students in the class working within a single set of project expectations, students are better able to connect to and learn from each other's experiences during class discussions and reflections. As the semester progresses, students continue to better understand how to operationalize elements of the assignment. By the end of the semester, many are able to look back on the project and tout its benefits. "I feel I can go into the nonprofit workforce with an excellent knowledge of what is going on. The class gave me a great foundation of knowledge to build on. Loved it!" If the plan design is left up to students and community partners, however, the delay can prevent this positive outcome. In a 15-week semester, confusion must be kept to a minimum. By working from the start from a designated list of elements to include in the plan, most students will be able to achieve understanding in time to produce a creative and useful plan.

Among those nonprofits that know they can advocate, many limit their policy involvement to one branch of government. Advocacy is much broader than legislative lobbying and the course is designed to teach students about all elements of the policy process. In the service-learning project it is important that the students are able to design a plan that analyzes how the organization could choose to be involved broadly in the policy process. Although students could help the organization lobby or do bill research and learn a great deal, they would not learn about the entire policy process. They would not be forced to think about the wide variety of opportunities available for nonprofit advocacy. For those students, only a small part of the curriculum of the course would be enhanced by the service. By designing the project and tailoring it to the needs of the community partners, I feel I am able to achieve the best blend of service *and* learning.

PUTTING STUDENTS INTO THEIR
SERVICE-LEARNING GROUPS

Another decision I have made is to have students work together in small groups, rather than individually. Some students express hesitation with this decision because they fear an unequal distribution of labor within the group and are resistant to meeting outside class. I try to allay some of their fears by including a peer review as 5% of their grade and allocate approximately 10 hours of class time over the course of the semester to in-class group work.

Another way to allay students' fears of working in a group is to let the students self-select the community partners they prefer to work with. The most successful approach has been to have students choose the subsector of nonprofit activities (e.g., arts, environmental, health) in which they have the greatest interest, allowing them to group themselves, and then match these interests to the nonprofits that want to participate in the project. One student said, "I would continue to allow students flexibility in terms of deciding on type of group/organization they want to do service-learning project for. Makes experience very valuable." The project was less successful when I selected one community partner for the entire class and let students choose which element of the overall plan they would work on.

I inform organizations that express interest in the project that the students will select from a list of nonprofits and that I will let them know if they are selected. Community partners also seem to place value on the selection process I use. For example, one commented in response to a question about their expectations of the project, "No specific expectations of the students because I did not know them. Higher than usual expectations because of the professor and the pre-project selection process."

CHOOSING THE COMMUNITY PARTNER

Choosing an appropriate community partner is essential to the success of the project. I suggest when I advertise the project (among my contacts in the nonprofit community and through the state nonprofit association) that it is likely most appropriate for nonprofits within a specified budget size range, which I use as a proxy for organizational capacity. I look for organizations that would not otherwise be able to accomplish the work of the project, but have the capacity to execute it once it is designed. This implementation choice also is based on balancing service with learning.

Students express being motivated by knowing they are making a real contribution to an organization. They want to know that the organization will really use their work. They also learn the most about advocacy when they are able to create an advocacy plan from scratch. When the organization does not do any advocacy at all, but expresses a basic understanding of its potential value to the nonprofit and its constituents, students are able to apply broad research skills and creatively apply knowledge from class in order to create a comprehensive plan. If, however, the nonprofit already has an advocacy plan in place, then students are largely directed to do research that simply updates elements of the plan. Creativity, too, is limited in this situation because they must work within existing expectations and are not allowed to utilize the implementation skills from class.

I have had some student groups work with very small organizations and others work with very large nonprofits, and have found that organizations in the middle seem to be the best match. Very small nonprofits, those with an annual budget of $25,000 to $250,000, often have very thin organizational structures. The people who work for the organization are already doing several jobs each. The resources, human and financial alike, are stretched so thin that the employees do not really have time to work with my students. In addition, the students can quickly see that their hard work on the project will likely never be used because the organization cannot put either the necessary money or man-hours behind the project. Although I work with the students to adapt the project to meet the needs and resources of the organization, the knowledge that their work will likely not be used is disheartening, and students lose motivation.

At the other end of the spectrum, when student groups have worked with very large nonprofit organizations, students often express that they feel that their work is unnecessary. When an organization has an annual budget in excess of approximately $3 million, they tend to have greater organizational capacity and either have internal expertise on advocacy or have the ability to hire consultants to create an advocacy plan. These larger organizations may also undervalue the quality of student work. They are more likely to see their participation in the service-learning project as a service they are providing to the students, rather than the more traditional view that students are serving the nonprofit. So, again, the constraints on organizational capacity in choosing community partners are meant to maximize student learning and maximize the utility of the service to the community partner.

CONCLUSIONS

In analyzing the context from the three times I used this project, I see several important differences. First, twice when I taught the class I used several community partners and once I used one partner. In the first two instances, I did my best to match the community partner's mission to the student's interests. Second, I have designed the learning objectives and the project twice and let the students with the community partner design them once.

Interestingly, the learning outcomes and the community partner respons-es were very positive in all three instances. Community partners were very pleased with the final projects. I, too, was very pleased with the work of the student groups, and the grades ranged from a low of B+ to a high of A+ on the projects. Nonetheless, student satisfaction and their evaluations of the projects varied immensely. Given this discrepancy, it seems important to return to the contextual factors to try to explain the variation in student satisfaction.

The ability of students to self-select into a group based on the mission of the organization should not be undervalued. First, students spend a great deal of time both in and out of class on these projects. Allowing them to make a difference for a cause they care about can be very important. Allow-ing them to work with others who have a shared interest is also beneficial. Although I have certainly had students who did not know anything about an organization at the beginning of a semester and learn to love it over the course of the semester, I have also seen students struggle to care because they never truly understood the work of the organization. This problem also points to the importance of good communication between the com-munity partner and the students, so that the students understand the im-portance of the organization's work.

Further, choosing one community partner for the entire class to work with limits the "real-world" feeling of the project. When fifteen students all work on various pieces of an advocacy plan, they are exposed to a smaller slice of the organization. They have less understanding of the nonprofit, they are less vested in the success of the project and the organization, and they do not fully understand the resource limitations of nearly all nonprof-its. Although initially this design feature seemed preferable for both instruc-tor and student, it proved more problematic than I could have imagined.

As discussed above, the number of partners made a difference for stu-dents. In addition, the student-led learning component was lessened when fewer students were enrolled in the course. In all classes I encouraged a great deal of in-class reflection on the service-learning. In the small class, however, there was very little participation in this function. Students, there-fore, did not learn as effectively from each other through sharing their service experiences.

The final contextual factor that proved important was the project design-er. Although I truly believe that the co-creation of knowledge could lead to superior outcomes for students and community partners, my experience demonstrates that the project design must be completed by the instructor prior to the beginning of the semester. The application of classroom con-cepts to real-world situations in a graded activity is intimidating. Regardless of their previous service-learning experiences, students are uncertain about the expectations of the professor and the community partner. A 15- or 16-

week semester is simply not enough time to support both the project design and the project application. In the student-designed project version of the course, my students were constantly frustrated by the fact that I was not telling them what to do. They were constantly asking what I wanted to see in the end. The more I said they could control the decisions of what to include, the more frustrated they became. In the other two versions of the course, when I designed the project and provided models and outlines to work from, students were much more comfortable with expectations and workload. They still expressed frustration with feeling lost, but these fears were significantly less and student evaluations were better.

In conclusion, the variation in the success of this project seems to point to several important considerations for service-learning classes. First, mission preferences of students should be incorporated into project selection. Second, students may be most comfortable with significant guidance on program design so that they can concentrate on application of the project specifications to the community partner. Third, student reflections should be shared in class frequently to maximize student-led learning.

CHAPTER 18

THE DOCUMENTARY, HUMAN RIGHTS, AND SOCIAL JUSTICE

An Experiment in Service-Learning

Hank Liese

ABSTRACT

Honors 3214, *The Documentary, Human Rights, and Social Justice*, is a two-semester, undergraduate service-learning class that introduces students to the landscape of human rights and social justice through a race-class-gender lens. Students learn basic filmmaking techniques, then partner with community agencies to produce mini-documentaries dealing with such issues as health care, homelessness, violence against women, immigration, and disability rights.

Finding Meaning in Civically Engaged Scholarship, pages 197–208
Copyright © 2009 by Information Age Publishing

THE SERVICE-LEARNING JOURNEY

I'm very fortunate to be on this ride. I never know where it's going to go next,
[but] these are the best rides to go on.

A student in my year-long, undergraduate service-learning course, *The Documentary, Human Rights, and Social Justice*, wrote those words in a reflection paper at the end of his first semester. He captured both the ambiguity and excitement of a new service-learning course, feelings not uncommon for instructors and students alike who choose to travel the path of engaged learning. Although I had introduced and taught the course a year earlier in the University of Utah's Honors College, I was still stirring the ingredients of course content, service, and reflection that characterize the service-learning experience, seeking the correct "mix" that would guarantee the perfect ride.

At this writing, I have just finished a third year of *The Documentary, Human Rights, and Social Justice*. After reading more than 200 student reflection papers and having numerous discussions with community partners, I have discovered there is no "perfect ride" in service-learning. I have also learned to tolerate ambiguity in teaching a service-learning course. The journey is just as rewarding as the destination, so enjoy the ride.

For me, there is a personal and professional journey-behind-the-journey, a five-year gestation period for the ideas and impulses that would result in Honors 3214, *The Documentary, Human Rights, and Social Justice*. My interest in documentary work started with my volunteer involvement in 2000 with the Center for Documentary Arts (CDA), formerly the Oral History Institute, in Salt Lake City. Working with CDA and its staff, I began to sense the power of documentary work (e.g., oral histories, radio, film) to advocate for vulnerable and oppressed populations and advance social change agendas—the raison d´être of my profession, social work. Yet I did not see many social work professionals harnessing the energy of documentary media—particularly film—toward these ends. How, I asked myself, could I incorporate documentary work into my classes and begin to teach future social workers the power of the medium?

One thing was certain: I couldn't begin to teach students how to do documentary work without first learning how to do it myself. Taking a year-long sabbatical during the 2003–04 academic year, I returned to the classroom at the University of Utah to study film. Three documentary film production classes later, I felt confident and comfortable enough to introduce filmmaking to my social work students, and service-learning was the vehicle I chose to do it. With seed money from the Lowell Bennion Community Service Center on campus, I purchased just enough equipment to get started, then took an existing Bachelor of Social Work (BSW) foundation course, *Human*

Behavior and the Social Environment, and "grafted" on a documentary service-learning component. This class, taught Fall Semester 2004 and Spring Semester 2005, was the "prototype" for Honors 3214.

Students in this pilot BSW course partnered with community agencies to produce short, 10–15 minute films and photo essays that focused primarily on the agency, its mission, and programs. The agencies could then use the films for public relations, marketing, and fundraising purposes. This was, essentially, the "service" students were performing in the community as part of their service-learning experience. Yet the social activist in me said something was missing. I wanted these student documentaries to be more hard-hitting, to go beyond mere public relations, to raise the awareness and consciousness of audiences in a position to do something about a particular issue, to take action to right a wrong, to alleviate suffering. My course, I realized, had to be about human rights and social justice.

In 2005, I applied for the Bennion Center's Public Service Professor award, an annual grant that allows faculty to propose and pursue a year-long service-learning agenda. My application laid out plans for creating and teaching *The Documentary, Human Rights, and Social Justice* as an undergraduate Honors course. Although it required a move outside the College of Social Work, there was more flexibility in the Honors curriculum to teach a course of this nature, and the director of the Honors program was most supportive of my "experiment." I was awarded the Public Service Professorship for 2005–06. What follows is a description of what, in many ways, has been the ride of my academic life.

DEVELOPING A COURSE "PREMISE"

> This past semester... has been one of the best semesters of my college career. This multi-disciplinary class has combined documentary film with social justice and taught them using a service-based approach... Advocating with these films has had a great impact on my life, and will act as a basis for what I hope to accomplish in the future. (student reflection)

At the University of Utah, service-learning courses are officially designated as such, and must meet a specific set of criteria. My first task after receiving the Public Service Professor award was to create my syllabus, take it before the Bennion Center's Service-Learning Class Committee, and demonstrate how the course satisfied these criteria. Unique to my course, I believe, is its approach to service. Students making films in the community are not performing the typical kinds of service one expects in a service-learning experience, e.g., volunteering and providing direct service at a local nonprofit agency. My syllabus begins with a quote from Robert Coles, whose *Doing*

Documentary Work (1997) is a required text for the class: "The experience of service can soon enough prompt a need for reflection—and so it is that documentary work can itself become a kind of service: the narrative work done among those vulnerable 'others' can enable us to stop and reflect who 'they' are, and what 'we' are trying to accomplish" (Coles, 1997, p. 251).

True, student films produced in my Honors course, as they were in my BSW service-learning course, can be and often are utilized by community partners long after they are completed, thus providing a valuable "service." But Coles connects documentary work to service on another level: service to the vulnerable and oppressed, whose voices are too often muted, if not silenced. Coles leads students to the underlying premise of the course, namely that documentary work can serve the larger causes of human rights and social justice. The Coles' quote is followed in the syllabus by the words of Paulo Freire in *Pedagogy of the Oppressed* (1970): "The dehumanization resulting from an unjust order is not a cause for despair but for hope, leading to the incessant pursuit of the humanity denied by injustice" (pp. 72–73).

Freire's call to action is followed by the words of Eleanor Roosevelt, which introduce students to the notion that human rights, often cast nationally and globally, are local issues as well: "Where, after all, do universal human rights begin? In small places, close to home—so close and so small they cannot be seen on any maps of the world. Yet they are the world of the individual person, the neighborhood he lives in, the school or college he attends, the factory, farm, or office where he works. Such are the places where every man, woman, and child seeks equal justice, equal opportunity, and equal dignity without discrimination. Unless these rights have meaning there, they have little meaning anywhere. Without concerted citizen action to uphold them close to home, we shall look in vain for progress in the larger world" (Reichert, 2003, p. 44).

RACE, CLASS, AND GENDER: AN ORGANIZING FRAMEWORK

From the very beginning, I knew the course offered something special. It offered the exploration of truth and the ability to promote that truth. (student reflection)

In the first semester of Honors 3214, students are introduced through readings, guest lectures, and documentary films to the "landscape" of human rights and social justice. One of the first reading assignments is the United Nations Universal Declaration of Human Rights, crafted in 1948, which they must apply in the first of six reflection papers spread throughout the semester. For this assignment, students are presented with a series of political cartoons dealing with current issues of human rights and social justice, e.g., torture and genocide, the health care crisis, the loss of U.S. jobs overseas. They select two or three of the cartoons and address the following: (1) What is the issue the cartoonist is addressing, as you understand it? (2) Why did you select this particular cartoon? For example, did something "speak to you" or "stir inside you" as you read the cartoon, or do you have a personal connection to the issue? (3) Which article(s) in the UN's Universal Declaration of Human Rights might apply to the issue featured in the cartoon, either directly or indirectly? (4) If you were going to make a documentary film addressing this particular issue, which two individuals might you interview to present the opposing sides (i.e., pro and con) of the issue?

Students are asked to view human rights and social justice issues through a race-class-gender lens, since most documentaries of this genre do the same. Course readings are taken largely from Andersen and Collins' anthology, *Race, Class, and Gender* (2007). Note Andersen and Collins (2007): "Studying race, class, and gender means recognizing and analyzing the hierarchies and systems of domination that permeate society and that limit our ability to achieve true democracy and social justice" (p. 11).

These issues and ideas are brought to life as students in Honors 3214 view and critique professionally produced documentary films throughout the first semester, as well as the work of students who have already taken the class. A highlight each of the past three years has been the viewing of the 2003 Oscar-winning documentary, *Born into Brothels*, followed by a question-and-answer session with the film's Executive Producer, Geralyn Dreyfous, a director of the Salt Lake Film Center. The past two years, Ms. Dreyfous has been joined in the class by Avijit Halder, one of the young men featured in the film, which chronicles the life of children who are born and live in Calcutta's red light district. With the help of Ms. Dreyfous, Mr. Halder was able to come to the U.S. and attend a private high school in Salt Lake City. Wrote one student in her reflection paper on *Born into Brothels*: "It was a privilege for me to speak with Avijit Halder and get his firsthand experience. [The film] was my favorite, because I can relate to the people in it. I feel that in my life, I also have been displaced by having to leave my home and come to a new place because of political and economic setbacks."

SETTING GUIDELINES FOR CLASS DISCUSSION

Perhaps the most poignant moment in the course was when James, a Lost Boy from Sudan, told us with such enthusiasm about the many individuals who have helped him in his long and difficult journey. What I realized then was that I could be one of those people, if not in any official capacity, just as a caring and mindful citizen. (student reflection)

Because Honors 3214 focuses on issues of race, class, and gender, the course can be used by students to satisfy the University's diversity requirement. Addressing diversity issues openly and honestly is critical in any class; equally important is creating a safe environment to do so. On the first or second day of class, students work together to develop *Guidelines for Class Discussion and Dialogue*, which are typed and distributed the following class period. Following are the guidelines students developed the first time I taught the course; each subsequent year, the guidelines have been similar:

1. Everyone has a right to an opinion. You don't have to agree with that opinion, but you should respect the other person's right to hold it.
2. When someone is stating his or her opinion or making a point, *listen* first, then respond.
3. Don't interrupt.
4. Don't dominate the conversation. There should be time for all points of view to be heard.
5. Focus on issues, not the person.
6, Use "I" statements when disagreeing (or agreeing) with another person.
7. Be honest.
8. Be respectful.
9. If an issue arises for you, try to talk about it when it comes up, as opposed to "letting it stew."
10. Keep what is shared in class confidential, especially matters of a personal nature.

FINDING COMMUNITY PARTNERS AND ISSUES

> When I found out this course was a year long I almost dropped it because I didn't think it would fit well into my graduation schedule. I signed up for the class for two reasons: I needed a diversity credit and I needed Honors credit for my degree. I stuck with the class because the idea behind the course is original and innovative. Not only would I get all the credits I needed, but working very closely with a small group of people on a creative project would be something totally new for me. (student reflection)

In many service-learning classes, community partners can be identified and recruited before the class begins, as the course content is already set. The first year I taught *The Documentary, Human Rights, and Social Justice*, I followed this pattern, selecting six organizations with which I was familiar and knew someone on staff. I prepared a handout for students that listed each agency and its mission and also suggested a range of possible documentary topics for each organization. The handout also included contact information for each agency's director. Of the six directors, I had previously worked with five in other capacities, which made my job of recruiting them somewhat easier, although it was still necessary to meet with each and essentially "pitch" the course, discuss mutual expectations between students and partners, and address any questions or concerns.

This approach, i.e., preselecting community partners and pre-identifying documentary topics, worked well. Over several class periods early in the semester, the 14 students in the first "cohort" of Honors 3214 discussed issues of interest to them, got to know their fellow classmates, and formed five groups of two to three students each to work with a particular community partner. To help students keep track of each other's interests, in both community partners and possible documentary topics, I prepared and continually updated a student "interest matrix," a handout that proved invaluable when it came time for students to make their final selections.

The last two years I have taught Honors 3214, I have taken a different approach recruiting community partners, one that recognizes the importance of student choice in selecting documentary topics. In Year One, these topics essentially were limited to the issues addressed by the community partners I had already selected. In Years Two and Three, students first formed their documentary groups based on common interests and decided upon a specific human rights/social justice issue to address in their films. Only then did I recruit community partners based on those topics. In hindsight, the Year One approach was more efficient in that students "hit the ground running" once they had formed their groups. With the student choice approach, community partners were not in place until well into the semester, and valuable time was lost in terms of student-partner contact and communication.

CLASS ASSIGNMENTS: THE ISSUE BRIEF AND THE DOCUMENTARY TREATMENT

I have enjoyed this course so far mostly because of the variety of information I have learned, the layout of the class, and the potential to help others. This class is completely different from any other class I have ever taken. Being a bioengineer, I am used to taking engineering and science-related classes where the professor lectures the entire time, and the homework assignments and the related readings are assigned according to the objectives and rigid schedule of the class. Therefore, I liked the personal choice aspect of the class and how at the beginning of the semester we were introduced gradually to documentary work. (student reflection)

Students meet in their groups to develop their story ideas, which they then share with their community partners. I tell students they need to be open to suggestions from their community partner, who may wish to take the film in other directions. After reaching consensus on their storyline with their agencies, student groups research their respective issues and prepare a four to five page *Human Rights/Social Justice Issue Brief.* In this assignment, students describe the nature and extent of the issue/problem they are addressing; discuss current policies, practice, or legislation that could be changed to address their issue; designate the target audiences for their documentaries; and summarize their "call to action," i.e., what they want to have happen after people view their films.

At the end of the first semester, students prepare a *Documentary Treatment and Dissemination Plan,* a five to six page paper that builds on their issue briefs. In this final assignment, they discuss the theme and significance of their proposed documentaries; present the elements of their films, e.g., whom they will likely interview, what cover footage (or "b-roll" in filmmaker parlance) they will obtain; and develop a preliminary dissemination plan, listing all the audiences they think should view their documentaries and why. Of the audiences they suggest, they are asked which they think are in the best position to bring about meaningful change vis-à-vis their particular issue.

AN INTRODUCTION TO FILMMAKING

> ... [L]earning about the nature of documentary filmmaking, the moral and ethical tensions, and the responsibilities as a filmmaker has been of incalculable worth to me. I feel I've grown a great bit during this class so far, in that I've been able to begin a foundation as a socially responsible filmmaker and a more informed voting citizen. (student reflection)

Perhaps the biggest challenge I have faced teaching this course is covering all the necessary content, basically in one semester (Fall), since Spring Semester is mostly spent "in the field," with students filming and editing their documentaries. The first year teaching Honors 3214, I waited too long to introduce students to the technical side of filmmaking and editing, a point made clear in students' final reflection papers. In the second and third years, I have had students working with the cameras, audio equipment, and editing software during Fall Semester so that no time is lost Spring Semester getting into production.

One of the assignments in the fall is a *Team Video Shoot,* a method I "borrowed" from the film production classes I myself took at the U. on my sabbatical. Here, students work in groups—preferably the groups they have formed for their projects—and take turns filming another group member being interviewed on camera. One member serves as the interviewee; a second conducts the interview; and the third, the videographer, does the filming. Each videographer must select a location for his or her shoot and set up the camera, tripod, and audio equipment on his or her own. Each videographer's filmed segment runs approximately 3–5 minutes and includes a minimum of three shot sizes—medium, medium close-up, and close-up— which gives students a feel for both shot composition and zooming. This year, for the first time, I had students capture (i.e., digitize) the footage they shot and edit a short film that was then shown and critiqued in a later class session.

The film equipment I use for Honors 3214 has been purchased with grant monies received over the past three years and includes five mini-DV cameras, five lavaliere microphone sets, five tripods, and two Mac G5 computers with Final Cut Pro editing software. I also use grant monies to purchase mini-DV tapes and blank DVDs for student use. Unfortunately, I do not have light kits for students to use, so they must shoot all of their footage with available light.

Although the class is taught in the Honors Center, the two computers are set up in my office in the College of Social Work, and students have easy access to them for capturing their video and editing their films. The camera equipment is also stored in my office, and students fill out and sign an inventory checklist whenever they use the equipment. The sign-out sheet carries the following language: "I agree to keep this equipment in my possession, using it for school business and not allowing others to use it while checked out in my name. I understand it is University of Utah College of Social Work property and will do all I can to protect the School's investment. I agree to the safe return of all equipment checked out and accept responsibility for replacing or repairing any items damaged through operator negligence." There has been very little equipment damage or loss in the three years I have been teaching the course.

Another required text for the class is Tom Schroeppel's (2005) *The Bare Bones Camera Course for Film and Video*, which does a good job presenting filming techniques to what are, for the most part, non-film majors. However, I have had at least one film major in each of the three years I have taught the course, and this has helped immensely during Spring Semester when the filming and editing begin. I have also learned that the "millennial" generation is quite techno-savvy, and many have already had experience shooting and editing films.

SPRING SEMESTER: ACTION!

> This course was the most unique one I have so far taken in college. The idea
> that documentary could be used for advocacy was completely new to me, as
> was the process. However, I felt that I benefitted from this course in a way
> that is entirely different from the usual class, and I feel I developed more as a
> person as well. What impacted me the most during the documentary process
> were the families that I got to meet and whose personal histories I began to
> understand. . . . They were some of the most interesting people that I have
> met, and I felt truly lucky to be able to capture parts of their personal stories.
> (student reflection)

As mentioned, Spring Semester is spent primarily in the field, with students
filming interviews, gathering coverage footage, capturing their video, and
editing their documentaries. Community partners play an important role
at this time identifying potential interview subjects for the students and,
in many cases, making necessary introductions, which smooth the way for
students by "legitimizing" their projects with interviewees, many of whom
are often wary of being filmed.

Class meets monthly instead of weekly during the semester, and class
time is usually spent getting project updates and, whenever possible, showing rough cuts of student films for feedback purposes. The two assignments
in the final semester are production of a 15–30 minute documentary film
and a final reflection paper on the filmmaking experience. In addition,
a *Peer Review Form* is used to allow students to rank the level of participation and contribution of each of their fellow group members. The form
uses a Likert-type scale and asks students to indicate the extent to which
they agree with the following statements: (1) This person was an active participant in the work of our group, (2) This person took the initiative when
necessary or asked to by the group, (3) This person followed through on
his/her assignments, and (4) This project could not have been completed
without the contributions made by this group member.

Although the syllabus outlines a schedule with specific dates and dead-
lines for filming and editing, every year, without fail, at least one or two
films are not in final form by the end of the semester. Students have been
willing, however, to come in after the semester ends to produce their final
cuts. The first year I taught the course, as Public Service Professor, rough
cuts of all five student projects (four films and one radio documentary)
were screened at the annual Public Service Professor lecture. The final cuts
where shown at a screening the following month for students and their
friends and families. These screenings were not held in Years Two and
Three, mainly due to the staggered completion of student projects.

STUDENT FILMS, STUDENT REFLECTIONS

> I admit I only entered the class to finish with general ed credit. Ironically, I left with more than just credit. I left with friends, my own movie, credit, and personal feelings that I never gave a chance to surface until this year. I consider myself a more educated person as far as worldly issues go. I feel more concerned with what is going [on] around me than I did a year ago. I have done a lot of growing up this past school year, and I think this was a great class to take during this time. (student reflection)

Documentaries produced to date by my Honors 3214 students have included, in Year One, four films covering refugee adaptation in Utah, rape and violence against women, the re-emergence of Gay-Straight Alliances (GSAs) in Utah high schools after a controversial 10-year absence, and the waiting list for disability services in Utah. Two students in Year One produced a radio documentary on homelessness. Year Two projects included five films covering diversity and campus climate at the University of Utah, refugee resettlement, end-of-life issues in hospice, homelessness, and healthcare. The three film projects in Year Three address the abortion issue (the two students working on this project took opposite sides of the issue, one pro-life, the other pro-choice), healthcare for people with disabilities, and immigration.

The Year One documentary on rape and violence against women is still being used for training purposes by the University's Women's Resource Center, who served as community partner on the project. The film on Gay-Straight Alliances was used the following year by that student group's community partner, the Utah Pride Center, for lobbying purposes when a bill was introduced in the Utah Legislature to ban GSAs in the state's high schools. (The bill, introduced and defeated the year before, passed this time. Although not banning GSA's outright, the bill makes it more difficult for these organizations to establish themselves.) Year One students working with the Disability Law Center (DLC) actually produced *two* films, a long one for Honors 3214 and a shorter version used by the DLC in public forums where the waiting list was discussed and debated.

Final student reflection papers these past three years indicate, I believe, the success of *The Documentary, Human Rights, and Social Justice.* For me, Honors 3214 was experimental not only because it was the first (and only) service-learning course I have taught, but also because of its unique approach, i.e., documentary filmmaking, to human rights and social justice issues. As the reflections that begin each section of this chapter demonstrate, the course raised students' awareness of local issues, of themselves in relation to those issues, and of the importance of advocacy and activism in bringing about social change. Students' increased self-awareness and personal growth were evident in their comments, as was the uniqueness of the class itself and what, in the end, students took away from it.

The theme of "generalizability," i.e., the notion that the things students learn in my class will stay with them for a long time, appears in several of their reflections. As an instructor, not only in this service-learning class but in all my classes, I am always optimistic that what I teach and what students learn from me and others will have a certain degree of staying power. I was heartened not long ago when I ran into a student on campus from Year One of Honors 3214. He was volunteering in several organizations and had just joined the Young Democrats. Since his documentary project for my class had taken him to the state Capitol to film a legislative session, I made a connection between his current volunteer and political involvements and taking my class. He confirmed that, indeed, *The Documentary, Human Rights, and Social Justice* class had set him on his current course. As is often said, "It doesn't get any better than that."

REFERENCES

Andersen, M. L., & Collins, P. H. (Eds.). (2007). *Race, class, and gender: An anthology* (6th ed.). Belmont, CA: Wadsworth/Thomson Learning.

Coles, R. (1997). *Doing documentary work.* New York: Oxford University Press.

Freire, P. (1970). *Pedagogy of the oppressed.* New York: The Continuum Publishing Company.

Reichert, E. R. (2003). *Social work and human rights: A foundation for policy and practice.* New York: Columbia University Press.

Schroeppel, T. (2005). *The bare bones camera course for film and video* (2nd ed., rev.). Tampa, FL: Tom Schroeppel.

CONCLUSION

Hank Liese and Marshall Welch

SUMMARY

This volume presented the landscapes traversed by nine faculty members as they discovered the challenges and rewards of civically engaged scholarship. Representing seven different departments and colleges at the University of Utah—English, Family and Consumer Studies, Social Work, Physical Therapy, Education, Political Science, and Architecture and Planning—these individuals, coming together as the Civically Engaged Scholar Cohort (CESC), each contributed two chapters. The first set of chapters (Part I) recounts personal journeys to civic engagement. The second set of chapters (Part II) describes professional experiences—e.g., service-learning classes, community-based research projects—that were, and for many authors remain, important milestones in their individual journeys.

As the Introduction notes, the book evolved from the gatherings and eventual writings of the CESC, which is now entering its third year together. Although three group members have moved to other institutions, the conversations and collaboration continue. "Cohort" implies companionship and aid, and both of these are evident in the workings of the CESC, as most of the authors make clear in their personal narratives. Perhaps most unique to this group is its interdisciplinary nature. The CESC has served to move many of its members from narrow academic silos to a multidimensional stage where the "pedagogy of engagement" plays out.

Finding Meaning in Civically Engaged Scholarship, pages 209–220
Copyright © 2009 by Information Age Publishing
All rights of reproduction in any form reserved.

This final chapter provides an overview of civic engagement as it is defined and portrayed in the professional literature. Institutional factors that support and promote civic engagement, and service-learning in particular, are discussed, along with the importance of community involvement in this work. Next, five common themes that appear throughout the book's chapters are presented. How authors navigated the retention, promotion, and tenure (RPT) process is discussed, and the chapter concludes with a final reflection on the Civically Engaged Scholar Cohort's journey.

CIVIC ENGAGEMENT

The narratives in this volume articulate how civic engagement is conceptualized and realized at a large, public research university. The chapters portray, through personal and poignant examples, the far-reaching impact of service-learning and other forms of civically engaged scholarship on students and faculty; on partner organizations and the larger communities they serve; on the University; and, indirectly, on the authors' own academic disciplines. Taken together, these examples map nicely with the characterization of civic engagement in the professional literature.

For Ernest Boyer (1996), the scholarship of engagement meant "connecting the rich resources of the university to our most pressing social, civic, and ethical problems..." (p. 19). Campuses, Boyer said, "should be viewed by both students and professors not as isolated islands, but as staging grounds for action... I'm convinced that ultimately the scholarship of engagement also means creating a special climate in which the academic and civil cultures communicate more continuously and more creatively with each other..." (p. 20). Carnegie Scholar Thomas Ehrlich (2000) described civic engagement as "working together to make a difference in the civic life of our communities and developing the combination of knowledge, skills, values, and motivation to make that difference" (p. vi). Similarly, Fogelman (2002) defined civic engagement as "an institutional commitment to public purposes and responsibilities intended to strengthen a democratic way of life in the rapidly changing information society of the twenty-first century" (p. 104).

In the introduction to a special issue of the *Journal of Public Affairs* devoted entirely to civic engagement and higher education, Saltmarsh (2002) noted that engagement "implies community-based public problem solving that not only generates new knowledge and higher order cognitive outcomes, but develops the civic skills of critical thinking, public deliberation, collective action, and social ethics" (p. viii). Clearly, Winemiller Basinger's service-learning course that partners students with local nonprofits, Kaufman's Family Literacy Center, Senbel's Westside Studio, Garrott's Neighborhood Democracy class, and Welch's hands-on, post-Katrina project in New Orleans encompass what Saltmarsh describes as community-based problem solving. For Cahill and her students, the goal of the Red Flags community-based research project is "action."

According to Bloomfield (2006, cited in Stanton & Wagner, 2006), a fundamental element of civic engagement is that "engagement is scholarly"; it involves not only the *act* of engaging, i.e., bringing together universities and communities, but also the *product* of engagement, i.e., disseminating evidence-based practices to larger audiences, both within the academy and the community at large. The chapters in this volume demonstrate the scholarly expertise of each faculty member. Utilizing sound theoretical methods within their courses, many authors were able to integrate the academic trilogy, essentially teaching what they research and researching what they teach while providing needed service. The engaged scholarship described by Cahill, Kaufman, Musolino, Welch, and Winemiller Basinger led to publications and, for several, extramural funding through grants. In addition, for most authors, using research and teaching to address community needs transcends traditional notions of service as shared governance on campus committees or being a good citizen to one's discipline by belonging to professional associations or serving on journal editorial boards.

For Jacoby (2009), civic engagement involves one or more of the following: (1) learning from others, self, and environment to develop informed perspectives on social issues; (2) working collaboratively and productively across difference for the common good; (3) participating actively in public life, public problem-solving, and community service; (4) assuming leadership and membership roles in organizations; (5) taking an active part in the political process; (6) developing empathy, ethics, values, and a sense of social responsibility; and (7) promoting social justice locally and globally. Nearly all the chapters, some more explicitly than others, incorporate most or all of the components Jacoby enumerates. Musolino described how her physical therapy course and professional preparation program attempted to cross-reference core values of her discipline's professional association with the core values of engaged scholarship enumerated by Holland (1997). Most of the chapters articulate how students developed empathy for those with whom they were working. In Kaufman's English course on literacy, Diener's child development class, Senbel's urban planning course, Liese's documentary film class, and Cahill's Red Flags project, students, many from affluent and privileged backgrounds, came to recognize their commonalities with "the other" from underserved communities.

This attention to and integration of key civic engagement concepts into service-learning courses is not an accident for this group of educators. There was a general awareness of the fundamental tenets and ethos of civic engagement at the University of Utah that may have served as an overt or subtle foundation for these authors' efforts. A group of faculty, some of whom are authors in this volume, spent more than a year in a study group to learn about civic engagement and the civic mission of higher education. As Liese notes in his first chapter, they collectively characterized their work as civically engaged scholars and defined civically engaged scholarship as:

> a dynamic and collaborative participatory process in which the rich resources of the university and community are combined to integrate research, learning, and service in identifying and addressing community-based issues and needs while promoting socially responsible knowledge. Faculty, staff, students, and members of the community forge relationships as meaningful partners in exploring those practices that produce tangible outcomes to benefit the partners and their communities and that disseminate new knowledge in a variety of ways. (Welch, 2002, p. 116)

With this definition of civically engaged scholarship as a theoretical foundation, it is relatively easy to see how the authors in this volume understand and promote civic engagement in their courses. The definition captures the efforts described in these chapters, in particular, the partnerships of faculty, students, and community agencies that produced mutually beneficial outcomes for all stakeholders. From a philosophical perspective, the chapters in Part I reveal both an understanding of and a desire to accomplish what Ernest Boyer articulated in terms of the "academy as citizen." Faculty saw their role as not only creating and disseminating new knowledge, but also providing their students an opportunity to co-create new knowledge and then apply it for the common good. In fact, this very language appears throughout the chapters. Winemiller Basinger described her course on nonprofits as a process in which her students and community partners co-created new knowledge. Musolino characterized her instructional objectives as "shared learning outcomes." Similarly, Cahill wanted her students and community partners to co-construct research, while Senbel's urban planning course incorporated what he called "participatory design."

INSTITUTIONAL SUPPORT AND COMMUNITY INVOLVEMENT

Research by Holland (1997) and Furco (2003) has identified a number of factors that support and promote service-learning. Prominent among these are (1) the organizational and/or institutional support structure and (2) community involvement. The authors of this volume acknowledged the value and need for institutional support and resources to do their work. Their institution, the University of Utah, had made a significant commitment, both philosophically and financially, to provide the necessary infrastructure to support this type of engaged pedagogy. Having a nationally recognized center for service-learning, the Lowell Bennion Community Service Center, proved facilitative for faculty, who received financial resources and technical assistance as they conceptualized and implemented their courses. Musolino described her initial trepidation over meeting with the Bennion Center's Service-Learning Class Committee when proposing her course, but came to understand and appreciate the committee's diligence to ensure quality. She, as did other authors, appreciated the one-on-one assistance provided by Bennion Center staff. In addition to receiving technical support, Kaufman acknowledged emotional support from both Bennion Center staff and like-minded colleagues, many of whom have contributed chapters to this volume; in fact, she characterized this group as a community and a "gift."

At the University of Utah, the Senior Vice President for Academic Affairs annually provides funds that the Bennion Center allocates for seed grants to help develop new service-learning courses and community-based research projects. The funds are also used for the Public Service Professorship, an annual faculty fellowship award of $10,000 to be used for a comprehensive, engaged project with the community as described in the chapter by Senbel. (Liese and Cahill were also recipients of the Public Service Professor award.) Not only is the financial support helpful to recipients, but the prestige that accompanies such an award promotes scholarly credibility; at the end of the academic year, each fellow delivers a formal campus-wide lecture on his or her project to colleagues and the community.

The Bennion Center also provides funds for teaching assistants, called Service-Learning Coordinators, to help faculty with their courses, especially faculty who are new to service-learning. Additionally, the Bennion Center has sponsored several book and discussion groups, one of which culminated in the operational definition of civically engaged scholarship cited above. This exchange of resources, information, and ideas helped create the community of scholars that became the Civically Engaged Scholar Cohort. Diener cites her involvement with this group, as well as interactions with Utah Campus Compact and University Neighborhood Partners, a campus-community partnership on Salt Lake City's west side, as critical in helping her derive and affirm purpose and meaning in her scholarship. In fact, the Bennion Center used a portion of its funding to defray the cost of faculty attending the Utah Campus Compact retreats that proved so pivotal in the formation and sustenance of this group of authors.

In addition to institutional resources and support, community partnerships are critical for the success of these authors' civically engaged courses and projects. For Winemiller Basinger, civic engagement is about participation in the third or voluntary sector, i.e., "nonprofit organizations that serve the public good through a specific mission." Winemiller Basinger notes that this third sector exists, in part, to fill the gap between the needs of society and what businesses (the private sector) and government (the public sector) choose to provide. "Not all civic engagement will occur in this third sector," she writes, "but this is the civic engagement that means the most to me."

For Senbel and his Westside Studio, the community partner acts as a "facilitator of access" into the community and also provides continuity for the Studio from year to year. Cahill benefits from the advice and resources of her community partners, who act as "informal advisors" to her and her Growing Up in Salt Lake City project. Garrott sees his work with community councils on Salt Lake City's west side as "a story of partnerships." What keeps his relationship with the Rose Park Community Council and its successful community festival going each year, says Garrott, is a sense of "civic friendship." "We share a *telos*," he writes, "a common public end, which Aristotle marks as one of the qualities of friendship found between citizens."

At the end of each semester, Diener includes her community partners in a reflection session in her service-learning class. During the session, she, her students, and the community partners discuss the benefits and challenges of the services that have been provided. "It helps for students to hear the perspective of the community partner," says Diener, "and vice versa. It also helps me to know how to facilitate the relationships, prepare the students, and what to focus on in our reflection sessions." Kaufman discusses the importance of "open communication, collaboration, a sense of community, and trust" in the community partner relationships in her Family Literacy Center at West High School. She believes that community partners must trust "that we from the University are not coming to the high school to impose a particular agenda, and the University service-learning students will be reliable."

Beyond faculty members' direct contact with community partners, the Bennion Center has a policy and practice of including representatives from the community on its various advisory committees. In this way, the community has a voice and makes a significant contribution to supporting service-learning. Additionally, the Bennion Center, in collaboration with two other institutions in the same geographical area, hosts and sponsors an annual gathering of community partners to network and provide technical assistance when working with faculty members and students. Informed community partners are empowered to work effectively with faculty members in the development, implementation, and assessment of service-learning. The Bennion Center also assists faculty members in identifying potential community partners and essentially coaches instructors on how to have a conversation that creates parity in the educational partnership. Indirectly, faculty receive support when they work with community partners who are informed and committed to service-learning.

COMMON THEMES

Five consistent and common themes emerged from these chapters. First, every author initially viewed and approached service-learning as a viable pedagogy that helps students discover their own role and responsibility in society as citizens. For Winemiller Basinger, service-learning "seemed common sense." Similarly, Kaufman engages in civically engaged scholarship "because it feels like the right thing to do." For several authors, the experiential aspect of service-learning is a traditional fixture within their professional disciplines, as Welch acknowledged in his work in teacher education and Diener in her field of child development. Experiential education also lends itself to preparing urban planners and addressing community development as described in the chapters by Senbel and Cahill. However, experiential education is not as common within English literature or political science, as both Kaufman and Garrott attest in their chapters. In fact, Kaufman acknowledged her initial reluctance to incorporate service-learning at a Family Literacy Center and did so only after the urging of a colleague. In time, service-learning became "grounded" in her own disciplinary work.

A second recurring theme is the relationship between civic engagement and political activism. At a more overt and disciplinary level, Garrott's service-learning was tied to understanding the political process in local government and decision-making. Other authors revealed another political dimension associated with service-learning and community-based research: their courses and projects were vehicles for addressing their personal and professional interests in social justice. Kaufman recalled her childhood interest in injustice in the context of her own Jewish heritage; for her, *tikkun olam*, repairing the world, "was something I was obligated to do," and she continues to "find ways to work against silencing and oppression and toward social justice."

Liese's service-learning course, *The Documentary, Human Rights, and Social Justice*, holds true to both his personal and professional social work values. Welch acknowledged a profound rekindling of his passion for social justice after his experience in New Orleans, which ultimately led him to leave the University of Utah after 20 years to work and teach at an institution in which social justice was key to its mission. Senbel's chapter suggests a deep personal struggle regarding privilege and exploitation. Initially, he recognized his own privilege and later came to wrestle with the ethical and moral dilemma in which service-learning does not always "deliver" in meeting the needs of the community. Similarly, Cahill described her struggle and concern that the "ivory tower is complicit in injustice." Diener's chapter pondered the political dynamics associated with women and tenure.

A third theme encompasses the notion of partnership and collaboration. Authors talked about the importance of connections—not merely cognitive connections with what was taught—but connections with students, colleagues, and the community. Cahill referred to her own engaged scholarship as a "pedagogy of collegiality" and noted that, as a community-based participatory researcher, she is "invested in the power of collaborative work at all levels." Kaufman refers to Johnston's (2006) notion of the "relationship landscape of classrooms," and quotes a student in her service-learning class who reflected that "connections must be made for learning to occur." Authors consistently recognized the value and role of community representatives and settings as contributors to co-creating new knowledge; the "service" in service-learning would not be possible without the involvement and contributions of community partners. Likewise, these chapters made consistent reference to connections with colleagues doing similar work, evidenced no more clearly than in the Civically Engaged Scholar Cohort that produced this volume. Liese captures this third theme when he writes, "For me, it is *all* about community—the community that develops between me and my service-learning students, the community of engaged scholars that I hold so dear, and the community that all of us who do this type of work seek to serve, and through that service to embrace, embolden, and, ultimately, empower."

The fourth commonality can be characterized as creating deeper educational and personal meaning for students and faculty alike. Musolino described how she had her students write a personal philosophy statement in the context of their discipline. One of Liese's students wrote in a reflection paper, "From the very beginning, I knew the course offered something special. It offered the exploration of truth and the ability to promote that truth." Welch recounts how he had "arrived" by attaining tenure and the rank of professor, yet still felt something was missing from his teaching and scholarship. Through service-learning, he discovered scholarship that could be applied to make a difference in the community as well as prepare professionals. Diener describes something similar when viewing her service-learning as transcending her research agenda. Kaufman realized this work allowed her to "investigate the sacred paths of life" and helped to "make scholarship matter." In his chapter, Senbel said he longed to go "beyond creating monuments to the ego" through architecture. Here, Senbel hints at the transcendent nature of service-learning and other forms of civically engaged scholarship. Ironically, working with others on behalf of others—putting, as Liese calls it, "service above self"—can run counter to the culture of isolation often found in the academy.

The fifth theme found in these chapters centers on the challenges faculty face in their civically engaged work. Diener found it difficult at times to prioritize her own needs and work over the competing demands of others—students, colleagues, and community partners. Kaufman felt similar time pressures. In the beginning, she didn't know "how we would meet the multiple needs that genuine service-learning demanded—my needs, my students' needs, the community partner's needs." In addition to time, Cahill mentioned finding the necessary support and resources to continue her work as another challenge.

Diener experienced other challenges in working with students and community partners. Most of her students work full-time, and many of them are parents; consequently, she felt that school in general, and her course in particular, might be a lower priority for them than she would like. Diener feels that when students resent the service-learning time commitment, it often shows in their "poor quality of work." Another challenge for Diener is ensuring good communication among students, the professor, agency staff, and clients. She also notes the high staff turnover of nonprofit agencies, which makes the partnership "a constant learning process and involves re-education each semester." Moreover, Diener notes, most community partners don't follow the University's calendar; thus, the "ebb and flow" of students doesn't always match the agencies' needs.

THE TIGHTROPE WALK OF CIVICALLY ENGAGED SCHOLARSHIP

The most frequently discussed challenge in this volume, however, was the difficulty faculty faced advancing their civically engaged scholarship while navigating the retention, promotion, and tenure (RPT) process within their respective colleges and departments. Garrott, a non-tenure track lecturer, termed civically engaged work at the University "a tightrope walk above manifest disincentives" and made the following observation: "Much of the book you hold is filled with stories of struggles to change the culture of retention and promotion within our departments and colleges... That burden, responsibility, and risk is not mine... Contrary to what many of this book's contributors have experienced, I haven't had to justify to my peers my concern with community."

The Bennion Center reviewed 52 individual departmental RPT criteria at the University of Utah as part of its ongoing programming support and planning. The results revealed that only five documents explicitly included or mentioned service-learning; four listed it under service, with only one department placing it under the heading of teaching. Therefore, it appears there is no explicit departmental or institutional motivation in the context of the formal reward structure for faculty to do this work. In fact, in some departments and colleges at the University, junior (untenured) faculty are advised *not* to get involved with service-learning as it may "hurt their chances" of receiving tenure.

Kaufman described how the University president, in a meeting with a group of civically engaged scholars, cautioned her to "be careful," but did not explicitly urge her to abandon her work. Winemiller Basinger revealed her anxiety about lower student evaluations in her service-learning courses and how they might impact her promotion and tenure review. Diener noted that, as she prepared her materials for her pre-tenure reviews, her concept of merit "did not match the University's concept of merit." Senbel writes that, as he was preparing his third-year tenure review documents, "it became obvious that my time and energy spent on the Westside Studio were not translating into proportionate output of tenure worthy publications." In their first chapters, both Liese and Kaufman discuss how they approached their final tenure reviews, writing detailed personal statements that carefully explained—often for the "uninitiated"—the meaning and value of civically engaged scholarship, then linked their work to traditional RPT expectations. Welch bemoans the fact that, after more than a decade teaching service-learning classes, his work is often "not valued and respected" by his colleagues.

RPT anxieties aside, it is clear the authors in this volume embrace the promotion of civic responsibility through engaged scholarship that creates, disseminates, and applies new knowledge toward the common good, in partnership with students and members of the community. However, the University of Utah's mission statement makes only a tacit and cursory reference to civic engagement when it states the importance of "fostering social responsibility." In contrast to other institutions, especially faith-based colleges and universities, the University of Utah does not explicitly or overtly promote civic engagement as part of its mission. The ethos of civic engagement articulated by the authors in this volume is, therefore, fundamentally counter to traditional academic culture at a public research university. Why, then, do these instructors teach service-learning when they are often not recognized and sometimes criticized for their efforts?

This same question was posed by Mundy (2004), who conducted a comprehensive national study of faculty from a range of disciplines and types of institutions to identify factors that predicted faculty involvement in service-learning. Her findings suggest that basic demographic factors such as age, gender, tenure status, discipline, and experience were not related to teaching service-learning. Instead, six factors seemed to predict faculty involvement: (1) being student-centered, (2) being community-oriented, (3) having administrative and collegial support, (4) having campus support, (5) perceiving service-learning as an effective pedagogy, and (6) being aware of promotion and tenure policies as they relate to service-learning. In her final regression analysis, Mundy found only one of these six factors was statistically significant: perceiving service-learning as an effective pedagogy.

It is apparent that the authors in this volume reflect Mundy's profile. As noted above, these scholars report they were initially drawn to service-learning because of its pedagogical appeal. However, over time, they recognize other value and purpose in this work. Almost all stated they drew personal satisfaction from their work that transcended the traditional scholarly devotion to their discipline. These instructors, while cognizant of tenure expectations, appear to do this work because they take pride in seeing tangible outcomes from their expertise and efforts in the community. Kaufman described this result as "making scholarship matter" in her life, as well as the life of her students and community. Winemiller Basinger noted her motivation to "make the world a better place," and Diener saw service-learning as "a way to connect with students and the community and succeed by touching real people's lives directly."

A FINAL REFLECTION

This book began with several definitions of the word *journey*, all of which apply to the Civically Engaged Scholar Cohort. The nine authors of this volume began their journey in the Utah desert, have had a long trip together (more than three years), and, as a group, have made the passage from one stage to another—more accurately, from one stage to several, with more stages likely to follow. Although each author's two chapters represent *individual* journeys, the writing, viewed *collectively*, captures the spirit, energy, and vision that define the CESC. We may have been searching for our identity in the desert, but we have solidified that identity in these pages.

This volume also began with a quote from Alice Walker (1993):

I believe we are destined to meet the people who will support, guide, and nurture us on our life's journey, each of them appearing at the appropriate time, accompanying us at least part of the way. (p. 3)

Walker captures what the CESC now knows to be true, in light of our years together socializing, dreaming, learning, writing, reflecting, rewriting—even "losing" three members to other institutions. Our "community of scholars" has become more—we are faculty colleagues but we are also friends, supporting, guiding, and nurturing one another as we reach higher in our personal and professional lives. The second half of Walker's opening quote says it best: "I think specific human beings, sometimes only in spirit, will present themselves in such a way that their presence will shape and reshape their hearts until we are more fully who we are" (p. 3).

REFERENCES

Boyer, E. L. (1996). The scholarship of engagement. *Journal of Public Services and Outreach, 1*, 11–20.

Bloomfield, V. (2006). Civic engagement and graduate education. *Communicator, 38*, 1–2, 6.

Ehrlich, T. (2000). *Civic responsibility and higher education.* Phoenix, AZ: Onyx Press.

Fogelman, E. (2002). Civic engagement at the University of Minnesota. *Journal of Public Affairs, 6*, 103–118.

Furco, A. (2003). *Self assessment rubric for the institutionalization of service-learning in higher education.* Berkeley, CA; Service-Learning Research and Development Center, University of California, Berkeley.

Holland, B.A. (1997). Analyzing institutional commitment to service: A model of key organizational factors. *Michigan Journal of Community Service-Learning, 4*, 30–41.

Jacoby, B. (2009). Civic engagement in today's higher education: An overview. In B. Jacoby (Ed.), *Civic engagement in higher education: Concepts and practices* (pp. 5–30). San Francisco: Jossey-Bass.

Johnston, D. K. (2006). *Education for a caring society: Classroom relationships and moral action.* New York: Teachers College Press.

Mundy, M. E. (2004). Faculty engagement in service-learning: Individual and organizational factors at distinct institutional types. In M. Welch & S.H. Billig (Eds.), *New perspectives in service-learning: Research to advance the field* (pp. 169–193). Greenwich, CT: Information Age Publishing.

Saltmarsh, J. (2002). Introduction from John Saltmarsh, guest editor. *Journal of Public Affairs, 6* (v–ix).

Stanton, T. K., & Wagner, J. W. (2006). *Educating for democratic citizenship: Renewing the civic mission of graduate and professional education at research universities.* Stanford, CA: California Campus Compact.

Walker, A. (1993). Part One: Introduction. In A. Walker & P. Parmar, *Warrior marks: Female genital mutilation and the sexual blinding of women* (pp. 3–4). New York: Harcourt Brace & Company.

Welch, M. (2002). Promoting civically engaged scholarship through a study/action group. *Journal of Higher Education Outreach and Engagement, 7*, 111–120.

ABOUT THE AUTHORS

The following is a list of authors who contributed to the book. Marissa Diener and Hank Liese served as the editors for the volume.

Caitlin Cahill, Ph.D., is an Assistant Professor in the College of Architecture and Planning. As the Bennion Center's 2007–08 Public Service Professor, her research interests include young people's well-being, globalization, citizen participation in community development, critical race and feminist theory, community-based and participatory action research approaches, and social justice.

Marissa Diener, Ph.D., is an Associate Professor in the Department of Family and Consumer Studies. A developmental psychologist, she is interested in individual differences in the socioemotional development of children. Dr. Diener is also interested in the role that culture plays in parenting and parents' beliefs about childrearing. She teaches several service-learning courses that bridge these interests.

Luke Garrott, Ph.D., is an Assistant Professor-Lecturer in the Political Science Department. He is a political theorist specializing in contemporary political thought and community studies. His Neighborhood Democracy service-learning class engages undergraduates in community-building activities on the west side of Salt Lake City. Dr. Garrott was elected in November, 2007 to a four-year term on the Salt Lake City Council.

Janet Kaufman, Ph.D., is Associate Professor of English and directs the English Education program. Working with service-learning and civic engage-

Finding Meaning in Civically Engaged Scholarship, pages 221–222
Copyright © 2009 by Information Age Publishing
All rights of reproduction in any form reserved.

ment in her courses, she has developed the Family Literacy Center in Salt Lake City. Bringing together her interests in teaching and poetry, she has also co-edited *"How Shall We Tell Each Other of the Poet?": The Life and Writing of Muriel Rukeyser* and *The Collected Poems of Muriel Rukeyser.*

Hank Liese, MSW, Ph.D., is Associate Professor and Director of Doctoral Studies in the College of Social Work. He was the 2005–2006 Bennion Center Public Service Professor and teaches a year-long Honors service-learning course, *The Documentary, Human Rights, and Social Justice*. He is active with civic engagement projects on a statewide level with Utah Campus Compact, comprising all 13 institutions of higher education in the state.

Gina Musolino, PT, MSEd, EdD, is newly appointed Associate Professor & Coordinator Clinical Education, School of Physical Therapy & Rehabilitation Sciences, College of Medicine, University of South Florida, Tampa, FL, following 8 years as Director of Clinical Education and Associate Professor (Clinical) in the College of Health, Department of Physical Therapy. Her research on teaching and learning has been published and presented at local and national levels. Dr. Musolino received the Feitelberg Journal Founders Award for her service-learning manuscript in the *Journal of Physical Therapy Education* and was recently honored as outstanding alumna of the year, Washington University, School of Medicine, Program in Physical Therapy.

Maged Senbel, Ph.D., is an Assistant Professor in the School of Community and Regional Planning at the University of British Columbia. As the 2006–07 Bennion Center Public Service Professor at the University of Utah, he directed the Westside Studio, which brought together students from architecture, business, and urban planning to work with neighborhood residents and community organizations on local development issues.

Marshall Welch, Ph.D., came to the University of Utah in 1987 as a faculty member in the Department of Special Education. He began teaching service-learning courses in 1994 and served as the Director of the Lowell Bennion Community Service Center from 2001 to 2007. He is actively involved in promoting service-learning at the national and international levels through publications, presentations, and workshops. Dr. Welch is now Director of the Catholic Institute of Lasallian Social Action at St. Mary's College of California.

Nancy Winemiller Basinger, M.P.A, Ph.D., is an Assistant Professor in the Masters of Public Administration Program, Department of Political Science. Her research and teaching focus on the interactions between nonprofit organizations and government institutions. Previous work has examined the advocacy efforts of disability groups to enact the Americans with Disabilities Act and the effects of nonprofits on the voting behavior of individuals.

Printed in the United States
149271LV00001B/21/P